The Economics of Biotechnology

This book is dedicated to

Megan, Daniel and Brian Gaisford,

Daniel and Ashley Hobbs,

Clifford William King,

and Marni's teachers

The Economics of Biotechnology

James D. Gaisford
Associate Professor of Economics, University of Calgary, Canada

Jill E. Hobbs
Assistant Professor of Agricultural Economics, University of Saskatchewan, Canada

William A. Kerr
Van Vliet Professor, University of Saskatchewan, Canada

Nicholas Perdikis
Senior Lecturer, School of Management, University of Wales – Aberystwyth, UK

Marni D. Plunkett
Research Associate, Excellence in the Pacific Research Institute, Canada

Edward Elgar
Cheltenham, UK • Northampton, MA, USA

Published by
Edward Elgar Publishing Limited
Glensanda House
Montpellier Parade
Cheltenham
Glos GL50 1UA
UK

Edward Elgar Publishing, Inc.
136 West Street
Suite 202
Northampton
Massachusetts 01060
USA

A catalogue record for this book
is available from the British Library

Library of Congress Cataloguing in Publication Data
The economics of biotechnology / James D. Gaisford ... [et al.].
    p. cm.
Includes bibliographical references and index.
1. Biotechnology industries. 2. Biotechnology—Industrial applications.
3. Biotechnology—Research. I. Gaisford, James D.

HD9999.B442 E25 2001
338.4'76606—dc21   2001031534

ISBN 1 84064 595 4

Printed and bound in Great Britain by MPG Books Ltd, Bodmin, Cornwall

Contents

List of Figures   *ix*
List of Tables   *xi*
Preface   *xiii*

1. Biotechnology   1
   1.1 What is biotechnology?   1
   1.2 The potential benefits of biotechnology   7
       1.2.1 Gains from technological change   7
       1.2.2. Producer benefits   9
       1.2.3 Consumer benefits   11
       1.2.4 Externality benefits   13
       1.2.5 Developing country benefits   13
       1.2.6 Realising potential benefits   14
   1.3 Biotechnological risks   15
       1.3.1 Risks to human health   15
       1.3.2 Risks to the environment   18
       1.3.3 Producer to producer externalities   19
   1.4 What are the issues?   20
   1.5 Who are the vested interests?   26

2. Intellectual property   35
   2.1 The changing nature of biological research   35
   2.2 The economics of protecting intellectual property   42

3. The environment   53
   3.1 Release and adoption under uncertainty   53
       3.1.1 Potential environmental externalities   54
       3.1.2 Modelling decision-making under uncertainty   57

3.1.3 Diverging policy approaches	59
3.2 Biotechnology as a negative public good	61
3.2.1 Aggregate GMO output as a negative public good	62
3.2.2 A framework for assessing environmental externalities	64
3.2.3 Assessing the impact of GMOs with external environmental costs	65
3.3 Biotechnology as a negative or positive public good	75
3.3.1 A GMO with external environmental benefits	75
3.3.2 The GM product has smaller external environmental costs than the non-GM	77
3.3.3 GMO inputs are overpriced due to imperfect competition	79
3.4 International regulation in the Biosafety Protocol	82
4. Consumer issues	89
4.1 Why do consumers care?	89
4.1.1 Evidence of consumer concerns	89
4.1.2 What are the consumer concerns?	90
4.1.3 The origins of consumer concerns	91
4.1.4 Regulatory responses	93
4.1.5 Imperfect information	94
4.2 Hidden quality and long-term food safety	96
4.2.1 Consumers	97
4.2.2 Non-GM farms: a competitive fringe	101
4.2.3 The single biotechnology firm	102
4.3 A single market with hidden quality – when market segmentation is not possible	107
4.3.1 Standard monopoly pricing	107
4.3.2 Pre-emptive and accommodating pricing	110
4.3.3 Biotechnology, agriculture and the 'Lemons Problem'	112
4.4 A general model without market segmentation	114
4.4.1 The farm sector	115
4.4.2 The biotechnology industry	120
4.4.3 The hidden quality problem revisited	123
4.5 Solutions to hidden quality – labelling options	126
4.5.1 Overview of identity preservation systems	126
4.5.2 Perfect identity preservation	128

4.5.3 Costly identity preservation   131
4.6 Cheating and its control   135
   4.6.1 Non-compliance in a mandatory GM food IPS   136
   4.6.2 Misrepresentation in a voluntary non-GM food IPS   139
   4.6.3 Consumer conundrums and policy   143

5. Ethical concerns   151
5.1 Ethical objections to biotechnology   151
   5.1.1 Biotechnology and ethics   151
   5.1.2 Religious attitudes towards genetic modification
      and biotechnology   152
   5.1.3 Specific religious objections   153
   5.1.4 Issues of safety   154
   5.1.5 Ownership and competitive issues   156
   5.1.6 Human ethics   156
   5.1.7 Ethical decision-making and the ethical matrix   157
5.2 An approach to formally modelling ethical concerns   160
   5.2.1 Ethical dimensions of food safety and environmental
      concerns   161
   5.2.2 Ethics and hidden quality   165
   5.2.3 Ethics and externalities   166

6. Who gets the biotechnology rents?   169
6.1 Capturing the rents   169
6.2 Biotechnology and the changing structure of industry   173
   6.2.1 Structural trends: merger, acquisition and alliance
      activity   173
   6.2.2 The changing structure of the input supply sector   174
   6.2.3 Insights from economic theory   175
   6.2.4 Changes in downstream feed and food processing
      industries   182
   6.2.5 The future structure of the biotechnology industry   185

7. International issues   187
7.1 Biotechnology and international trade   187
   7.1.1 Hidden quality: a GM import embargo versus
      unlabelled imports   188
   7.1.2 Revealed quality: labelling of GM imports versus an
      embargo   192

7.1.3 External costs: GM imports as negative public
      goods   198
7.2 The World Trade Organisation and trade in genetically
    modified products   200
7.3 International protection of intellectual property   207
7.4 Biotechnology and the international distribution of
    income   215
    7.4.1 Classification of technical progress   216
    7.4.2 Neutral technical progress, the terms of trade and
          income distribution   216
    7.4.3 The effect of capital-saving technical progress   218
    7.4.4 The effect of labour-saving technical progress   218
    7.4.5 The effect of growth on income distribution   219
    7.4.6 Alternative or additional views on income
          distribution   219
    7.4.7 Conclusion   221

8. Economics and the future of biotechnology   223
   8.1 The nature of biotechnological change   223
   8.2 Pushing the limits of economic analysis   224
   8.3 Public policy role   227
   8.4 Developing country issues   228
   8.5 Crystal ball gazing . . .   229

References   231
Index   243

Figures

1.1	Gains from technological change	8
2.1	Intellectual property rights	46
2.2	First generation GM plants	49
2.3	Second generation GM plants	50
3.1	GM food as a superior new product	66
3.2	Substantively equivalent GM and non-GM foods	69
3.3	Substantively equivalent products with larger social costs	71
3.4	Coexistence of GM and non-GM products	73
3.5	Social benefit of a GM Product exceeds the private benefit	76
3.6	Lower environmental cost GM products	78
3.7	Imperfect competition in the GMO input market	81
4.1	Quality effects in consumer demand	100
4.2	Standard monopoly pricing	104
4.3	Pre-emptive and accommodating pricing	105
4.4	A drastic innovation in biotechnology	109
4.5	A general model with a constant price	116
4.6	A general model with a price decline	118
4.7	A biotechnology industry with two firms	119
4.8	Perfect product identification	129
4.9	Costly non-GM food identification with no cheating	133
4.10	Non-compliance with a mandatory GM food IPS	137
4.11	Misrepresentation with a voluntary non-GM food IPS	141
5.1	Consumer GM food decisions	162
5.2	Producer GMO decisions	164
5.3	GMO development by biotechnology firms	167
6.1	Biotechnology rents	170
7.1	A pooling equilibrium in international trade	190
7.2	A separating equilibrium with labelled GM food imports	193

7.3   A possible decline in non-GM food price   197
7.4   Foreign monopolisation if intellectual property rights
        are enforced   211

Tables

5.1   The ethical matrix   158

Preface

Biotechnology is a major issue as we make the transition from one millennium to another. There is hardly a day that goes by that a story concerning biotechnology does not feature prominently in the news. Those stories encompass the entire spectrum from biotechnology being touted as humankind's saviour to it being the seed of our ultimate destruction. Biotechnology stirs strong emotions among some as witnessed by the (sometimes violent) protests that are recorded for the nightly news. Many people are simply mystified. Governments have had difficulty designing policies to regulate all facets of biotechnology from research protocols, to testing, to protection for intellectual property, to licensing for release into the environment, for food safety and for international trade. It is an issue that has the makings of a major international trade confrontation between the United States and the European Union. It pits developed and developing countries against each other. The ethics and trustworthiness of the scientific community, regulators, policy-makers and politicians have been questioned. Some of the world's largest corporations are strategically manoeuvring to position themselves to capture future market shares in what they perceive as a major potential industry. Others fret over the increased influence those firms may have over their lives and the lives of their children. There is little consensus regarding any aspect of biotechnology.

From the point of view of economists, biotechnology represents a technological change with potentially monumental impacts. As with any major technological change, it will create winners and losers and it will force many individuals to change the way they do things. While some individuals relish change, most find it unsettling. Change can sometimes look like chaos, a state that tends to bring forth strong emotions and often leads to poorly designed policy responses. We believe that economics can help provide a degree of order to what may sometimes appear as a chaotic state of affairs. Dealing with the many facets of biotechnology, however, often points out the limits of economic analysis and, hopefully, provides an incentive to expand the limits of our discipline.

While we have attempted to deal with a wide range of issues that are posed by the large-scale technological change that biotechnology represents, there are some limits to our investigation. We have not explicitly dealt with the human medical and pharmaceutical aspects of biotechnology. In part, this is because medical/pharmaceutical aspects of biotechnology have been, in general, far less contentious than the other aspects of biotechnology. The innovative process for medical and pharmaceutical applications of biotechnology appears to be following a pattern that is similar to other innovations in those fields. The technology remains largely within controlled laboratory and professional environments and its distribution regulated within the medical and pharmacy systems. Further, this aspect of biotechnology is not within our areas of experience or interest as economists, and is best left to others. Many of the topics discussed in this book, however, do have relevance for medical/pharmaceutical biotechnology. The discussions relating to the protection of intellectual property, research, the distribution of the rents arising from the new technology, ethical issues and international trade problems can all provide insights for medical/pharmaceutical biotechnology. In the future, these aspects of biotechnology may become much more bound up with agrifood applications as new crops with health attributes are developed and the boundaries between the two become blurred.

This book focuses on biotechnology that has applications in the agrifood industrial complex. This is where biotechnology has been most contentious as its commercialisation requires the widespread release of genetically modified organisms into the natural environment and the incorporation of its products into human foods. It has also meant significant changes in the conduct of research, in farming, in the organisation of food supply chains and in the protection of intellectual property. International trade problems have centred on trade in foods and fibres that result from biotechnological production. We hope that the insights provided by the application of economics to the various issues pertaining to the introduction of biotechnology into the agrifood complex will be of interest to policy-makers, researchers, business practitioners, NGOs, consumers, academics and students.

We would like to thank the management and staff at Edward Elgar for their interest, support and assistance with this project. We are grateful to a large number of colleagues, students and friends who have provided input into various aspects of this book and who have patiently listened to our discourses on the topic in all manner of formal and less formal venues.

Carol Lau and Tim Folkins deserve special recognition. Finally, we would like to thank Dale, Helen, Laurie, Pam, Daniel, Brian, Megan, Jill and Bill, our families, who endured our long absences in front of computer screens.

Nicholas Perdikis, Aberystwyth, UK; **James D. Gaisford** and **Marni D. Plunkett**, Calgary, Canada; **Jill E. Hobbs** and **William A. Kerr**, Saskatoon, Canada, June, 2001.

1. Biotechnology

1.1 WHAT IS BIOTECHNOLOGY?

The 'new information economy' that is emerging at the start of the third millennium is founded on three rapidly evolving technologies. The first, and oldest, is the widespread use of computers for information processing and enhanced decision-making. The second is the ability to transfer and acquire information globally at low cost via the Internet and its complementary technologies. Accessing, understanding and utilising productively the information contained in the genetic material of living organisms represents the third, and least developed, foundation of the information economy. This technological revolution, which involves a wide range of scientific processes, is commonly termed biotechnology. Biotechnology involves the use of information on genetically controlled traits, combined with the technical ability to alter the expression of those traits, to provide enhanced biological organisms, which allow mankind to lessen the constraints imposed by the natural environment.

The boundaries that can be pushed back through the use of biotechnology are wide-ranging. Biotechnology has the potential to heal the sick, prevent illness, extend the lifespan, feed the hungry, nourish the malnourished, reduce environmental damage, make productive resources out of hitherto unusable materials and replace the consumption of non-renewable resources with renewable resources. As with any new technology, along with the potential benefits, uncertainties are also created. The products of biotechnology may represent risks to health and the environment. While some individuals are risk lovers, most of us are not. Technological change inevitably creates winners and losers. Further, the use of a new technology requires some individuals to change the way they do things. Rapid rates of change, such as those that are the hallmark of the transition to the information economy, make many individuals uneasy. The science that underlies biotechnology is complex, difficult to explain and still being explored. As information is incomplete and public understanding of the technology poor, the unease that some individuals experience as a result of changes brought by the technology is open to manipulation and exploitation. In periods of disequilibrium, the images created by terms such as 'Frankenstein foods' can have a widespread influence on the acceptance of the technology and its future development.

The commercialisation of a new technology creates rents, along with competition for these rents. As a result, questions arise regarding the size of the available rents and their distribution. The question of rents becomes particularly complex and emotive when the products involved pertain to human health or basic human needs. The manipulation of genetic material to produce outcomes that cannot be achieved in nature and the patenting of life forms both generate considerable ethical debate. Policy-makers, firms, advocacy groups and individuals are all being forced to grapple with the changes, potential changes and uncertainties brought by this technological advance. Economics can be useful in shedding light on all these concerns and in analysing the effects of alternative policy proposals.

As with any new technology, terms and concepts need to be explained. Modern biotechnology, which had its origins in the 1970s, is comprised of an array of new techniques – genomics, tissue culture, micro-propagation, marker-assisted breeding, gene splicing and transgenics – that allow breeders to selectively modify living organisms at the molecular level. A genome is the complete set of instructions for making any living organism whether it be bacteria or a human being. The genome of any individual contains the blueprint for all cellular structures and activities for the lifetime of the organism. It is encoded within a set of molecules called DNA, or in the case of some viruses, RNA. Each molecule of DNA/RNA contains many genes (for example approximately 50 000 in a cereal). Genes are the basic physical and functional units of heredity. In a cereal, for example, only about 10 per cent of the DNA is used in coding genes while the remainder includes control sequences that identify when and where particular genes are expressed.

There is a universal genetic code that applies to all living organisms from the simplest organism to humans. Individual species arise from the particular combinations of genes they encompass. The code allows a segment of DNA to specify the structure of a particular protein. A gene is expressed when the protein is synthesised. The amount of protein produced may vary depending on cell type, timing, environmental stress and so on, thus allowing for individual differences.

Scientific breakthroughs in the 1960s generated two ideas that provide the foundation of modern biotechnology. The first is that, as the genetic code is inscribed in molecular terms on DNA, it must be possible to decipher the message. This has been accomplished using physico-chemical methods and is commonly known as genome mapping. In the year 2000, for example, an extremely large international scientific project (the Human Genome Project) finished preliminary mapping of human genes. The second idea underlying biotechnology is that, as the genetic code is universal, gene transfers can be used to introduce genetic information into an organism (Paillotin, 1998). The transfer of genetic material between species is known as transgenics.

Some of the confusion in terminology arises because genetic modification can be considered a continuum. Traditional selective breeding is one form of genetic modification. If perceived from this perspective, almost all commercial crops and domesticated animals have undergone some genetic modification. The major differences that modern bio-technology brings are that genome mapping allows scientists to precisely select the genes, which will lead to the expression of desirable traits. The old selective breeding technology could only achieve progress through hit-and-miss experimentation. Large samples were selectively bred and then the progeny where the traits were expressed were selected for further experimentation. It was like trying to drive from A to B where there are a large number of roads, most of which end in dead ends, and there are no road signs and no maps. If you have enough time you will eventually get to where you are going, but you will have gone down a lot of blind alleys in the process. Biotechnology provides the map. When biotechnological procedures are used for within-species modification, this map can be used to engineer organisms in a faster and more precise way than could be achieved through selective breeding. Within-species genetic modification reduces the cost and increases the precision of what could be achieved through natural selective breeding.

The second advancement provided by biotechnology is the ability to transfer genetic material between species at the molecular level (for example inserting a fish gene into a tomato). This transgenic transfer goes beyond that which can be achieved through nature and is at the heart of much of the controversy surrounding genetically modified (GM) organisms. The ability to undertake transgenic modifications of organisms, however, holds the greatest potential for scientific advancement. Confusion arises because both within-species genetic modification – improving wheat using only wheat genes – and transgenics – improving corn using a gene from a bacteria – are both achieved using biotechnological procedures. Many of those who perceive threats from biotechnology are only concerned about transgenics. Others, however, are worried about the technology itself – genetically engineering humans using within-species modification or the cloning of existing individuals. On a practical level, this difficulty with terminology can confuse the regulatory process, for example, food processing technology may remove transgenic material from the product consumed. Some consumers may only be concerned about ingesting transgenic materials and, thus, they have no need for the product to be labelled if these materials have been removed. If, on the other hand, consumers object to the technology itself and do not wish to purchase products produced using biotechnology then labelling will be requested.

In this book the term *genetically modified organism* (GMO) will be used to mean any organism that has recombinant DNA – that is, it has had DNA transferred to it from another organism. *Genetic modification* is the process of creating a GMO. A *genetically modified product* is a product (or group of products) arising from a GMO, for example, GM canola or GM foods (GMFs). As most of the interest is in transgenic GM products, we will use the terms GMO and GM products to refer to organisms or products that are transgenic. Within-species genetic modifications will be directly identified if differentiation is required.

The first commercial products of transgenic technology entered agri-food supply chains in the late 1980s. Over the intervening period, research has produced a range of microbes, crops and animals using biotechnological methods. More than 40 genetic modifications related to 13 different crops[1] were produced in one of twelve countries by 2000. International trade has made transgenic foods and fibres available in a large number of countries. Some countries have also approved one or more varieties of GM drugs (for example, bovine somatotropin (rBST) for milk production), microbes, trees (for example, poplar), and fish (for example, salmon). Approximately 40 additional crops and a range of microbes and animal species have been genetically modified and were awaiting regulatory approval at the end of 2000 (OECD, 2000). Hundreds of products are in the advanced stages of development and thousands more are on the drawing board. The technology is becoming refined and standardised; the learning-by-doing phase is well advanced. Gene mapping continues and its technology is constantly improving.

By the end of the twentieth century approximately 100 million acres of GM crops were produced. While commercial production was taking place in 12 countries, 99 per cent of the commercial activity was in three countries – the USA, Argentina and Canada (James, 1999). Soybeans accounted for over half the 1999 global acreage, corn (also known as maize) approximately one quarter and cotton and rapeseed (also known as canola) 10 per cent each.

The so-called 'first generation' or 'first wave' products of bio-technology comprise almost all of the existing commercial GM products. First generation crops are those which improve the efficiency of existing crops. Their primary benefits are agronomic through the reduction of costs or losses. The most important agronomic improvement thus far is herbicide tolerance whereby commercial crops are bred to resist specific chemicals so that herbicides can then be used to kill weeds. Seventy-one per cent of the acreage planted to GM crops was seeded with herbicide tolerant varieties in 1999. Approximately one quarter of the acreage is in pest-resistant varieties. These GM products do not alter output in ways that benefit consumers directly other than the decrease in price that could arise from increased efficiency and possible benefits from reduced chemical use.

'Second generation' (second wave) GM products will be those that alter the final composition of the product in ways that benefit the consumer directly. In other words, it will be possible to enhance existing desirable product characteristics (for example, improve the nutrition content of rice) or to add new characteristics desired by consumers (for example, corn which can reduce the probability of heart attacks). While in the beginning, these second generation products may serve mass markets, progressively they are likely to be tailored to specific market niches. Further, there is considerable potential for the engineering of new crops that can be used as industrial inputs such as specialised oils, fibres and chemicals. Crops may be developed for direct pharmaceutical uses. Over the longer run animals may be engineered to provide replacements for human organs.

The advances available from biotechnology are likely to alter both the organisation of agricultural production and the industrial structure of the agrifood sector in fundamental ways. The distinction between the traditional food and fibre industry and other sectors such as pharmaceuticals and health care will become progressively blurred as GM products are engineered to provide characteristics that reduce health risks or provide curative properties in combination with nutrition.

A technological change of the magnitude that appears likely in the case of biotechnology will bring about considerable changes in the global economy. While the development of the technology and gene mapping have been very costly and required a high degree of scientific and technical capability, its application requires less resources and sophistication. Reverse engineering, in particular, will be within the technical capabilities of all but the poorest of nations. As a result, it will not be possible to limit the spread of the technology.

Biotechnology has the potential to alter fundamentally the constraints that have traditionally defined the interaction of humankind with the biological environment. While the changes that have been brought by this aspect of the knowledge economy have so far been modest, biotechnology has far greater potential than either the information processing or information transfer revolutions. Unlike the other aspects of the new knowledge economy, it also has large potential unknowns. Combining the DNA of different species produces new organisms that must then be incorporated into the existing physical environment. It cannot be known for certain how these new organisms will be accepted in the environment or how they will individually or collectively alter it.

The scientific community, for the most part, has embraced the technology although there is an ongoing debate within the scientific community regarding the technology. Biotechnology, however, has altered the nature of biological research. The technology allows new and valuable organisms to be developed by scientists. These new organisms are the product of intellectual endeavour, hence, scientists have an interest in protecting GM products through intellectual property laws. The granting of the right to patent life and the protection of biotechnological intellectual property in other ways has meant that much of the research has moved from the public sector to the private sector. In turn, this has led some to suspect that the scientific community has lost its objectivity, particularly where potential hazards are concerned. The public, as well as public policy-makers, are being asked to make a host of judgements regarding the desirability, the efficacy and the economic impacts of biotechnology when information is incomplete and distributed asymmetrically.

Rapid rates of technological change mean that economies are in disequilibrium. Economists tend to think that economic systems evolve towards a new equilibrium, although this is a debatable point. Applying economic analysis to the broad range of issues raised by biotechnology, hopefully, will provide some insights into what the future will hold and the choices that are available.

1.2 THE POTENTIAL BENEFITS OF BIOTECHNOLOGY

1.2.1 Gains from Technological Change

Economic theory predicts that, *ceteris paribus,* technological change should lead to a gain in net social welfare. Figure 1.1 illustrates this prediction. Technological change shifts the industry's supply curve to the right from S to S'. Under the neoclassical assumptions of competitive markets and perfect information, equilibrium price falls from P_e to P_e' and quantity rises from Q_e to Q_e'. Consumers benefit from both a price effect and a quantity effect. The gain in consumer surplus is shown by area P_eABP_e'. For producers, although prices have fallen, quantity supplied has increased. While producers lose area P_eACP_e' of the old producer surplus, they gain area DCBE. The total new producer surplus is represented by area P_e'BE. The gain in consumer surplus plus the gain in producer surplus more than offsets the loss in producer surplus and there is a net gain in social welfare.

Clearly, this is a simplified model; in particular, five simplifying assumptions are made.

1. Only price and quantity effects are considered, to the exclusion of potential *quality* effects from the technological change. It is assumed that consumers always benefit from higher quantities of the good; there are no adverse quality effects that would shift consumer demand to the left.
2. Consumers have perfect information and can detect any quality differences between products of different technologies.
3. Downstream markets are competitive, allowing perfect pass-through of price changes to consumers.
4. Producers are homogeneous and are willing and able to adopt the new technology.
5. There are no externality effects from the technology.

The effects of relaxing these simplifying assumptions will be examined

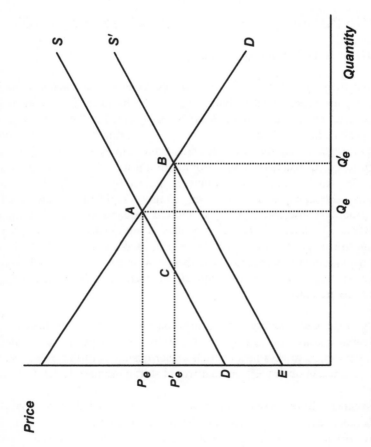

Figure 1.1 – Gains from technological change

8

in later chapters. We begin, however, by focusing on the potential benefits of biotechnology, which underlie the neoclassical economic prediction of gains to society from technological change. These include producer benefits, consumer benefits, positive externality benefits and benefits to developing countries.

1.2.2 Producer Benefits

As discussed in section 1.1, the first generation of biotechnological products involved those with enhanced 'input traits'. These products provide direct benefits for agricultural producers and only indirect benefits to consumers. Producer benefits include both agronomic (production) benefits and economic benefits.

The primary agronomic benefits of input trait GM crops, such as herbicide-tolerant and pest-resistant varieties, are yield increases and/or a reduction in input usage. Weed control practices for conventional crops require both pre-emergent and post-emergent herbicide applications. Selective herbicides are applied after weeds have emerged and are targeted to certain weed types; however, this practice only controls a limited group of weeds (Fulton and Keyowski, 1999). With herbicide-tolerant crop varieties only one herbicide application is needed, rather than multiple applications. The effectiveness of weed control is enhanced by enabling the use of a non-selective herbicide (for example Roundup) to which only the Roundup Ready crop is resistant. Agronomic benefits to farmers include improved weed control, greater flexibility in weed control and increased yields due to the reduced competition with weeds for moisture and nutrients (Fulton and Keyowski, 1999). Farmers growing conventional crops are discouraged from using the same selective herbicide on the same field over a prolonged period of time because it can encourage the development of herbicide-resistant weeds.[2] Instead, they are supposed to rotate herbicide use within a group of herbicides with the same selective weed-killing abilities. The use of herbicide-tolerant varieties may reduce the need for herbicide rotation (Mayer, 1999).

Reduced soil erosion is another potential agronomic benefit, given that pre-emergent chemical applications are no longer necessary. Fewer chemical applications can result in higher moisture conservation and can reduce impacted spoil problems caused by repeated use of heavy machinery on the land. Reduced chemical applications benefit farmers who have adopted conservation farming practices such as the 'zero' or 'no tillage' system in which minimal passes are made over the land with machinery, leaving the soil as undisturbed as possible during seeding and chemical application. Zero tillage systems are becoming more popular in some areas as a means of reducing soil erosion and maintaining higher levels of soil organic matter (Fulton and Keyowski, 1999).

Crops genetically engineered to include resistance to specific insects, such as *Bt* (*Bacillus thuringiensis*) corn or soybeans, reduce yield losses from pest damage without the need for chemical pesticides. The resulting agronomic benefits are similar – simplified pest control, reduced soil erosion and yield increases. Koziel et al. (2000) estimate yield gains from *Bt* corn of up to 8 per cent. Potential production benefits from livestock biotechnologies include better growth rates, higher milk yields and improved disease resistance.

These agronomic and production benefits result in potential economic benefits for producers by reducing costs thereby increasing expected profits. In the case of herbicide-resistant and pesticide-resistant crops, there are direct savings in chemical costs plus savings in labour, fuel and machinery depreciation costs from reduced spraying. There is also an opportunity cost saving in management time with fewer chemical applications. The potential for increased profits is the economic motivation behind producer adoption of the new technology. Carlson et al. (1997) estimate average cost savings of US$2.80 to US$14.50 per acre from the reduced use of pesticides with *Bt* corn. The same authors estimate the potential average increase in profits for US farmers from the use of Roundup Ready soybeans at US $5.65 per acre.

It is questionable, however, whether these economic benefits will accrue to all producers. A comparison of 1999 costs and gross returns from conventional canola and three herbicide-tolerant varieties showed that, although herbicide costs were lower with Roundup Ready canola, seed costs were higher. Overall, estimated gross returns per acre were found to be smaller with the Roundup Ready canola variety due to lower yields (Fulton and Keyowski, 1999). Despite this, there has been rapid adoption of GM canola in Canada. Herbicide-tolerant varieties of canola grew from 4 per cent of Canadian plantings in 1996 to 72 per cent in 1999.[3] This apparent contradiction can be explained if one acknowledges that producers and farms are heterogeneous, with different management abilities and/or agronomic potential to benefit from biotechnology (Fulton and Keyowski, 1999).

Similar adoption trends are evident for other GM technologies, including rapid adoption by farmers of herbicide-tolerant soybeans, *Bt* cotton and rBST in dairy production. The rapid adoption of these new technologies in countries in which they have been approved for use suggests that there are potential benefits, both tangible and intangible, to some farmers.

1.2.3 Consumer Benefits

Input-trait and output-trait biotechnologies offer different potential benefits for consumers. While input-trait GM foods primarily benefit producers through increased technical efficiencies, consumers only benefit indirectly in the form of lower prices. If biotechnology leads to lower production costs for producers and an increase in supply, *ceteris paribus*, prices fall. The decline in prices provides the consumer surplus gain illustrated in Figure 1.1. Declining real prices for food has been a long-run outcome of general technological change in the agricultural industry. In reality, the extent to which these cost savings are passed on to consumers in the form of lower prices depends on the competitiveness of downstream food processing and retailing industries. Oligopolistic downstream industries can capture the increased rents from technological change resulting in imperfect pass-through to consumers of decreases in farm output prices. Rationalisation and increased concentration of food processing is evident in the agrifood sectors of a number of countries. Food retailing also tends to be highly concentrated. Where significant downstream concentration levels exist, consumer price benefits are likely to be smaller.

Input-trait GM crops also generate a potential quality benefit for consumers if there is a reduced use of agricultural chemicals since this will lower the risk of chemical residues in food. The risk that residues are present reduces consumer utility. Studies have shown a positive willingness-to-pay among consumers for reduced levels of chemical residues in food and/or labelling policies to inform consumers of potential residue problems (Caswell, 1995).

While there appear to be only limited, indirect benefits to consumers from input-trait biotechnologies, the second generation of 'output-trait' products offers several direct consumer benefits. By definition, output-trait products are modified to appeal directly to different consumer segments. Potential consumer benefits include enhanced food safety, health, quality and convenience. Through biotechnology, allergenicity problems could be alleviated by removing food genes which create allergic reactions, for example, the production of a non-allergenic peanut. In developed countries, as consumers have become more affluent, 'healthy' foods have become an important consumer trend. There has been a growth in food segments with reduced fat content and those marketed with a health appeal. Foods genetically engineered to have a lower fat content, for example, high-starch potatoes that absorb less fat when fried, could be targeted directly at the health-conscious consumer segment (House of Lords, 1998).

Foods that positively enhance health are a small, but rapidly growing, segment of the food industry. 'Functional foods' or 'nutriceuticals' offer a myriad of future consumer benefits, from prevention of specific cancers to a reduction in blood cholesterol. While some of these products are produced through conventional means, others are products of biotechnology.

Industrial crops are being genetically engineered to produce pharmaceuticals at a fraction of the cost of industrial production methods. Again, consumers will benefit if these cost savings are passed on in the form of lower retail prices for pharmaceuticals. Canola, for example, has been modified to produce hirudin, a blood anticoagulant.

Modification of output traits will facilitate product differentiation, enabling products to be tailored to the needs of different consumer segments. Through biotechnology, the taste of products could be enhanced, for example, producing better tasting fruit through a slower ripening process. There may be 'convenience' modifications that reduce preparation time for consumers, such as seedless watermelon or tender-stemmed broccoli (House of Lords, 1998). While some of these benefits would eventually be available through traditional plant breeding methods, genetic engineering considerably speeds up the process of scientific discovery, enabling new products to be developed more rapidly and potentially at a lower cost.

The traditional neoclassical economic model suggests that consumers benefit from technological change partly due to a fall in prices, as shown in Figure 1.1. This model is limited, however, by its underlying assumptions of homogeneous consumers consuming homogeneous goods in a world of perfect and costless information. In reality, consumers are heterogeneous; some will benefit from certain biotechnologies, whereas others will not. Likewise, products are heterogeneous; indeed, this is the source of an important benefit for consumers – the potential to improve specific quality attributes of food products. This quality benefit could outweigh any price benefits. The situation is further complicated when one relaxes the assumption of perfect information and recognises that, without some form of signalling, consumers may not be able to perceive these product quality differences. These issues are explored in Chapter 4.

1.2.4 Externality Benefits

Possible positive externalities from input-trait GM crops include environmental and health benefits as a result of the reduced use of agricultural chemicals. Farmers' motivations for growing these varieties are likely to be agronomic and economic rather than for the public health or environmental benefits these technologies may offer. *Ceteris paribus*, the private marginal benefits from input-trait varieties may be less than the social marginal benefit. Left to the private market, there will be an underinvestment in GM varieties and a loss in social welfare if these externality benefits are not realised.[4]

1.2.5 Developing Country Benefits

Several of the benefits from biotechnology affect producers in developing countries in a manner similar to those in developed countries. The different economic circumstances in developing countries, however, create additional potential benefits including production, economic development and health benefits.

Crops that can be genetically engineered to increase their drought resistance, disease resistance or pest resistance offer production benefits in the form of increased yields. These benefits can be particularly important in bringing into production new farmland that was previously underproductive and in increasing food production. Less reliance on chemical inputs may also be beneficial. Genetic modification of crops to enable them to capture nitrogen from the air, for example, would reduce farmers' reliance on expensive fertiliser inputs. Of course, this benefit is dependent on farmers realising a cost saving from substituting GM crop varieties for chemical inputs.

Resource-poor farmers in developing countries may not commonly use chemical inputs for weed and pest control. Instead, family labour is often substituted for these inputs; in some developing countries it is estimated that approximately 60 per cent of farmers' time is spent weeding (Spillane, 2000). Herbicide-tolerant crops would reduce the opportunity cost of labour, freeing up this labour to be used in other activities.

Inadequate storage and distribution infrastructure is a perpetual problem in developing countries, leading to substantial post-harvest losses for perishable commodities. The introduction of genes that delay ripening or spoilage could reduce these losses. These improvements to production and storage offer potential for greater long-run stability in local food supplies (Gray et al., 2001).

Given the importance of agriculture to developing country economies, these production benefits can generate tangible economic development benefits. Increased incomes for small farmers from productivity gains are an important means of economic development in poor countries. These changes facilitate the transition from a subsistence to a commercial, agricultural system upon which further economic development can be based.

Biotechnology offers the promise of health benefits from nutritionally enhanced foods. Where serious nutritional deficiencies exist in a society due to inadequate diets and/or low incomes, foods can be genetically engineered to enhance nutrition traits to compensate for these deficiencies. Vitamin A deficiency and iron deficiency are major causes of blindness in some less-developed countries. Through biotechnology, a new strain of rice has been developed that is enhanced with Vitamin A. The potential to genetically engineer foods to deliver vaccines could enhance the effectiveness and scope of vaccine and medicine provision in developing countries.

1.2.6 Realising Potential Benefits

A number of political, economic and social factors, particularly in developing countries, affect the adoption and/or distribution of new technologies and influence whether these benefits will be realised. Adoption of biotechnological advances is complicated by the potential risks (whether perceived or real) and by the influence of vested interest groups. These issues are discussed in greater detail later in this chapter.

The distribution of the benefits from biotechnology depends on whether the genetic modification of a product involves an input trait or an output trait – although the potential for stacking of multiple GM traits in a single product may eventually blur this distinction for an individual product. It also depends on the extent to which benefits are private, accruing directly to the producer or consumer of the product, or whether there are significant public externality benefits. Controversy surrounds the distribution of the benefits from biotechnology between lifescience companies, farmers, food manufacturers, distributors and consumers; in particular, who will capture the rents from investment in the technology. This issue is dealt with in Chapter 6.

1.3 BIOTECHNOLOGICAL RISKS

The introduction of the biotechnology industry into the global economy has focused attention not only on the potential benefits of biotechnology but also on its potential risks. This has been particularly so in Europe where initial efforts to introduce the products of biotechnology have met with considerable opposition. The principal objections to agrifood biotechnology and the work being carried out in other areas of the biotechnology industry are the potential adverse impact they may have on human health, the environment and other production processes.

1.3.1 Risks to Human Health

The public's concerns regarding both the products and the methods of biotechnology with respect to human health are twofold. First, there are concerns regarding the potential for the escape of 'bugs' from laboratories which, once in the atmosphere, could multiply and pose a threat to human health. In many countries, the risks from accidental release have been minimised by stringent regulations aimed at limiting the likely occurrence of biohazards. Human error, however, cannot be eliminated and concerns remain. These risks are not unique to biotechnology and arise with any research that entails the use of materials which pose a biohazard.

The second major concern regarding public health arises from the potential detrimental effects on personal health from consuming products of biotechnology. It is in this area of GM foods that consumer worries have been most widely expressed. The dubbing of GM products as 'Frankenstein foods' by the media conjures up in the public's mind a whole host of negative consequences and outcomes (Greenpeace, 1998).

Whether public fears are well founded is open to debate. It is probably fair to say that the majority of the conventional scientific community do not see the consumption of GM foods as constituting a potential risk to the public. The Royal Society's evidence to the House of Lords Select

Committee examining European Community regulations of genetic modification in agriculture pointed out that (House of Lords, 1998):

1. GM products are often identical to their conventional counterparts, for example sugar produced from GM sugar beets.
2. As a result of processing, the majority of GM foods will not contain viable genes or DNA and so these cannot be passed on.
3. While 'foreign' DNA can survive in human saliva for 20 minutes and in the stomach for eight seconds there was no evidence to suggest that such DNA was incorporated into the genetic material of human cells. Those who gave evidence on this topic were firm in their belief that DNA could only be passed on if there was sexual compatibility. If such compatibility did not exist then this 'natural barrier' would prevent the transfer of genes between species. As a result, eating GM food was safe for humans and other creatures. In other words, there would not be any harmful side effects and Frankenstein's ghost could be laid to rest.

If the weight of scientific opinion was not enough to allay the public's fears, then the existing regulatory process would ensure the protection of human health. In the European Union (EU), and particularly the UK, for example, a whole battery of regulations and advisory committees exist to protect consumers from the products of biotechnology. For example, all GM products, whether grown in or imported into the EU, are subject to assessments under the EC's Novel Food Regulation, which also meets the World Health Organisation's standards. In the UK, the principal body that deals with assessments and applications for assessment is the Advisory Committee on Novel Foods and Processes (ACNFC). This body is made up of members of the scientific community as well as representatives from consumer groups. There is also a member assigned to examine ethical issues. To cover cognate areas, some of the scientific members also belong to other regulatory committees that look at issues of toxicology and other aspects dealing with the medical aspects of food.

The House of Lords Committee, and certainly the Chair of the ACNFC, considered the testing of novel foods to be rigorous (Burke, 1998). The Chair went on in her evidence presented to the House of Lords Select Committee to suggest that if the common potato was examined using the current level of scientific rigour its approval would be unlikely. GM foods were tested for a variety of things, but in particular, stability, toxicity and allergenicity. Other developed countries have their own testing procedures that may be more or less stringent or based on a different scientific approach. No country will license products it considers dangerous.

Risks to human health can usually be attributed to the properties of the host food and of the transgenic material. By checking the track record of the gene in the new genetically altered food, conclusions can be drawn as to the effect of the new food on human health, for example allergies. This procedure may be appropriate where a specific gene or transgenic material have already been in use in a food. It is less appropriate where this has not been the case. Here, there may be greater potential risks to human health. In this case, the need for a cautious approach in product approval becomes apparent. In the case of allergies, where the allergenic mechanisms are not well understood, it may be prudent not only for tests to be carried out but databases compiled for comparative use by other researchers.

There has also been speculation regarding the potential negative effects on human health of the use of antibiotic-resistant marker genes. Marker genes are used to track the presence of a modified gene. The fear is that this genetic material could lead to humans becoming resistant to antibiotic therapy. To reduce this uncertainty, it has been proposed that antibiotic-resistant marker genes not be used in commercial biotechnology applications.

Whether the risks to humans can be minimised using current scientific procedures and regulatory processes has been questioned. Some recent studies suggested that the prolonged consumption of genetically modified foods could affect vital organs. This was suggested in the case of mice. Lacewings and ladybirds feeding on GM crops, or insects that have eaten these crops, may have also been adversely affected. A recent study by the UK Advisory Committee on Animal Feeding Stuffs suggested that transgenic material could be passed on to animals feeding on GM feedstuffs (Barnett, 2000). This implies that these genes may be able to withstand the heating process during the manufacture of animal feeds. It was speculated that humans eating animal products fed this way could also absorb the transgenic material. No official scientific tests have been undertaken to examine this speculation.

While there may be criticisms regarding the way in which scientific studies have been conducted, a few scientists also believe that the process of genetic modification disrupts the host gene function and results in unpredictable outcomes. If this is the case, then consuming GM foods could lead to unwelcome outcomes. As there is a well-publicised debate within the scientific community over this issue, it is not surprising that a portion of the general public perceives that the risks associated with biotechnology are high. The growth in the demand for organically grown products is not unrelated to consumer fears over GM goods. Of course, fears regarding the quantities of pesticides and agrichemicals used in modern farming have also had an important influence on the demand for organic products.

1.3.2 Risks to the Environment

Risks to the environment are even more difficult to assess than the effects on human health. The main channels by which the environment can be affected are via an accidental or deliberate release of GMOs into the atmosphere. Some genetic modifications, particularly output-trait modifications, are unlikely to pose serious risks, for example, the slow ripening of fruits and vegetables. At the moment, most of the uncertainties surrounding GMOs and the environment relate to input traits that alter the agronomic performance of plants. The potential risks are associated with outcrossing, pest resistance, stress tolerance and multiple tolerance.

Outcrossing is the accidental transfer of modified genes to other organisms. Gene transfer can take place between micro-organisms, in this case, problems can only arise when the transfer is to a pathogen or if the result of this transfer is a pathogen. Transfers from micro-organisms to higher organisms, such as plants, seem to take place only with a limited number of bacteria. Current conventional scientific knowledge suggests that transfer from plants to bacteria is very unlikely.

Outcrossing among plant species, however, may pose a risk to the environment if weeds are sexually compatible with a herbicide-tolerant crop. An example of this would be wild oats and oats. If transfers did take place, then there could be detrimental effects on natural vegetation. If the recipient of the resistance – the weed – could not now be eradicated by existing chemical products, or needed larger chemical applications than hitherto, farmers or others attempting to reduce the population of resistant weeds would have to alter their weed control practices. In addition to higher chemical application rates it could result in the use of less-specific herbicides or herbicide combinations that adversely affected a wider spectrum of wild vegetation. The result could be increased chemical pollution of the soil and of rivers, with harmful consequences for wildlife and plant communities. These problems could be compounded if crops are genetically modified to tolerate a range of herbicides through the stacking of multiple GM traits. In this case, greater uncertainty would exist regarding the interaction of GM plants with the natural environment. Research on these issues remains sparse and inconclusive, with causal mechanisms being highly speculative.

Another environmental concern involves the development of 'stress-tolerant' plants. If plants are developed to withstand hostile conditions, they may adopt the characteristics of weeds in some environments. Stress-tolerant plants, or their outcrossed wild relatives, may also pose risks to the composition of the plant communities into which they have been introduced. The artificially hardier plants may crowd out other indigenous species altering local habitat or ecosystems. Further, heightened stress tolerance could result in additional land being brought under cultivation, reducing or eliminating natural habits. In the absence of a strong environmental protection regime the reduction of natural habitat could threaten indigenous fauna and flora.

One objective of input-trait biotechnologies is to produce crops that are resistant to specific pests. This has been achieved by introducing genes that produce toxins, such as from the bacteria *Bacillus thuringiensis* (*Bt*). These toxins are effective against a wide variety of insects but in particular against Lepidoptera (for example, butterflies and moths). Currently the toxins derived from *Bt* are used in a wide variety of pesticides. After being applied to crops they usually dissipate over time and are absorbed by the soil. There is speculation regarding two environmental risks that could arise when *Bt* genes are incorporated directly into crops. First, insects may become immune to the toxins. This might be the case because, unlike plants sprayed with *Bt*-based insecticides, those that have toxins in their genetic make-up 'express' their resistance more uniformly over time and for longer. As a result, insects will be in contact with the toxin longer than is otherwise the case. Second, the toxins may kill non-targeted insect species that make a positive contribution to the natural environment or are aesthetically pleasing to humans. Thirdly, the toxins may be so effective in killing off the insects that they deprive higher life forms a source of food, thereby damaging the ecosystem. Chapter 3 explores these environmental issues in more detail.

1.3.3 Producer to Producer Externalities

There is a concern that gene transfer from GM crops could contaminate the non-GM crops of neighbouring farmers. If the non-GM crops were grown for markets requiring GM-free foods, the value of the crop would be seriously compromised. The Soil Association, a body representing the interests of organic farmers in the UK, has expressed strong concerns regarding this issue.

Another externality from the introduction of GM production can arise if consumers do not have sufficient information to determine whether or not a particular product is genetically modified. If there is a negative consumer reaction to a GM crop, producers of non-GM varieties of the same crop may also suffer a declining market. Reversing this negative externality may require a costly consumer information campaign or expensive systems to ensure that products are kept separate. These issues are explored in Chapter 4.

1.4 WHAT ARE THE ISSUES?

When new technologies can be adopted profitably they create change. In response, some individuals will alter their working practices and/or their lifestyles. Some of these changes will be embraced voluntarily while others will be only reluctantly accepted, often through the subtle discipline of market forces. In some cases these two events affect the same individual in both ways. The owner of a new automobile in the early 1900s who was just laid off from his buggy whip factory due to declining demand is an obvious example. The involuntary changes imposed on individuals sometimes leads to violent reactions to new technologies such as the Luddite attacks on factories in the nineteenth century or anti-nuclear protests in the twentieth century. The uncertainties surrounding new technologies often lead initially to precautionary regulations, which are mirthful in retrospect. Regulations that required early cars to be preceded by a flagman and to not exceed 10 miles per hour come to mind. On the other hand, the failure to adequately regulate other new technologies, on occasion, has led to considerable environmental damage. The industrial pollution of inland waterways and over-fishing of common property resources are but two examples.

As outlined in the previous sections, new technologies often have the potential to provide a range of benefits, yet they may also entail a number of potential risks. In the early days of a technology, both the benefits and risks may be poorly understood. As a result, they may be either overestimated or underestimated. This lack of transparency enables claims that simultaneously hype exaggerated benefits and discount risks or that play up the risks and dismiss the benefits. Citizens and policy-makers are often faced with considerable costs if they try to make new technologies less opaque to improve their ability to make decisions. Asymmetric and incomplete information raises the prospect that there may be over- or underinvestment in the technology and the possibility for unwarranted rents to be created and captured as well as opportunities for fraudulent gains.

The changes brought by new technologies inevitably create losers as well as winners. While society's welfare is expected to increase from the spread of the new technology, without adequate compensation (which is almost never provided) those who perceive that they will lose can be expected to resist the change. If either the expected benefits are overestimated or the costs underestimated, in part due to externalities, the technology may not in any case provide the expected gain in societal welfare. In some instances the technology will fail but society bears the cost of the disruption associated with a period of disequilibrium. In other cases, the technology survives but only because others bear the costs associated with negative externalities. The development and adoption of the new technology creates vested interests who will resist changes that threaten those interests. The opaque nature of technological change, particularly a large-scale technological change, such as biotechnology, thus raises a host of issues to which economic analysis can be applied.

The application of biotechnology embodies a number of elements that are not typical of past technological changes. The technology is biologically based. The basic science that underlies the new technology was completed at approximately the same time that governments in most developed countries had become mired in a period of sluggish economic performance, ballooning government deficits and soaring debt service costs. Regaining control of government finances became a priority. Expenditures were capped or reduced, including those made in support of research. Past biological-based technological changes, such as the development of hybrid corn in the USA (Griliches, 1957) and the crops of the 'green revolution' (Pearse, 1980), were financed by governments directly or indirectly through international research centres. In part, this was because biological innovations reproduce themselves through natural breeding, thus allowing farmers to retain part of their crop for seed. As a result, it was difficult, if not impossible for private developers of new varieties to capture sufficient returns to justify their research and development (R&D) expenditures. This market failure (due to non-excludability) moved biological-based innovations into the category of public goods where government intervention could be justified. The fiscal difficulties that began in the late 1970s, however, meant that governments were no longer willing to shoulder this financial burden. Governments were, however, cognisant of the potential of biotechnology.

The precise nature of genetic manipulation, as opposed to the experimental nature of plant breeding, made it more likely that private returns could be made from the development of products derived from biotechnology. Further, initial breakthroughs could be made in small labs rather than requiring extensive research facilities. As a result, governments made conscious decisions to move the development of biotechnology into the private sector, primarily by extending the system of intellectual property rights to cover both biotechnology methods and products. The privatisation of biological research brings forth a variety of issues. There are ethical issues surrounding the ownership of life forms and questions regarding the efficacy of monitoring private scientific activity (for example, the cloning of humans). The privatisation of scientific activity also raises questions about the objectivity of the scientific establishment. The reduction of university budgets, combined with the privatisation of research, has led to an interest by universities in the private funding of research, calling into question their intellectual freedom and independence.

The creation of private intellectual property rights in biological products has brought forth additional concerns. These relate to the industrial organisation of agrifood supply chains and industrial concentration in the sector. To facilitate the protection of their intellectual property, some firms supplying agricultural inputs have altered the way they organise transactions with farmers. They have moved to a system of contracts as opposed to traditional spot market sales for seed. Among other things, the contracts often specify that farmers cannot retain part of the crop for next season's seeding. The move to contracts, however, also changes the nature of the transaction relationship to 'one-on-one bargaining' from the 'public offer price accept or not accept' tatonnement system that characterised input spot markets. The absence of a transparent pricing mechanism for inputs creates asymmetric information that puts farmers at a disadvantage in one-on-one bargaining.

While small laboratories can make the genetic breakthroughs that underlie new biotechnological products, the commercialisation of those products often requires considerable financing and large-scale distribution systems. In particular, the process of regulatory approval may be both costly and slow. As a result, the commercialisation of biotechnology has fallen to large agribusiness firms, which are often transnational in their operations. In some cases, existing agrochemical giants have been reengineering themselves as 'lifes cience' companies to capitalise on the opportunities presented by the wholesale creation of new intellectual property represented by biotechnology. This has led to concerns regarding increasing levels of industrial concentration in the agrifood sector and the exercise of market power.

The alteration of biological life forms at the genetic level has created uncertainties regarding how the new life forms will interact with the natural environment. Decision-making, both private and regulatory, under uncertainty is not an exact science. Decisions will also be affected by the risk preferences of private individuals and those who are embedded in regulatory systems. Risk lovers will make entirely different decisions from those who are risk averse. Given the biological uncertainties that currently surround the technology, large externalities may exist from the release of new biological products into the natural environment. This means that private adoption decisions may impose large costs on those who are more cautious. On the other hand, considerable forgone opportunities may accompany an overly cautious approach. Thus, given the possibility of negative environmental externalities, government intervention in the decisions regarding the release of GMOs is justified. Governments have been forced to make difficult regulatory decisions. There may also be significant first-mover advantages from early adoption of the technology that must be factored into the government decision processes.

Differing risk preferences of governments regarding GMOs has led to different timetables for domestic approvals among countries. Products that have not been licensed for domestic release may also have to be prevented from entering the market through imports. The imposition of import barriers brings forth accusations of protectionism from firms in countries where GMOs have been licensed. As the failure to license a technological improvement puts producers at a competitive disadvantage, trade barriers do have a protectionist element. The World Trade Organisation (WTO) and other international trade forums may be called upon to judge whether the imposition of trade barriers is consistent with international trade obligations.

The creation of economically superior varieties using biotechnology has also raised questions regarding the effect of the new products on biodiversity. Even if there are no environmental externalities that threaten biodiversity, GM crops may be sufficiently economically superior to alternative crops that they will lead to increased monoculture production and, hence, reduced biodiversity. This could increase the costs associated with weather or pest-induced crop failures and raises the spectre of localised food shortages, particularly in some developing countries. Alternatively, biotechnology may well lead to a multitude of niche market crops that would actually result in an increase in biodiversity, albeit engineered rather than natural.

The genetic modifications that produced the new products have led some to question the safety of the products when consumed by humans or animals. There has been considerable speculation, but little evidence, that human biochemistry is not sufficiently well understood to fully comprehend how ingested GMOs will interact with it. Again, uncertainty underlies the process of decision-making. As governments often shoulder a degree of the responsibility for human health, they have been forced to deal with the human health uncertainties created by the new technology. The degree of trust in the regulatory system responsible for human health, and indeed the scientific community that sets and administers its standards, differs both between individuals and among societies. As in the case of environmental uncertainty, governments in different countries have dealt with human health uncertainties in a variety of ways. Further, individual consumers and consumer organisations have been demanding the ability to choose for themselves through labelling of GM products. The decision to license or not license GM foods has considerable ramifications. Further, labelling may carry considerable costs associated with verification of the label's claims, has ramifications for the relative competitiveness of GM and non-GM products and has the potential to create perceptions of risks when they do not actually exist.

The long supply chains that characterise modern food production and distribution systems create the potential for asymmetric information between producers and consumers. As a result, questions arise regarding adverse selection and how the information asymmetry may be removed or reduced. Segregation of supply chains for GM and non-GM products is one alternative. This leads to questions regarding monitoring, acceptable levels of contamination and legal responsibility. Important economic questions surround each of these issues. Alternatively, testing may be required prior to sale. This raises questions regarding the efficacy of testing procedures.

In addition to issues relating to human health and environmental uncertainty, consumers may also have ethical concerns with the technology itself. To some individuals, biotechnology is unnatural or a process which 'messes with God's work'. This may manifest itself in requests for the right to know how products have been produced. As processing may remove all evidence of GMOs from GM products, this removes the testing option for verification of labels.

Ethical concerns may lead some groups of consumers to paternalistically call for the removal of the choice from all consumers through product bans. This raises issues of consumer sovereignty.

The advent of the new technology also raises a large number of issues that have an international dimension. Some of these have already been alluded to. Differences in policy decision-making under uncertainty leads to differences among countries in both the products that are approved and in the rate at which approvals take place. New technologies also have considerable distributional effects that governments may wish to delay having to deal with. For example, the increased efficiency that arises from the use of biotechnology may accelerate the exit of farmers from production. The technology may also favour adoption by large farms to the detriment of small farms. Governments expend considerable resources attempting to slow these trends. They may also wish to extend protection for farmers when products are traded internationally. While the imposition of trade barriers to protect human health or the environment may be legitimate, it has been agreed at the WTO that the capricious use of these barriers to extend economic protection to domestic producers is not allowed. As a result, trade barriers put in place against the products of biotechnology will be subject to close scrutiny and may be the subject of international disputes.

Given the high proportion of the value of GM products accounted for by intellectual property, piracy is likely to be a major international issue. The potential for rapid commercialisation of new GM products appears large. This means that each new product will have a relatively short product life cycle. As a result, firms will require access to the largest markets possible for their products. Intellectual property piracy reduces the markets available, lowers private returns to investment in biotechnology and slows the rate of technological change. Since developed country governments see the creation of new intellectual property as a major determinant of their relative prosperity, they will want strong international protection for intellectual property. Developing country governments have been relatively ambivalent regarding the protection of intellectual property, given that they produce so little of it (Kerr et al., 2000). In the case of the early products of biotechnology, seeds for farmers and human pharmaceuticals, they may well see the high prices that arise from the granting of intellectual property protection as antipathetic to their development goals or the welfare of their citizens. Developing countries reluctantly agreed to put intellectual property regimes in place during the Uruguay Round. The provisions of the WTO's Agreement on Trade Related Aspects of Intellectual Property (TRIPS) may be tested by the advent of biotechnology. Even if intellectual property regimes are put in place by developing countries, questions will arise regarding the enforcement of those regimes. If TRIPS does not prove to be effective, alternative incentives for the protection of intellectual property internationally will have to be considered.

There are a number of other issues that are likely to arise for developing countries and for their relationship with developed countries from the advent of biotechnology. The technical capability of developing countries to assess and control the use of the products of biotechnology may lead to them becoming dumping grounds for products that developed countries will not license. Biotechnology may increase the role of transnational corporations in developing countries, raising worries about their influence in the local economy and with their governments. If international markets for GM products are restricted either through prohibitions on imports or labelling requirements, developing countries may find their exports threatened given their poor capacity to regulate or segregate the use of GMOs.

On the other hand, biotechnology may hold the key to feeding the expected large increases in developing countries' populations, improving nutrition levels and reducing stress on their ecosystems. As a result, policies in developed countries that inhibit investments in biotechnology may considerably reduce developing countries economic well-being over the long run.

It should be clear that the advent of biotechnology provides a large number of complex issues that have considerable economic ramifications. Biotechnology provides fertile ground for economic research and for policy input by economists. There are also a large number of groups that have a vested interest in how the biotechnological revolution unfolds.

1.5 WHO ARE THE VESTED INTERESTS?

As suggested above, while technological change can be expected to be welfare-enhancing, it will also create winners and losers. Both winners and losers have a vested interest in how the technological change unfolds. A technological change on the scale of biotechnology is not likely to leave too many people untouched, but clearly some economic actors will find themselves more directly affected than others. The disequilibrium created by technological change can also create opportunities to act strategically to try to ensure that one is a winner, and for that matter, that the amount by which one wins is increased. Of course, potential losers can attempt to alter the evolution of the change so that they instead become winners, to ensure that some of the gains are transferred to them by way of compensation or to stop, or slow the technological change to protect their interests.

Technological changes often mean that the policy and regulatory frameworks that govern the existing state of technology are no longer appropriate and a new institutional framework is required. Venues for policy and regulatory development often become the battlegrounds for potential winners and losers. It is important, therefore, to identify those with vested interests prior to examining closely the economic issues surrounding biotechnology.

Most of the interest in those who are expected to be winners from the advent of biotechnology has centred on the transnational firms that are attempting to strategically position themselves to take advantage of the long-run potential of the new technology. There are, however, a large number of other vested interests that have a stake in how the technological change unfolds, and who are attempting to affect the outcome.

If one has any doubts regarding the impact that biotechnology is expected to have on the future of agribusiness and related industries, one has only to examine the merger and acquisitions activity in the agro-input supply industry over the last few years. In particular, chemical supply firms, which were already extremely large transnational corporations, arguably with considerable market power, have been engaging in aggressive merger and acquisitions activity to strategically position themselves to be winners in the biotechnology era. For example, Monsanto (a chemical company) spent a total of US$4.8 billion in 1998 to acquire three firms it considered as vital components of its biotechnology strategy. DuPont (another chemical based firm) spent US$1.7 billion in 1997 to acquire a seed company – Pioneer Hi-Bred International. A number of other transactions in 1998 approached the billion US dollar mark (Shimoda, 1998). This strategic activity is also driven by the realisation that if a firm does not act strategically to adapt it may well become a loser. Standing still is not an option. According to Shimoda (1998, p. 62):

We are moving into a new century in which breakthroughs in the understanding of biology at the molecular level will create waves of new technologies and products. The technologies and products are expected to redefine the growth and value creation potential of agriculture. These dynamics are expected to drive an accelerating wave of strategic corporate actions. We will witness the birth of new companies and industries, the need for companies to redefine themselves in order to remain competitive and take advantage of new business opportunities, and unfortunately, the demise of some companies and industries which do not understand the magnitude and potential impact of this developing technology wave, which is about to turn into a tsunami.

The agrochemical companies were, perhaps, the first to see the threat to the status quo provided by biotechnology. First generation biotechnology products are agronomic. They provide production advantages to farmers. The most important of these changes relate to reduced use of agricultural chemicals, particularly herbicides and pesticides. Sales of some chemicals were projected to decline up to 40 per cent. According to Hayenga (1998, p. 46):

> Industry experts expect that biotechnology-based solutions to weed, fungal and insect problems will comprise 10–20 percent of the global $45 billion crop protection market. . . . Forty-five percent of cotton produced in 1998 was genetically engineered for insect resistance, herbicide resistance, or both.

It is probably not surprising that the large agrochemical transnationals such as Monsanto, Dow, DuPont, Hoechst, Schering, Ciba and so on began to reinvent themselves as 'life science' companies. Once the decision was made by these large agribusiness firms to enter the biotechnology business defensively, then further strategic initiatives were required to ensure that they would be able to capitalise on the new technology. They began to acquire rights to existing intellectual property in biotechnology and to strengthen their life science research capability. The new life science companies also began to vertically integrate down the supply chain, in particular acquiring seed companies. Seed companies provided the delivery mechanism for the biotechnology and are particularly important when the GM crop was engineered to be tied to the use of one of the firm's existing chemical products (for example the herbicide Roundup). Further, as intellectual property comprises a rising proportion of the value of GM crops, the acquisition of the seed companies allowed the lifescience firms to better protect their intellectual property (Kalaitzandonakes, 1998).

Thus, it seems clear that large transnational life science firms have a vested interest in the biotechnology revolution. Given their investments and strategic positioning, it would also seem that they have a vested interest in having the revolution progress as fast as possible. The wider the markets for their products, the higher their rates of return on investment and the greater probability that other potential claimants to the rents available from biotechnology will be passed by before they can position themselves to challenge the life science firms. Rates of adoption of the biotechnology products commercially available in North America have been very rapid relative to previous commercial technologies. If, as in the past, successive waves of new biotechnological products follow similar patterns of diffusion, the life science companies appear well placed to capture a substantial portion of the potential rents available from crop biotechnology. Their ability to capitalise equally well on other aspects of biotechnology, such as agricultural pharmaceuticals and animal products, will depend upon the strategies of drug and animal industry firms. One crucial area for further strategic behaviour will be in the innovation process itself.

While the large life science and pharmaceutical firms are directly investing heavily in R&D, it is probably not in their interest to attempt to monopolise research. Small- and medium-sized research labs, as well as universities, seem well placed to contribute to the research process. They can be quick, nimble and unconventionally innovative. As well, they are able to tap high-risk venture capital. Given the apparent importance of biotechnology in the knowledge economy, public policy-makers should see that encouraging small- and medium-sized biotechnology research establishments as well as the R&D activities of large life science companies provides a vehicle for diversifying society's research portfolio.

One way for firms to attempt to capture the rents from biotechnology will be to acquire intellectual property rights to the underlying genetic innovations, either the genetic material itself or the scientific technologies required for further progress. Thus, firms wishing to use genetic material or scientific technology to produce innovations with commercial application would have to pay royalties to the holders of these intellectual property rights. As the genetic material and scientific techniques have public goods (non-rivalrous) aspects, public policy-makers will have to find the right balance between the private endowment of property rights and public goods. Freedom to operate is already an issue with biotechnology research firms that must acquire the right to use a range of biotechnology-related inputs in their research. They have a vested interest in having a system for acquiring those rights, which is transparent and efficient. Further, university research establishments now see biotechnology as a major potential source of present and future research funds, particularly given the unwillingness of governments to fund them at historic levels. They see a vested interest in acquiring the rights to the intellectual property their personnel create on a shared basis. This alters the previous public good character of university research. While biotechnology is not the only area where the privatisation of university research has become an issue, it has the potential to have a significant impact on research in the life sciences.

While there are groups that are strategically positioning themselves to benefit from biotechnology, there are others who feel they have a lot to lose from the advent and spread of the technology. Resistance to biotechnology has been vocal and sometimes destructive or violent. The fields of farmers doing GM crop trials have been vandalised and some of the protests at the Seattle Ministerial meeting of the WTO in autumn 1999 were anti-GMO. The press has found willing audiences for pieces on 'Frankenstein foods' and protesters in costumes depicting characterisations of GM products have been popular for television news clips. Beyond the more extreme expressions of anti-GM sentiments, there is a broader segment of society that has reservations regarding biotechnology. Resistance to GMOs has been most strongly manifest in the EU but groups that question GMOs can be found in almost all countries.

A large number of surveys have been undertaken and they tend to show considerable unease regarding biotechnology – although the results of surveys must be interpreted carefully both due to bias in survey design and in the population samples to which they are administered. Perdikis (2000) reports the results of a number of surveys in Europe. A European Public Concerted Action Group survey in 1999, for example, found that 74 per cent of those surveyed believed that GM foods should be labelled, 60 per cent wanted public consultation regarding new developments and 53 per cent felt that existing regulations were insufficient to protect individuals. A poll conducted in the UK in 1998 found that 77 per cent of respondents believed GM crops and food should be banned and 61 per cent said they would prefer not to eat GM foods. A member survey of the National Federation of Women's Institutes (an association with 265 000 members in England and Wales) showed that 98 per cent of those surveyed wanted more debate on GMOs and 93 per cent wanted GM foods labelled. Surveys have also shown that there is considerable confusion among consumers regarding GMOs.

The organisations that have been leading the campaigns against GMOs represent groups that tend to have strongly held preferences. These groups existed prior to the commercialisation of GM products but have identified them as new additions to trends they already did not like. First, there are those who were already concerned about the healthfulness of the food they consume. They are concerned about food additives, chemical residues and pharmaceutical use in animal production. They are major proponents of organic food products. In their perception, GM foods are just another example of 'unnatural' food. Second, there are those who have strongly held preferences for the environment. They see GM crops and other organisms as further examples of irresponsible treatment of environmental risks and disregard for future generations. Greenpeace and Friends of the Earth have been particularly active in the anti-GM campaign.

Third, there are individuals who have ethical concerns regarding the technology itself. They are concerned about altering nature and the future abuse of the technology (for example genetically engineering humans). Finally, there are those who are worried about the power and influence of transnational corporations in the economy and society. Given that most of the commercialisation of GM products is being undertaken by transnational corporations, and that the technology appears to be strengthening their position, these individuals believe that biotechnology should be opposed. In biotechnology, these four groups, who tend to hold strong preferences, have found common ground. As a result, they have been able to keep the issue in the press and on the public agenda to a far greater degree than has been possible in the case of an issue of interest to only a single group (Perdikis and Kerr, 1999).

Public concerns regarding GMOs have been able to effectively stop the licensing of GM products and imports into the EU. There have also been a number of commercial responses to the strong adverse consumer reaction to GM foods. Some firms moved to protect their vested interests in their reputations as purveyors of safe and high-quality foods. For example, by April 1999, all the major supermarket chains in the UK had committed to the elimination of any GM foods from their own brand products. All claim that their decision was made in response to consumer preferences.

The major UK food manufacturers Unilever and Cadbury agreed to ban GM inputs from their product lines. In 1997, Unilever declared itself free of GM products in both Germany and Sweden. Nestlé also promised to do away with GM ingredients and, where it cannot provide that guarantee at present, it will label the product clearly, thus allowing consumer choice. It is important to note that, for the most part, the commercial response has been to ban GM materials rather than following a strategy of strict labelling whereby consumers can choose. This suggests a level of consumer concern that exceeds the need simply to be better informed. In the USA, on the other hand, most retailers and food processors have not acted to remove GM foods from their shelves. Gerber and Heinz, baby food manufacturers, announced in 1999 that they would use only non-GM foods in their products (Nelson et al., 1999). Some major fast food chains and potato processors have announced they will not purchase GM potatoes. The adverse reaction of some consumers and environmentalists to GM foods has induced other firms in biotechnology supply chains to act strategically to protect their vested interests.

Farmers are caught in the middle. While farmers can see the agronomic benefits from the use of GM seeds, they face considerable uncertainty if they commit to growing them. Changes in the buying preferences of a major food processor can have significant price effects. Lack of transparency and consistency in government policies increases farmers' risk.

Farmers are also concerned that the new technology will alter their relationship with input companies and their customers in ways that are not advantageous (Klein et al., 1998). The agro-input companies may be able to tie farmers to a bundle of inputs (fertiliser, herbicide, pesticide) for which the crop has been specifically engineered. Input suppliers will also want to monitor farmers more closely to protect their intellectual property. Buyers may want to ensure that non-GM crops are not mingled with GM crops, again demanding the right to monitor more closely what is transpiring behind the farm gate. Second generation GM products with attributes that consumers desire may well be produced for niche markets supplied by a single firm – leaving the farmer to deal with a single buyer. All this suggests reduced independence for farmers; independence is something farmers are often thought to value highly (Klein and Kerr, 1995). Input suppliers and processors may form tied relationships to engineer and market GM products leaving the farmer in the middle. According to Nelson et al. (1999, p. 73):

> Not only might the farmer lose freedom of choice among suppliers and buyers, and hence, be likely to see margins squeezed, but the role of the farmer would become more that of a manager and less of an independent business owner. In

this respect, the GM revolution could be one of a series of developments that change the agricultural sector permanently.

Other actors along the agrifood supply chain may also have their vested interests threatened. If it becomes necessary to segregate GM and non-GM foods in the transport and distribution chain, for example, then some of the sunk capital in those sectors may no longer be appropriate (for example grain elevators with limited segregation ability or ship cleaning systems, which allow a considerable degree of cross-contamination from load to load).

Developing countries may particularly be affected by the introduction of GM crops and other organisms. As suggested above, on the one hand, GM crops may decrease the use of chemicals reducing pressure on their environments. Second generation crops engineered to provide better nutrition and/or reduced incidence of human illness also hold great appeal. On the other hand, the poor regulatory and enforcement capabilities of many developing countries may allow GM products that are unable to be licensed in developed countries to be introduced into their markets. If some markets require non-GM products, developing countries may be hard pressed to verify that their crops are GM-free, thereby threatening export markets. It may be that only transnational corporations have the capacity to provide certification, thus allowing them to monopolise the trade of some developing countries – something those countries may not see as being in their interest. Further, as experience from the green revolution suggests, there may be considerable ramifications for the distribution of income in developing countries, for example between rich and poor farmers, which may arise as a result of major technological changes (Marks et al., 1992).

As outlined in this chapter, biotechnology can provide considerable benefits, may entail unforeseen risks and, as with any technological change, creates winners and losers. In the process, it may alter considerably the structure of the industries it affects. All of these are issues where insights can be obtained from the application of economic analysis.

NOTES

1.   Rapeseed (canola), flax, maize (corn), melon, papaya, potato, rice, soybeans, squash, sugar beet, tobacco, tomato, cotton.
2.   See Chapter 3, however, for a discussion of similar resistance concerns from genetically engineered crops.

3.   Transgenic canola represented about 55 per cent of Canadian plantings.
4.   The *ceteris paribus* qualification is particularly important here. For now we are ignoring any potential 'negative' externalities from GM products. These are discussed in section 1.3 of this chapter and in Chapter 3.

2. Intellectual property

2.1 THE CHANGING NATURE OF BIOLOGICAL RESEARCH

A considerable proportion of biological research has historically been carried out in the public sector. The USA was the major producer of biological research in the twentieth century. It has an extensive system of public (land grant) universities and government research establishments at both the federal and state level. Most other developed countries have established public institutions to conduct agricultural research and, in addition, fund universities to do both basic and applied research. Latterly, systems of publicly funded international research centres were set up to provide biological research for developing countries.

Some biological research is undertaken by inquisitive farmers. In pre-scientific societies there has always been a long process of domestication for both plants and animals. In crops, these are known as 'landrace' varieties. In many developing countries landrace varieties tailored to local conditions are still important, although scientific varieties have made considerable inroads since the green revolution of the 1960s and 1970s and its aftermath. Landrace varieties were collected in 'gene banks' to provide the genetic diversity required for traditional plant breeding. In recent years much of this material was collected and treated as a public good by internationally funded research stations. These gene banks are now important sources of genetic material for biotechnological work at the molecular level. As genetic research has progressively moved from the public to the private sector, the genetic material in 'public good' gene banks has become increasingly valuable and its ownership and the rights to its use have become increasingly complex issues.

In developed countries, private sector research has concentrated on delivery mechanisms such as seed, semen, seedlings and cuttings for grafting. This private sector research was often engaged in adapting and commercialising the more basic research conducted by the public sector. While private sector research did have some legal protection for its products, private firms relied more on efficient division of labour, economies of scale in preparation, storage and logistics and lower monitoring costs for quality control to provide their profits. In any case, given that publicly funded research was treated as a public good, often provided at zero or nominal cost, the value of the intellectual property provided by private firms was relatively small.

Most non-biological innovative activity in developed economies has taken place in the private sector. This is because legal regimes have been put in place to reward successful innovations, largely through the use of patents. Patents allow those who are willing to take the risks inherent in the creation of new products to capture the benefits, albeit for a limited period. The limits put on patent duration is a recognition that new knowledge has public goods' aspects. Public goods have two characteristics, they are non-rivalrous and non-excludable. New knowledge has both of these characteristics. It is non-rivalrous because its consumption by one individual does not prevent its use by others. A new computer program can be used by anyone with a compatible computing system. New knowledge is non-excludable because once it is understood by one person, that person can communicate it to others. Patents and other forms of protection for intellectual property provided by governments represent attempts to make that which is inherently non-excludable, exclusive.

The major reason why the outputs of biological research have not traditionally been made exclusive and, therefore, 'privatised' is the ability of biological entities to reproduce themselves. As a result, while exclusivity could be granted by governments, in practice it was impractical to enforce. After a farmer had purchased seed once, he or she could simply hold back part of the harvest and use it for seed in the next planting season. Further, farmers could sell or otherwise share part of their crop with other farmers who could then use it for seed. The monitoring and enforcement costs associated with attempting to enforce property rights in biological products were seen to outweigh the benefits conferred by the property rights.

In most cases, biotechnology has not altered this inherent problem with biological products and a considerable proportion of the evolving changes in agrifood supply chains can be seen as strategic positioning of the owners of the intellectual property in biotechnology to be better able to capture the benefits available. Of course, genetic manipulation at the molecular level may itself provide the ability to privately create exclusivity. The identification of the so-called 'terminator gene', which can prohibit the germination of crop outputs, thereby preventing saving some of the crop for seed, greatly increases the potential to capture any rents arising from investments in research and development. Needless to say, the commercial use of the terminator gene has been controversial with farm groups protesting that this removes one of their major defences against the abuse of market power. Intellectual property rights had long been granted for plant species, primarily flowers, fruits and vegetables that could be bred to not reproduce using conventional (non-biotechnological) methods.

Without the ability to capture the rents from biological research, private firms would not invest in those activities. Governments, however, could see that there were large potential benefits from investing in biological R&D. Given the inherent public goods nature of new knowledge creation, government intervention in these activities could be justified on the basis of correcting a market failure. As suggested above, most governments in developed countries directly created and administered agricultural research establishments and/or provided public funding to the private or university sector for these activities. A large number of assessments of these public research expenditures have been undertaken over the last half century (Griliches, 1958; Nagy and Furtan, 1978). While differences in methodology led to a range of rates of returns being found for public sector investments, one consistent result has been that estimated rates of return have been in excess of private rates of return on investment (Peterson and Hayami, 1977). Further, the results of the assessments suggest that governments were consistently underinvesting in biological research (Davies and Kerr, 1997).

With research primarily produced as a public good, the benefits were divided between producers and consumers. Consumers received their benefits largely in the form of lower prices. Producers benefited through improvements in efficiency that translated into lower costs. The elasticities of supply and demand in the particular market determine the division of the available benefit.

While the public-funding-based research establishment has its roots in the nineteenth century, it expanded rapidly during the long period of consistent real growth experienced by developed economies during the 1950s, 1960s and early 1970s. Sustained levels of real growth meant increased government revenues while the ruling economic paradigm was loosely based on Keynesian intervention. The result was a dramatic growth in the role of the government in the economy. Social policies were put in place whose solvency relied on the continuation of sustained economic growth.

In the late 1970s, in part as a result of the Organisation of Petroleum Exporting Countries (OPEC) oil price shocks, previous growth rates were no longer manifest. Governments, confident that sustained real growth rates would return, turned to deficit financing to continue their social programmes. The result was ballooning deficits, spiralling debt and debt service charges that comprised an increasing proportion of government expenditures. Faced with progressively difficult fiscal realities, governments grudgingly conceded that the sustained rates of growth of the past were not likely to return and began to address their fiscal difficulties directly. Expenditures were reined in. One result was closer scrutiny of all government programmes, including expenditures on biological research.

Research, particularly pre-biotechnology breeding, carries with it a high degree of uncertainty. In times of fiscal difficulty, governments desired a greater degree of surety in being able to select 'winners' *ex ante* than could be provided by the biological research establishments that they were funding (Davies and Kerr, 1997). Governments began to seek ways to shift part of the burden of the risks associated with biological innovation to the private sector. For example, government research stations and publicly funded universities were encouraged – sometimes required – to seek out private sector collaborators or joint venture partners for their proposed research. Private sector partners required, in return, private intellectual property rights in research outputs. This moved the biological research establishment from being providers of public goods to being risk-sharing partners for the private sector. The subsidisation of private risk would still encourage more rapid rates of technological progress than if research was conducted in the private sector, but private firms often had different research priorities than public institutions. In general, their research was targeted more to projects with shorter pay-back periods and a higher degree of expected appropriability. This change in orientation was often difficult for research establishments and their personnel given their long-standing orientation toward the provision of public goods.

Beyond the 'privatisation of risk' motive, governments faced with the need to cut expenditures often viewed their research establishments as soft targets because reduced expenditures in these areas only meant future opportunities forgone rather than reductions in existing service levels. Governments were cognisant that there were opportunities forgone and were willing to facilitate those opportunities being provided in the private sector. At the same time as governments were dealing with their financial exigencies, the technological breakthroughs underpinning biotechnology were coming to fruition and private firms could see greater opportunities for profitable research. As a result, governments in developed countries were willing to extend and/or strengthen their intellectual property regimes in the life science area. Given the potential of biotechnology, however, it seems unlikely that governments would have been willing to expand their public research establishments sufficiently to support the current level of research activity in biotechnology even if they had not been giving priority to fiscal management.

The initial stage of commercial biotechnology research is predominately laboratory-based and does not require a large-scale research establishment. Given that the technology was new, it could be characterised as high risk but with potential high returns. With scientific knowledge being far from complete and with the rapid advancement of knowledge and the technologies needed to support it, biotechnology became a vehicle for venture capital and ripe for highly speculative investments. Along with high risk came a high propensity for failure. Small biotechnology companies, similar to small software companies in the computer industry, do not have the resources to carry their innovations to commercialisation. Instead, they only wish to develop a 'winner' whose rights, possibly along with the innovative firm's human capital, can be sold to another firm with the resources to commercialise the innovation. Most of the attention pertaining to research in biotechnology has focused on these second stage firms because they have tended to be large and operate in relatively concentrated industries. As a result, there are concerns that market power can be used to extract additional rents from innovations that can be characterised as public goods. Further, there is an ongoing controversy in economics as to whether market power and industry concentration increases or inhibits innovation (Arrow, 1962; Jorde and Teece, 1992; Mansfield, 1986).

While small venture capital biotechnology research firms remain a significant and important part of the innovative process in biotechnology, the large firms are also increasingly involved in both basic and applied biotechnology research (Brennan et al., 2000). The involvement in applied research is simply the natural result of the acquisition of intellectual property from venture capital or university labs, which have undertaken the innovative step. Applied research is required to bring the technology to the commercialisation stage. The movement of the large firms into basic research is, in part, simply prudent diversification as there is no clear answer as to whether innovation is best accomplished in large research establishments or small venture capital facilities. While the latter benefit from innovative activity being freed from the inevitable bureaucracy that accompanies a large organisation, small firms often fail even if they have a good idea because they cannot raise sufficient capital to complete the innovative process. Large, well-funded facilities do not face the same constraints. Further, while internal corporate bureaucratic processes can inhibit innovative creativity, the order they can bring to the process may lead to research proceeding in more logical progressions. There are clear trade-offs and large firms are wise to diversify their research portfolio between acquisition of innovations and self-development.

It may also be prudent to acquire the human capital along with their innovations so that those scientists with proven track records can be employed in-house. In this way the venture capital research system acts as a sorting system for scientists. It also seems clear that many scientists are not comfortable in the entrepreneurial role that is often entailed when working in small venture capital labs. They may prefer the 'calmer' atmosphere of larger research establishments.

Finally, vertically integrating backward into primary research may simply be a defensive strategy in a period of poorly defined property rights. Property rights in life sciences are relatively new. Innovations in biotechnology often require the use of a combination of patented inputs and procedures. In the wake of the aggressive acquisitions and merger activities of the large life science companies there has been a spate of lawsuits that put forth conflicting claims over the rights to the intellectual property embodied in the acquired innovations. Litigation has been costly and slows down the commercialisation of the innovations acquired. To avoid these delays and costs firms increasingly keep more of their basic research in-house.

Innovative activity is notoriously difficult to measure. Brennan et al. (2000) suggest that field trials are a reasonable proxy for innovation. For the USA, they observed two trends during the 1990s. There was an increase in the number of firms conducting field trials as well as an increase in the percentage of trials conducted by the four largest firms. This is consistent with both the spread of a new technology, whereby new firms learn about it, as well as the moves by large firms to gain control of the technology. The four largest firms, despite considerable entry of new firms, were successful in keeping their share of field trials between 60 and 75 per cent of the market throughout the decade. In the latter half of the decade, the four leading firms slightly increased their share of trials while the total number of firms conducting trails tailed off to some degree.

Patents can also be a proxy for innovative activity although they suffer from both pre-emptive speculative activity for technologies whose potential is poorly understood and strategic defensive banking of patents to discourage entry of competitors. Thus, they may overestimate the true extent of innovative activity. In spite of these limitations, patents do provide an indication of activity and insights into the degree of concentration. For example, controlling the enabling technology may be more important than controlling the genetic material itself. Patents on key transformation technologies for grains are controlled by DuPont and Monsanto. DuPont has an exclusive licence for gene gun technology. Monsanto held patents on the use of agrobacterium for transforming grain, although the US Federal Trade Commission forced the firm to give control of some of this technology to the University of California at Berkeley (Brennan et al., 2000). Patent concentration is less extensive in the actual genetic material, for example, in the late 1990s approximately 40 per cent of genes used for pest resistance were controlled by the four largest firms, with the largest firm, Dow, controlling 20 per cent. The top four firms controlled 40 per cent and 50 per cent of corn and soybeans patents, respectively, while this climbed to 70 per cent in tomatoes (Brennan et al., 2000). In the late 1990s, however, the data suggested:

> . . . a dramatic increase in concentration among a few firms in innovation output. Based on these results, it is felt that innovation activity is heavily concentrated among a few firms as a result of merger activity over the last decade (Brennan, 2000 et al., p. 166).

Although it is probably too early to confirm this trend definitively, it would appear that the privatisation of biological research is creating an industrial structure that may be of public concern because the ability to extract monopoly rents expands beyond that expected from the granting of patents to knowledge with public goods' attributes. In particular, there is a dynamic aspect to the private innovation process that may perpetuate concentration in innovation activities.

The final aspect of research privatisation is the involvement of public universities and their partial conversion from being providers of public goods into owners of intellectual property. According to Foltz et al. (2000, p. 624) for the USA:

. . . much of the driving force in ag-biotech research is the creation and utilization of property rights by universities in order to shore-up ever shrinking agricultural research budgets.

As yet, patents are still a small source of universities' revenues. The change in emphasis is important, however, because it has ramifications for the justification of public expenditures on higher education, the impact of commercial priorities on academic freedom, the possible capture of public research establishments by large lifes cience firms and the continuation of the university sector's role as an independent check in the democratic system, particularly as it relates to the prudence of commercialising new biotechnologies. While these broad concerns are beyond the scope of this book, they do point to the far-reaching effects that may result from the privatisation of biological research.

2.2 THE ECONOMICS OF PROTECTING INTELLECTUAL PROPERTY

The development of a new biotechnology-based commercial variety has three phases. The first is the collection of genetic material upon which to search for genes with commercial potential. There are three sources of this material in the case of the development of new plant varieties. These are: (1) landraces – traditional varieties developed and adapted to local conditions by farmers over long periods; (2) wild varieties of commercial crops and closely related weeds; and (3) sources of genetic material which previously had no commercial value. This latter category has become very important with the advent of transgenics and extends to all sources of genetic material – plants, animals, bacteria and so on. There are already large quantities of the first two categories held in the world's international gene banks as a result of concerns over the reduction of biodiversity in the last half of the twentieth century. These are treated as an international public good by international agreement. All three categories can also be acquired through prospecting activities, for example gathering collections.

Once a collection of genetic material is available, modern techniques of gene mapping can be used to isolate genes with commercial potential. This is a new phase in the development of commercial varieties arising from the advent of biotechnology. In the third phase, the genetic material with promising commercial potential is inserted into an existing commercial crop (or possibly a species that had no previous commercial value) and laboratory trials are undertaken which, if they show commercial potential, are moved to field trials. If those trials are successful and the regulatory hurdles for licensing are cleared, then commercial quantities are produced, marketed and distributed. The final phase is similar to traditional plant breeding with the exception that direct insertion of genetic material replaces traditional cross-breeding techniques.

Technological development in agriculture raises the question whether the ideas and information resulting from investments in R&D and other creative activity can be owned in the same way as physical assets. The notion of intellectual property extends the definition of property and ownership to encompass ideas, inventions and creative expressions (Sherwood, 1990). Governments often act, individually or collectively, to uphold ownership over new ideas by conferring intellectual property rights. Copyrights, trademarks and patents are the three most prominent means of protecting intellectual property. Patents are supposed to be used to protect only new products or production processes. The objective of granting property rights is to prevent other individuals or commercial enterprises from unlicensed production of or use of the product or process for the duration of the patent.

Intellectual property has long been controversial in the agrifood sector. At the outset it is important to ask why governments bestow intellectual property rights. The ideas and information that arise from R&D are similar in economic respects to public goods such as national defence (Gaisford and Kerr, 2001). As suggested in Chapter 1, public goods are 'non-rivalrous' and 'non-excludable'. A new technology is non-rivalrous in the sense that any firm can make use of it without detracting from the simultaneous use of it by other firms. Use of information by one firm does not preclude use by others as is the case with private goods. A new technology is non-excludable in that it would be difficult, costly and ultimately impossible to prevent other producers from using it in the absence of intellectual property protection from governments. Public goods, however, lead to a 'free rider' problem. In the case of a new technology, each producer has the incentive to free-ride on the innovations of its rivals because copying a technology (for example via reverse engineering) is typically less costly than performing the original R&D. This dramatically reduces the incentive to invest in R&D.

The protection of intellectual property is a second-best solution to the problem of underinvestment in R&D. Patents afford temporary monopoly rights whereby an innovating firm becomes the exclusive user of the technology. While the temporary monopoly increases the incentive to invest, it does so by introducing a new distortion. In order to maximise profits, a monopoly will supply less than the efficient output. Thus, there is a trade-off; the longer the duration of the patent or copyright, the smaller the underinvestment problem relating to innovation but the larger the undersupply problem relating to production.

The trade-off arising from intellectual property rights can be illustrated using Figure 2.1 for a firm engaging in producing a new commercial product. The demand and marginal revenue curves for a new product that has reached the stage of commercial production are D and MR respectively. The firm must engage in costly R&D prior to the commencement of production but these costs are sunk and unchangeable by the time commercial production occurs. Total production costs, however, vary with output. For simplicity, the production cost per unit of output (that is the marginal and average cost of production) are assumed constant and equal to Pc as shown by the MC, AC curve in Figure 2.1.

First, suppose that there is no patent for the new product and that the products can be copied instantaneously without cost. If one firm were to develop the new product, it would be unable to recover any of its R&D costs as other firms enter and produce the competitive quantity Qc and sell at the competitive price Pc. In this extreme case, there would be not be any R & D because no firm would want to be the first to innovate. Nevertheless, the innovation is socially beneficial provided that the present value of the consumer surplus (A + B + C dollars) in perpetuity exceeds the costs of R&D.

Now suppose that patent protection is introduced so that an innovating firm will maximise profits by producing Qm and selling at price Pm. Its revenue exceeds its production costs by A dollars. The firm's *ex ante* decision prior to engaging in research and development activities is then: Proceed with R&D if:

$$\sum_{t=1}^{T} \frac{E(A)}{(1+r)^t} > R + D$$

Do not proceed with R & D if:

$$\sum_{t=1}^{T} \frac{E(A)}{(1+r)^t} < R + D$$

(2.1)

Where:

E (A) is the expected value of the monopoly rents from the new product prior to the investment in R&D;

R + D are expenditures for research and development of this new product;

r is the appropriate interest rate;

T is the duration of the patent or the length of the product's life cycle, whichever is shorter.

If the product life cycle is longer than the duration of the patent, then there will be a greater incentive to invest the longer the period for which the patent is granted. Innovation, while socially beneficial if the present value of A + B + C exceeds R + D costs, would not proceed if R + D costs exceed the present value of E (A).

Since the monopolist receives A dollars per period and the new consumer surplus is C dollars per period, the total surplus is A + C dollars per period over the life of the patent. While this is clearly better than nothing at all, it remains inefficient. As long as the product life cycle exceeds the duration of the patent, after the patent expires and other firms enter, industry output will rise to Qc and price will fall to Pc and the consumer surplus will increase to A + B + C dollars per period.

This classic trade-off associated with intellectual property protection can be put into the context of modern agricultural biotechnology. Let us start with a firm in the third phase of developing a new biotechnological product. Currently, there are two types of biotechnology product. The 'first generation' biotechnology products have improved agronomic properties but do not have distinguishable attributes valued by consumers. 'Second generation' biotechnology products have attributes valued by consumers. First generation biotechnology products can be examined using Figure 2.2. Prior to the innovation, a non-genetically modified variety exists and we assume that it is produced competitively. The price is Po. If a successful product with superior agronomic performance is developed, production costs will fall, from MCo = ACo to MCn = ACn. Depending on the demand

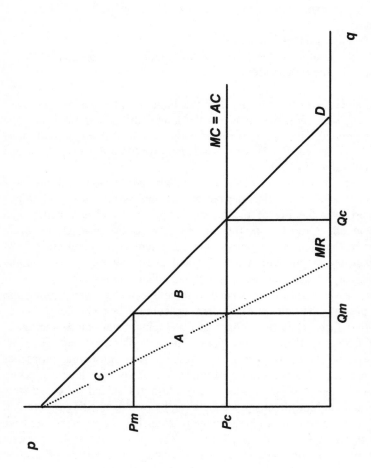

Figure 2.1 – Intellectual property rights

curve's properties over the segment between the cost of the existing variety and the new variety, if the firm is granted intellectual property rights it will price its product to maximise profits somewhere between Po and Pc, for example a price of Pn in Figure 2.2. It will receive monopoly profits equal to A per period and a distortion of B dollars per period is borne by society to induce the innovative activity. Note that the firm cannot charge a price to users of its new variety that is higher than MCo because farmers still have the option of purchasing the old variety. Farmers using the technology can be no worse off.[1] The decision for the firm *ex ante* to the commitment of resources is exactly the same as in the classical case in equation (2.1) except that A is now defined as in Figure 2.2.

The case of second generation biotechnology products can be explored using Figure 2.3. Prior to the introduction of the new product, there is an existing product (depicted in the left-hand panel) with demand curve Do sold competitively at price Pc. An innovative second generation product has new or improved characteristics that some consumers value more than those of existing products. This represents a new commodity and is depicted in the right-hand panel of Figure 2.3. We assume that this product represents no agronomic improvement, therefore the production costs of the old and new varieties are equal (MCo = ACo = MCn = ACn).[2] Some consumers would switch from the existing to the new variety shifting the demand curve for the existing variety from Do to Do'. If the firm producing the new variety has intellectual property rights it will produce quantity Qm and price at Pm. The increase in society's surplus is A + C per period and distortion B is the cost borne by society in each period to induce the innovative activity. Again, however, the investment choice of the firm is as in equation (2.1) with A defined as in Figure 2.3.

We can now examine the question of extending intellectual property rights or other forms of ownership to the first two phases of the biotechnology process – collecting genetic material and isolating genes. Up to now we have assumed that the firm in phase three could obtain its genetic material as a free public good. If some form of ownership is conferred on natural genetic material, then those obtaining the ownership rights can charge for its use leading to a gene cost, G_c. If patent protection is extended to the products arising from phase two then there will be an isolation cost, I_c, for the firm in phase three to use these products.[3] In this case the *ex ante* decision for a firm undertaking phase three becomes:

Proceed with R&D if:

$$\sum_{t=1}^{T} \frac{E(A)}{(1+r)^t} - G_c - I_c > R + D$$

Do not proceed with R&D if:

$$\sum_{t=1}^{T} \frac{E(A)}{(1+r)^t} - G_c - I_c < R + D$$

(2.2)

Clearly, introducing gene costs and isolation costs reduces the likelihood that firms in phase three will undertake the innovative process. This means that some innovative processes will not be undertaken if these costs exist. For every decision not to invest resulting from the existence of these costs, there will be no ownership revenue for the owners of phase one and two materials. The higher these costs, the less innovation at phase three. Thus, it is important to examine the justification for extending some form of ownership rights to phases one and two.

There is no intellectual property content to phase one – the collection of genetic material (except possibly knowing what plants or other material to collect). These are naturally occurring materials. The issue, however, has often been couched in terms of intellectual property rights – collective intellectual rights for those farmers currently using landrace varieties developed by their progenitors (and possibly in iterative ways by the current generation). The argument has been applied to farmers in developing countries in particular. This seems tenuous intellectual property at best. The goods themselves have public good attributes. When used in biotechnology they are non-rivalrous. Using a gene in one biotechnology product does not preclude its use in another. Further, they also seem virtually non-excludable – it is difficult, costly and, ultimately, impossible to prevent their use by others. While some landrace varieties may remain locally isolated, by now most have been distributed widely – particularly when it is remembered that biotechnology requires only minute amounts. Further, it would be almost impossible to prevent smuggling – certainly requiring the use of scarce resources in developing countries that would far outweigh any benefit.

In a similar fashion, there have been movements to endow countries with ownership rights to their wild varieties, closely related weeds and previously non-commercial sources of genetic material. Again, these sources of genetic material have public goods characteristics. The debates surrounding the provision of ownership rights to naturally occurring genetic materials are almost always couched in terms of 'North–South' (developed-developing country) inequities.

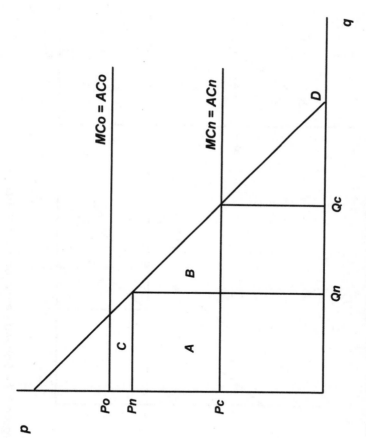

Figure 2.2 – First generation GM plants

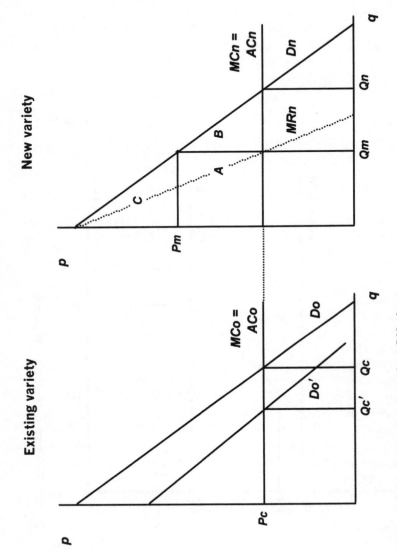

New variety

Existing variety

Figure 2.3 – Second generation GM plants

50

Firms from the 'North' who use this genetic material without paying a fee are often accused of biopiracy. The gene banks of the international centres established to preserve biodiversity are now, ironically, sometimes portrayed as an elaborate plot by Northern governments to steal Southern genetic property. Non-government organisations (NGOs) and others who argue the case of developing countries tend to focus on the areas represented by A in our diagrams – revenues that in many (if not most) cases accrue to (multinational) firms from developed countries. Developing countries receive very little of the global returns from R&D. Giving ownership rights to genetic material to developing countries is an attempt to appropriate some of area A for developing countries. While this may be laudable on equity grounds, as we have seen it simply adds an additional distortion which will reduce the rate of innovation. It also begs the central question of how to redress the imbalance in the proportion of returns to global R&D which accrues to developing countries; that is introducing a new distortion rather than fixing the problem.

The second phase of the biotechnology process (isolating genes) is more complex. Is simply being able to identify something that naturally occurs actually producing anything new? Arguably, it is not. The output of this phase would seem to have public goods' attributes. The use of an identified gene in a biotechnology product (for example corn) does not preclude its use in another product (potatoes) – it is non-rivalrous. Exclusion also seems unlikely as reverse engineering is fairly straightforward. In fact, the now relatively simple technology of gene isolation and its non-rivalrous nature suggests that granting patents could lead to large profits.

For human genes, this process has taken place in the large international publicly funded 'Human Genome' project. For genes of agronomic interest, however, this process has been left primarily to the private sector. In the absence of the foresight to publicly fund this research, property rights have been extended to those isolating genes. The USA, the EU and Japan all have legislation granting intellectual property protection to the outputs of the second phase. This is consistent with accepting a distortion to induce private investment. It adds an additional distortion to the development of commercial biotechnology. Given the potential size of the distortion relative to the costs of isolating genes, extending the protection in this case may lead to large distortionary losses. One suspects that if property rights were not granted in the products of the isolation process, firms in the third phase of biotechnology development would have had an incentive to search directly for genes with commercial value so that they could reap the benefits from owning intellectual property rights in final products. This would have preserved part of the public good aspect by allowing others with an interest in using the gene in another final product access to that gene – albeit with the same costs associated with identifying the desirable genes. If these costs are significant, one would expect private sector open access gene sharing systems to develop to eliminate the cost of duplicating effort.

Legally extending private property rights to biotechnology does not necessarily mean that those rights will be respected given that, in most cases, the products of biotechnology retain the ability to biologically reproduce. To a certain extent, the changes to the industrial structure being observed in the biotechnology sector can be explained as attempts to better secure the rents that should be available from owning intellectual property rights. These issues are dealt with in Chapter 6.

NOTES

1. This abstracts from short-run problems, which could arise if the old variety has been withdrawn from production and there is a start-up lag. The existence of the existing technology, however, makes these markets contestable.
2. Note, it would be easy to incorporate an agronomic improvement as well by lowering $MC_n = AC_n$. This would not change the analysis except to increase the size of areas A and B.
3. Note, the firm in phase two might have to purchase the genetic material from the owner in phase one. This would mean that G_c would be incorporated into I_c. For simplicity we keep them separate. Note G_c and I_c are themselves determined through monopoly pricing. We do not explicitly build their price determination into our model.

3. The environment

3.1 RELEASE AND ADOPTION UNDER UNCERTAINTY

Transgenics represents a fundamental technological change. The ability to move genetic material among different species (squash to rice) or between life forms (bacteria to animals, animals to plants and so on) separates biotechnology from traditional biology where natural barriers (normally) restricted genetic material to the same species. This means that organisms with genetic structures with which we have no experience are being released into the natural environment. Given the complexity of natural ecosystems, it is not possible to know with certainty whether or not the new organisms will interact with those in the existing environment in ways that will have consequences that are undesirable, or for that matter catastrophic. For many products of biotechnology, it is likely to be the case that satisfactory information will only become available once a new organism is allowed to interact with the environment over a long period of time. In other words, the only way to determine if there is a risk to the natural environment is to risk the natural environment.

Laboratory tests, computer simulations and limited releases under controlled conditions can be used to provide information to determine if certain interactions with the environment are within acceptable tolerances, but not all. Some potential interactions will not be amenable to control situations and, further, not all potentially undesirable interactions can be conceptualised *ex ante*. While this is also true for non-biotechnological genetic manipulations, the long experience with many new products suggests that these unknowns are manageable. As yet, there is insufficient experience with biotechnology to provide a similar degree of comfort. Certainly, there are a sufficient number of examples of unforeseen environmental consequences from human activity to suggest that a degree of caution is prudent.

Policy-makers are faced with considerable uncertainty when they make decisions regarding the entry into the natural environment of products of biotechnology. Even though it has been recognised for decades, decision-making under uncertainty lacks transparent and deterministic decision rules with a solid grounding in economic theory. *The New Palgrave – A Dictionary of Economics* (Eatwell et al., 1987) under its *Risk* entry states:

> The most fundamental distinction in this branch of economic theory, due to Knight (1921), is that of risk versus uncertainty. A situation is said to involve risk if the randomness facing an economic agent can be expressed in terms of specific numerical probabilities. On the other hand, situations where the agent cannot assign actual probabilities to the alternative possible occurrences are said to involve uncertainty.

Decision-making under uncertainty cannot be perfect (that is, where mistakes never occur). One needs to be careful to fully characterise a mistake. For example, one might think that simply denying the release of a GMO into the environment would remove the possibility of a mistake because no damage to the environment can take place. However, this introduces a bias into the decision-making because it fails to consider the benefits forgone from releasing the GMO into the environment. These benefits may be both economic and environmental. Of course, a negative effect on the environment can also have economic costs. In a similar fashion, a decision process under uncertainty should not be biased towards release of the GMO by only considering the benefits. Either of these biases can increase the probability of making a mistake. Hence, decision rules that consider both costs and benefits will be superior to those that are inherently biased. Again, in situations of uncertainty, a decision rule that completely eliminates mistakes cannot be devised.

Another desirable characteristic of a decision rule in situations of uncertainty is that the decision process should be transparent and follow a due process to reduce the probability that it is open to political interference or capture by vested interests. In other words, as a system that eliminates mistakes cannot be designed, whatever system that is chosen should be allowed to operate so as to minimise the uncertainties associated with the decision process itself and to prevent bias from creeping in *ex post*.

3.1.1 Potential Environmental Externalities

The potential negative externalities that may arise from the release of GMOs into the environment were discussed in Chapter 1 along with some of the expected environmental benefits. These are summarised briefly here. Currently, the most common modification to agricultural crops that results in environmental benefits is the addition of genes to create resistance to certain insect pests or to tolerate specific herbicides. In terms of pest resistance, the most commercially successful genetic modification has been to transfer genes from *Bacillus thuringiensis (Bt)* to agricultural crops. *Bt* produces toxins that are lethal for some insects. This means that the plant itself kills the pest, reducing the need to use chemical insecticides. The reduced use of chemical insecticides in some circumstances can be seen as bringing an environmental benefit.

In the case of herbicide tolerance, crops such as cotton, corn, flax and canola have been modified to permit them to resist broad-spectrum herbicides such as bialaphos, bromoxynil, glufosinate and glyphosate. Herbicide tolerance enables farmers to use herbicides more effectively, killing weeds with fewer chemical applications – again providing an environmental benefit. Future GM crops are expected to be resistant to major diseases and environmental stresses such as frost or drought. The latter may reduce fertiliser use or the need to irrigate. In the case of the former, the use of fungicides and other agents that inhibit the onset of disease can be reduced.

The potential environmental costs of GM crops can be grouped into three major concerns (Mooney and Klein, 1999). First, there may be evolutionary resistance in target organisms. The continuous use of specific herbicides can lead to an increase in the herbicide-resistant weed population. This is a general problem associated with herbicide use (Holt and Le Baron, 1990). The resistance to a single herbicide may accelerate the process of increased resistance in weeds but there is nothing unique to the gene modification technology for this environmental concern. There is considerable existing information on resistance in weeds so existing regulatory systems should be sufficient to deal with the problem. Insects can also evolve to resist toxins such as those produced by *Bt* and indeed there appears to be evidence that some insects are becoming resistant to *Bt* sprays (Tabashnik, 1994). Sprays incorporating *Bt* are used by organic producers and in integrated pest management systems. If *Bt* resistance became widespread it would reduce the profitability of organic production and the use of integrated pest management systems (Mooney and Klein, 1999). Again, however, resistance in insects is not unique to GM technology with a large number of insects showing signs of resistance to insecticides (Georghiou and Lagunes-Tejeda, 1991).

Second, there is the possibility of outcrossing with wild and weedy related plants. Cross-pollination between GM crops and wild varieties could transfer resistance, which could make these plants more difficult to control. This could lead to altered plant community compositions, changing food availability for species higher in the food chain and reduced biodiversity. These are also problems that can arise with cross-bred plants, but exactly how these changes will be manifest is less well understood because transgenic interactions are new.

Third, there is the possible contamination of 'terminator' genes with other domestic crops. These genes can be added to crops to prevent seed germination. If farmers typically retain some of their crop for seed then cross-contamination could have economic consequences if obtaining commercial replacement seed is more costly. Sterile seeds, however, cannot contaminate the gene pool as the trait cannot be passed on.

Environmental groups have also expressed worries about possible increases in monoculture production and reduced biodiversity. If a particular GM crop proves to be markedly superior to existing varieties and no GM rivals are invented, then less other crops will be grown. Again, this is not a problem that is specific to the technology and could as easily happen in the case of a markedly superior non-GM crop. Another possible environmental concern regarding the release of GM crops into the environment that has received considerable attention in the media is that pest-resistant crops or those genetically engineered to produce pharmaceuticals could kill non-target (for example, Monarch butterflies) or even beneficial insects and fungi (Rissler and Mellon, 1996).

It seems clear that, even on narrow environmental criteria, there are both benefits and costs associated with GM products, hence it would be unwise to concentrate solely on costs. Of course, there are also wider economic benefits and costs that will be important in any assessment. The discussion of environmental concerns also suggests that any assessment of GM technology should focus on the characteristics of the plant itself and the environment to which it is to be introduced rather than on the method of genetic manipulation by which it was produced. The environmental issues do not pertain exclusively to transgenic crops but are also associated with plants bred using traditional methods. As genetic engineering has the advantage of being more precise, quicker and less costly than traditional methods, the pace of genetic innovation is increasing. This means that more resources will have to be made available for testing and approval of GM products.

3.1.2 Modelling Decision-making Under Uncertainty

Isaac (2001) suggests that it is useful to classify concerns into three types of risks: (1) recognisable risks; (2) hypothetical risks; and (3) speculative risks. Recognisable risks are those where there is sufficient information to attach probabilities. In the case of hypothetical risks, there is sufficient information upon which to base a testable hypothesis but the research has not yet been done. Finally, speculative risks are those which can be imagined but for which no hypothesis and/or test can yet be devised. It would seem that most of the environmental concerns relating to GMOs fall in the first two categories. Speculative risks are those where uncertainty cannot be removed.

According to Mooney and Klein (1999, p. 439):

> The economic benefits of GM crops are reasonably well known. However, the costs of undesirable and perhaps irreversible environmental outcomes are harder to estimate. The economics discipline is well suited to assessing tradeoffs and can contribute to development of public policy by providing a rigorous and defensible framework to evaluate costs and benefits associated with introducing GM crops as well as insights into investment decisions under uncertainty.

Following Mooney and Klein (1999), assume that the benefits from the release of a GM crop that accrue at time period t, B_t and some of the costs Cc_t are known with certainty. Some of the environmental costs Cu_t occur with probability P_t. The discount factor is $Dis_t = 1/(1 + r)^t$ where 'r' is the social rate of time preference. The decision rules relating to the release of GMOs into the environment become:

Release the GMO if:

$$\Sigma_t \, Dis_t \, (B_t - Cc_t - P_t \, Cu_t) > 0;$$

Do not release the GMO if:

$$\Sigma_t \, Dis_t \, (B_t - Cc_t - P_t \, Cu_t) < 0.$$

In other words, if the discounted benefits of release exceed the discounted probability weighted costs of release, then the net benefit rule indicates that the crop should be released.

The potential economic and environmental costs and benefits can be estimated using standard methods. Where magnitudes are uncertain, sensitivity analysis can be used to evaluate the importance of the underlying assumptions.

In the case of hypothetical risks where probabilities have yet to be determined or where the risks are speculative, according to Mooney and Klein (1999, p. 441):

> Even without obtaining the objective probability of an adverse event, the economic framework can improve decisions by identifying a threshold probability level, on a case by case basis, at which the net benefits from the release are positive.

Given information on the potential benefits and costs, the framework can be used to determine a threshold probability P^*, below which there are net benefits from the release of a GM product. If P^* is close to 1 and the qualitative likelihood of an adverse event is low, then releasing the crop may result in a positive net benefit. On the other hand, if the qualitative likelihood of an event is high and P^* close to zero, then releasing the GM crop may result in negative net benefits. In this way the likelihood of making a mistake can be reduced. Of course, there will be cases, P^* near zero and qualitative likelihood low, where uncertainty regarding a mistake remains (Mooney and Klein, 1999).

The release of GM crops, however, may lead to long-term instability of local ecosystems, changes in wildlife habitat or in the composition of plant communities – events that might be considered 'irreversible'. According to Henry (1974, p. 1006), an event can be considered irreversible if 'it significantly reduces for a long time the variety of choices that would be possible in the future'. An outcome that cannot be reversed can constrain future actions (Miller and Lad, 1984) and lead to welfare losses over the long term (Fisher and Krutilla, 1974). Unfortunately, the benefit-cost framework developed above does not provide insights into decision-making when irreversibility is present. Mooney and Klein (1999) show that the net present value from planting a GM crop when irreversible environmental damage is present is less than would be the case where damages are reversible. Thus, the GM crop is less desirable. As a result, precaution is prudent. Precaution suggests a degree of bias towards non-release.

3.1.3 Diverging Policy Approaches

Current decision-making criteria vary among countries. In particular, there is a disparity between North America, where GM product releases are well advanced and in the EU where release of GM products effectively has been put on hold. The non-standardisation in decision-making under uncertainty is important because it has considerable ramifications for international trade.

In North America, neither the USA nor Canada has passed specific laws pertaining to the release of GM crops. This reflects a product-based decision process rather than a process-based system. In the USA, the United States Department of Agriculture's (USDA) Animal Plant Health Inspection Service (APHIS) and the Environmental Protection Agency (EPA) are the most important arms of government involved in decision-making. In Canada, three federal government departments are involved, Agriculture and Agri-food Canada, Health Canada and Environment Canada. Prior environmental assessments form the basis of both countries' risk-based approach. Before approvals are granted, risks that GM crops might pose to humans, non-target organisms and the environment are assessed. In the USA, the EPA, under certain circumstances, will undertake a benefits' assessment, but not the net-benefits' assessment described above, to evaluate whether releasing the crop will result in positive economic benefits. According to Mooney and Klein (1999, p. 439), in the North American system:

> One of the major concerns in the release of GM-crops is that off-farm environmental effects of biotechnology will not be effectively internalised in private decisions. Incomplete or non-existent markets for 'environmental services' means that individual production decisions can result in externalities that alter the provision or quality of environmental services and lead to inefficient use of society's resources. These economic consequences are not counted in the decision criteria currently used by the agencies to determine whether or not a GM crop can be released.

Perdikis (2000) has described the US approval as a 'Why not?' system implying a lack of precaution. On the other hand he describes the EU approach to approval as 'Why?'. As suggested above, precaution may be prudent in the case of GM products. Unfortunately, the EU's attempts to operationalise precaution appear to be mired in a system that is biased against release and has neither transparency nor due process. Thus it is open to political interference and capture by vested interests. To be fair, having enshrined the 'precautionary principle' in domestic environmental legislation, the European Commission, the body responsible for devising the mechanism for operationalising the principle, has had great difficulty in coming up with an acceptable system and, as yet, has not put one in place. The 'precautionary principle' is popular with environmental groups internationally because of its bias against changes to the status quo. It is an understandable position for people with strongly held preferences for environmental protection but it is a poor basis for public policy.

The precautionary principle is biased because it only considers potential costs, ignoring potential benefits. As envisioned by some economists, the precautionary principle exhibits large subjective elements. For example, Perring (1991, p. 161) describes decision-making under the precautionary principle as follows:

> . . . to each future state they [decision makers] attach a measure of the potential surprise that they imagine they would experience if that state actually occurred. . . . The set of choice options – in this case the set of policies available to the decision maker – is ordered by an attractiveness function that registers the power of each . . . outcome to command the attention of the decision maker. . . . Outcomes will generally attract greater attention, the smaller the potential surprise they involve and the extent of damage they imply.

To see the difficulties associated with decision-making under the precautionary principle, it is informative to read carefully the discussion by Streinz (1998, p. 421).

> Whereas this [precautionary] principle is recognized 'in principle' at least in some branches, especially environmental law, it is difficult to fix the concrete emanations, the application of the principle in practice. The reason for this is that the precautionary principle should be applied explicitly in situations of recognized uncertainty, when a risk assessment has been made, but could by the limits of scientific recognition not lead to a clearly science-based decision, whereas serious risks which cannot be excluded need preventative ie 'cautious' action. To determine the situations which justify the application of the precautionary principle, and, if decided to do so, to determine the extent of 'caution' are political decisions, even if they may be partly based on scientific evidence. In this context it must be emphasized that the reference on 'science' is not necessarily a reference to objective data and presumptions.

There are no answers as to how much science is enough, what costs to the environment (or human health) are acceptable, when uncertainty no longer exists and so on. With an absence of transparency over these issues, the question arises as to what will be the basis of 'political decisions'. Once decisions have a political element the criteria can no longer be confined directly to the issue of environmental safety. Even more important, the political decision-making process can be influenced by other interests. Again Streinz (1998, p. 421) is instructive:

> It [the precautionary principle] can be shaped to support any cause, when protagonists are arguing about the future, which does not exist except in their imaginations.

A recent European Commission document (Commission of the European Communities, 2000) concludes ultimately that decisions under the precautionary principle will be 'political decisions'.

Isaac (2001) predicts that a regulatory regime targeting speculative risks would result in no new technology ever being approved because speculative risks can always be found. Until a more balanced and influence-free method of integrating precaution into decision-making regarding the release of GMs into the environment is developed, it will be difficult to resolve a range of issues pertaining to biotechnology and the environment.

3.2   BIOTECHNOLOGY AS A NEGATIVE PUBLIC GOOD

Naturally enough, environmental concerns relating to biotechnology centre on the release of GMOs into the environment. This means that the main focal point for these concerns is in the agricultural domain at the farm level rather than the upstream biotechnology firms. By contrast, the consumer and ethical concerns discussed in Chapters 4 and 5 may be more broadly based and also implicate biotechnology applications in medicine and even the innovative activities of biotech firms themselves.

Agricultural production that utilises GMOs may lead to adverse or beneficial effects on the environment that do not go through the market. Such non-market effects are known as 'externalities' and they give rise to 'external costs' or 'external benefits'. It should be emphasised that we will be considering environmental costs, and subsequently benefits, that are truly external to firms, such as perceived threats to biodiversity or anticipated harm to Monarch butterflies. For example, consider the case where the use of genetically modified (*Bt*) corn threatens Monarch butterfly populations, which are valued by the public. The costs of higher butterfly mortality to a single firm resulting from its own application of *Bt* corn will be negligible in comparison to costs that can be imputed to society as a whole. Consequently, any profit-maximising firm will ignore the external costs associated with damaging butterfly populations in its decision-making.

It should be emphasised that many environmental costs and benefits are internal to the firm. Consider the case where the use of a pest-resistant GM crop leads to fewer chemical applications and less use of machinery on the land. This crop may confer benefits, in terms of reduced soil erosion. This potential benefit from using a GM product, however, is largely internal to the firm. That is, a farm operator will take into account the benefits of reduced soil erosion because of the resulting effect on land values. These capital gains on land will be directly reaped when the operator is also the land owner. Even if the operator is not the land owner, land rents stand to be higher when the GM product is used, given full information. Analogously, if the use of a GM product were to reduce land values, the environmental costs would be internal to firms.

3.2.1 Aggregate GMO Output as a Negative Public Good

Clearly, we need to be able to understand how external environmental costs or benefits are determined. From an economic standpoint, the environment can be seen as an array of interconnected amenities or naturally occurring pure and impure public goods. As suggested in the previous chapter, pure public goods are defined to be fully non-rivalrous and non-excludable. Many aspects of environmental amenities such as access to clean air are almost completely non-rivalrous in that one person's use or 'consumption' does not detract from use by other people. Similarly, access to the air is also virtually non-excludable in the sense that no individual can be prevented from consuming it. Other aspects of the environment such as enjoyment of a beach or scenic walkway may not be fully non-rivalrous in that they are subject to congestion, particularly at high levels of multiple use. The beach and scenic walk may also be subject to exclusion by various costly means.

The quantity of environmental public goods declines with the amount of damage to the environment and increases with the amount of damage abatement. Thus, if the agricultural use of GMOs causes environmental damage, it reduces the quantity of environmental public goods and the damage itself can be seen as negative public good or a 'public bad'. In the next section we analyse other situations in which the application of GMOs may confer environmental benefits and, thus, be a positive public good. In situations of either type, the extent of environmental impact will typically depend on the particular GMO and its aggregate input and/or output level in agricultural use. Other features, such as the geographic concentration of agricultural applications of a GMO or its interaction with other GMOs may also be important in the determination of environmental damage. Nonetheless, for clarity we will assume that environmental damage is simply an increasing function of aggregate or sector-wide GM food output.

Since each individual potentially values the environment, each individual is potentially adversely affected by the aggregate output of the GMO when the environment is damaged. Since each individual will value an amenity differently, each is therefore affected differently both by damage to the amenity and efforts to mitigate the damage. Nevertheless, both the total and the marginal external cost of environmental damage to society can be found simply by aggregating across individuals. While this is conceptually clear enough, the actual measurement of the marginal and total external costs associated with aggregate GM food production is, in practice, difficult and costly because preferences are not directly observable.

The assessment of the magnitude of external costs to the environment that arise from GMOs must typically be made in the context of uncertainty or more precisely incomplete information. The environmental outcomes associated with a particular GM food, like those of a particular pharmaceutical, may either be certain or be uncertain and subject to particular objective probabilities. The problem, as emphasised earlier in this chapter, is that these objective probabilities are virtually never known when a GMO is first introduced. Further, the degree of informational imprecision varies enormously with the environmental issue at hand. On the basis of laboratory experiments there may be considerable information on the effect of *Bt* corn on butterflies at the time of release, whereas there may be much less reliable information on the long-term implications for biodiversity of introducing an array of GM crops.[1]

At a superficial level, incomplete information does not pose serious analytic difficulties. Each rational person would simply form 'subjective probabilities' over the set of apparently possible outcomes, and each person's external cost at a particular point in time would be based on a personal assessment of expected environmental damage and a personal attitude towards risk-bearing. As new information becomes available over time, individuals would simply update their subjective probabilities in accordance with *Bayes' Rule* with these probabilities eventually converging on their objective or true values (Gravelle and Rees, 1992, pp. 403–4). There are, however, three major problems associated with this formulation of rationality. First, the evidence that people actually adhere to *Bayes' Rule* is mixed at best (Varian, 1992, pp. 190–94). Second, even if people are assumed to behave in this manner, the empirical measurement of external costs is difficult, costly and imprecise. Finally, actual and measured external costs are likely to be highly time-dependent, especially early in a product's life when subjective probabilities may change rapidly in light of new information.

3.2.2 A Framework for Assessing Environmental Externalities

It is enlightening to analyse the economic implications of external environmental costs and benefits from the agricultural use of GMOs in spite of the inherent measurement difficulties. As a starting point, we will defer an array of consumer and ethical issues for treatment in subsequent chapters and focus on environmental issues. More specifically, we will assume that if a GM food is shown to be substantively equivalent to a non-GM food given the available information, all people treat the two products as perfect substitutes. We will also begin with a number of extreme but temporary assumptions concerning the underlying market structure and the environmental externalities themselves:

1. The environmental externalities associated with the production of GM crops are assumed to be negative or harmful rather than positive or beneficial.
2. It is assumed that production of the non-GM crop does not generate negative or positive externalities.
3. All stages of supply chains are assumed to be competitive. In particular, biotech-input suppliers, as well as farm-level producers, are for the moment assumed to be competitive.

Later in this chapter, we will examine the important implications of relaxing each of these extreme assumptions.

When the environment is damaged, the demand- and supply-determined market output of the GM food can be compared with the efficient output of the GM food. The efficient output can be found by adapting the requirement for the provision of public goods, which is sometimes known as the *Samuelson Rule* (see Gravelle and Rees, 1992, pp. 525–8). In particular, the society-wide marginal external cost of environmental damage due to the GM food is equated with the net private benefit of the GM food. The marginal external cost of environmental damage to society, as we have seen, is the sum of each individual's marginal external costs. The net private benefit of the GM food, in turn, consists of the marginal benefit to consumers, represented by the height of a demand curve in partial equilibrium analysis, minus the marginal private cost of GM food producers, represented by the height of the competitive supply curve. Alternatively, the optimum sector-wide output of the GM food can be found where the marginal benefit or demand for the GM food consumption is equal to 'marginal social cost' of GM food. The marginal social cost of GM food production is defined to include both the private marginal costs of the producers and the marginal external costs of the GM food to society as a whole.

3.2.3 Assessing the Impact of GMOs with External Environmental Costs

Inasmuch as people value the environment, the marginal social cost of production is higher than the marginal private cost when the environment is damaged. Figure 3.1 shows a case where the GM food is substantively superior to its non-GM counterpart and, therefore, treated as a new product. In other words, there are objective, scientifically documented characteristics of the GM food that are valued by consumers. Most frequently, such a GM food may have an engineered output trait such as a health benefit or a longer shelf life that is valued by consumers. Alternatively, the GM food could have an input trait that reduces the need for agricultural chemicals and leads to lower chemical residues.

In Figure 3.1, the S'; MPC' curve is the supply or marginal private cost for the GM food, and the MSC' curve indicates the marginal social cost of producing the GM food inclusive of environmental damage. Consequently, the vertical distance between the marginal private and social cost curves represents the marginal external costs of environmental damage associated with each output level for the GM food. As depicted in Figure 3.1, the marginal social and private costs diverge as output increases. Consequently, marginal external costs are increasing in industry output, Q, which is

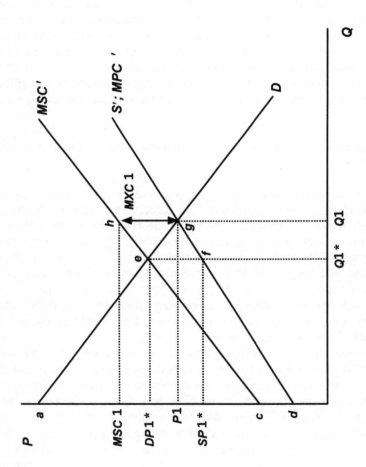

Figure 3.1 – GM food as a superior new product

66

typically the case. Since firms do not pay the external costs, they do not take such costs into account when they make their production decisions. In Figure 3.1, the market equilibrium is at *g* in the absence of intervention by government. Output of the GM food equilibrates at Q1, the price is P1, the marginal social cost is MSC1 and the marginal external cost is distance MXC1.

The total surplus associated with the market equilibrium is equal to a dollar value given by area *a-g-d*, which consists of producer and consumer surplus, minus area *c-h-g-d*, which measures the total external environmental costs. Consequently, the total surplus associated with the market equilibrium is equal to area *a-e-c* minus *e-h-g*. This immediately leads to an important conclusion. Even in the absence of any corrective government action, the introduction of the GM food may be warranted in the sense that it is beneficial to society. Such a gain from introducing the GM food will arise whenever area *a-e-c* exceeds *e-h-g* as it does in Figure 3.1. Equally, if the external damage is large enough that area *e-h-g* exceeds *a-e-c*, the introduction of the GM food would be unwarranted in the absence of corrective government action because it would be harmful to society.[2]

The efficient outcome is at *e* in Figure 3.1 where the output is Q1*. Here, the marginal social benefit given by the demand curve is equal to the marginal social cost. The government could intervene to reduce output to this efficient level. For example, it could impose a so-called 'Pigouvian tax' equal to the difference between SP1* and DP1*. Such a Pigouvian tax is equal to the marginal external cost associated with efficient output (see Gravelle and Rees, 1992, pp. 520–22). With such a tax in place, consumers would pay a demand or consumer price of DP1* and producers would receive a supply or producer price of SP1*.

The government could also issue tradable permits for GM food production equal to Q1*. The market value of a permit for the production of a single unit of the GM food would be equal to the marginal external cost at the optimum given by the difference between SP1* and DP1*. Once again, the demand price would be DP1* and the supply price would be SP1*. Either the Pigouvian tax or tradable permits are superior to the direct regulation of output because they allow more cost-efficient farms an opportunity to produce additional output, while less efficient farms produce less. In essence, direct regulation amounts to a system of non-tradable permits. The total surplus associated with the efficient output of the GM food is equal to a dollar value of area *a-e-f-d* of producer surplus, consumer surplus and government (or permit) revenue minus *c-e-f-d* in total external costs associated with environmental damage. Consequently, the corrective action yields a total surplus of area *a-e-c* dollars generating a potential efficiency gain of area *e-h-g* dollars over the market outcome. Note that the total surplus is enclosed by the demand and marginal social cost curves in the presence of the GM food externality.

This analysis implies that the presence of external costs associated with GMO release into the environment does not create an automatic case for prohibiting GM food production. While the efficient output of the GM food is less than the market output, the efficient output typically remains positive. Larger marginal external costs do lead to smaller efficient output levels by shifting the marginal social cost curve upwards. Nevertheless, the intercept of the MSC' curve given by *c* would have to rise up to or above the intercept of the demand curve at *a* in order to warrant a ban on GM food production or a prohibitive Pigouvian tax of *a* minus *d*.

If there were no transaction costs associated with government intervention, the introduction of higher quality GM foods accompanied by appropriate corrective measures would typically be beneficial. In reality, however, we have seen that there are likely to be significant transaction costs associated with designing, implementing and administering the corrective policy. If the transaction costs associated with corrective policy are in excess of area *e-h-g* dollars, then it is counterproductive for the government to attempt to correct the externality. If it is also the case that area *e-h-g* exceeds area *a-e-c* then society would have been better of without the introduction of the GM food.

Figure 3.2 examines the case where the GM food and its non-GM counterpart are substantively equivalent and treated as perfect substitutes by consumers. Prior to the introduction of the GM food there is an initial equilibrium at point *n* where the demand curve, D, and the supply curve S° intersect. We assume that the introduction of the GM food on the supply side of the market fully displaces the production of the non-GM food so that the non-GM food is no longer produced. This product displacement requires a lower resource cost in GM food production so the market supply curve shifts downwards from S° to S'. Consequently, a new, post-GM food equilibrium will be achieved at *g*. The equilibrium market quantity rises from Q0 to Q1, the price falls from P0 to P1 and external costs rise from zero to MXC1.

The introduction of the GM food causes a change in the total surplus from its initial level of area *a-n-b* dollars to *a-e-c* minus *e-h-g* dollars.

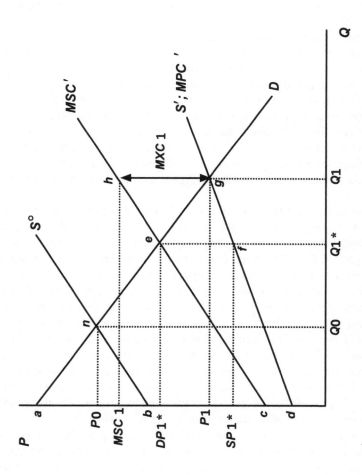

Figure 3.2 - Substantively equivalent GM and non-GM foods

69

Provided that area *b-n-e-c* exceeds area *e-h-g* as it does in Figure 3.2, the introduction of the GM food is beneficial to society even if a policy to correct the distortion is not implemented. On the other hand, if the distortion were larger such that area *e-h-g* exceeded *b-n-e-c* and corrective policy was not forthcoming, possibly because transaction costs rendered implementation impracticable, society as a whole would be worse off after the introduction of the GM food.

Now suppose that a Pigouvian tax of DP1* minus SP1* can be costlessly introduced to achieve the efficient outcome at *e* where the output is Q1*. The total surplus would then be equal to area *a-e-c* dollars. This clearly represents an unambiguous efficiency gain of *e-h-g* dollars over the *laissez-faire* market equilibrium after the GM food is introduced. The key question is whether the efficient outcome in the GM-dominated market is superior to the initial equilibrium prior to the introduction of the GM product. This may or may not be the case. In Figure 3.2, the social costs of production have fallen with the introduction of the GM food because the MSC' curve lies everywhere below the S° supply curve, which also represents initial marginal social costs. Under these circumstances, there is an unambiguous efficiency gain of *b-n-e-c* dollars when the GM product is introduced in conjunction with a Pigouvian tax that addresses the externality.

Social costs, however, could rise with the introduction of the GM product. In Figure 3.3, by contrast with Figure 3.2, the marginal social cost curve, MSC', lies above the original supply curve, S°. Since private costs still fall (that is, the S' curve lies below the S° curve), production may again switch entirely to the GM product. Suppose that the government restricted the output of the GM food to a maximum of Q1*, which is the efficient output conditional on complete product displacement. Due to the higher social costs of production with the GM food, there is an efficiency loss to society of *c-e-n-b* dollars from the introduction of the GM product and the displacement of the non-GM product. Even when the GM product is introduced with a simple corrective measure that seems to address its external costs, society may be worse off. A broadly defined Pigouvian tax that is set at a prohibitive level so as to prevent the introduction of the GM food, however, would be an appropriate corrective measure.

While we have so far assumed that the GM product completely displaces the non-GM product, this is neither necessary nor, as we have seen, necessarily desirable. Alternatively, suppose that the non-GM product

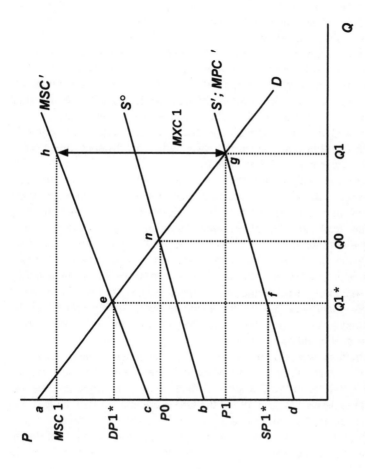

Figure 3.3 – Substantively equivalent products with larger social costs

remains in production after the introduction of the GM product and consider the proportions of the two types of output that are used in the production of any given aggregate quantity. In Figure 3.4 the aggregate output is held fixed at Q' and the proportions of the GM product and non-GM product are allowed to vary. Equivalent diagrams could be constructed for alternative aggregate outputs. In Figure 3.4, the quantity of the GM product is measured moving to the right from Og, while the quantity of the non-GM product is measured moving to the left from On. The MPCg and MSCg curves show the marginal private and social costs of the GM product over the range of possible proportions of the two types of the product. Likewise, the MCn curve shows the marginal cost of the non-GM product, which we have temporarily assumed does not impose external costs.

If Q' were produced prior to the introduction of the GM product, the price would be P0. When Q' is produced after the GM product is introduced, the equilibrium composition of the market is at j where the marginal cost curve for the non-GM product intersects with the marginal private cost curve for the GM product. Consequently, the total output is comprised of Q1g units of the GM product and Q1n units of the non-GM product in equilibrium. Since the two types of product are perfect substitutes for consumers, the price is P1.

The marginal social cost of the GM product, MSC1g, exceeds the price because of the external costs associated with environmental damage by the GM product. In comparison with the initial situation, the introduction of the GM product leads to a social resource saving inclusive of external costs equal to *y-e-c* minus *e-h-j* in the production of Q' units of total output. In Figure 3.4, this resource saving is positive and the introduction of the GM product is beneficial even in the absence of corrective government policy measures to address the external environmental costs. On the other hand, if the external costs were higher, the social resource saving could well be negative (that is, *e-h-j* could be greater than *y-e-c*), and the introduction of the GM product could be harmful.

The efficient composition of the market, however, is at e where the marginal cost curve for the non-GM product intersects with the marginal social cost curve for the GM product. Efficiency requires, therefore, that the total output consist of Q1g* units of the GM product and Q1n* units of the non-GM product. The market overproduces the GM product relative to the non-GM product for any given level of aggregate output. The imposition of a Pigouvian tax on the GM product equal to the difference between P1* and

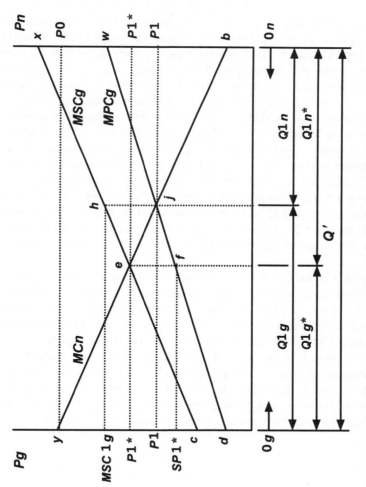

Figure 3.4 – Coexistence of GM and non-GM products

SP1* would generate an efficiency gain of *e-h-j*. In such a situation, P1* would be the price paid by all consumers and received by non-GM producers, while SP1* would be the supply price received by GM producers.

It is useful to conclude this section by briefly considering alternative configurations of Figure 3.4 that would have given rise to complete, rather than partial, product displacement. On the Pn axis, if the intercept of the marginal cost curve for the non-GM product at *b* had lain above the intercept for the marginal private cost curve for the GM product at *w*, then the entire Q' units of output would have been comprised of GM product in equilibrium. On the one hand, if point *b* were also above the intercept of the marginal social cost curve at *x*, then no output of the non-GM product would be warranted on efficiency grounds. This is the situation analysed in Figure 3.2. On the other hand, if point *b* had lain between points *x* and *w*, then some output of the GM product would still be warranted on efficiency grounds even though none would have been produced in the absence of corrective policy. Finally, continue to consider the situation where point *b* lies between points *x* and *w* on the Pn axis, but now suppose that on the Pg axis it is also the case that the intercept of the marginal social cost curve for the GM product at *c* lies above the intercept of the marginal cost curve for the non-GM product at *y*. In this situation, as in Figure 3.3, efficiency requires that no GM production is introduced, whereas in equilibrium the market will be completely dominated by the GM product in the absence of policy.[3]

We have found that the introduction of a new biotechnology gives rise to complex results despite the fact that we began with three rather heroic simplifications. We have seen that society may be better off after the introduction of the GM product even if corrective policies are not implemented or cannot reasonably be implemented. By contrast, even if output is regulated to account for marginal external costs to the environment, the introduction of a GM product may be harmful to society. Thus far, however, there has been a general presumption that competitive markets will overproduce GMs relative to the efficient levels. We now consider some crucial limitations of this presumption.

3.3 BIOTECHNOLOGY AS A NEGATIVE OR POSITIVE PUBLIC GOOD

The presumption that GM crops will be overproduced in the presence of environmental externalities is not robust to variations in any of our initial three extreme assumptions. If a GM product gives rise to external benefits, if the GM product generates lower external costs than its non-GM counterpart, or if the biotech firms that create GMO inputs are imperfectly competitive, then the GM crop may be underproduced rather than overproduced relative to efficient levels. We will consider each of these cases in turn.

3.3.1 A GMO with External Environmental Benefits

Genetic engineering typically focuses on providing direct or indirect benefits to farmers, rather than beneficial external effects for which farmers cannot be charged. Nevertheless, the possibility of external benefits from GMOs cannot be ruled out. While external benefits could simply be treated as negative external costs, it is more conventional to add the marginal external benefits to the marginal private benefits given by the demand curve to derive a 'marginal social benefit' curve such as MSB' shown in Figure 3.5. Since the marginal social benefit and demand curves converge, the marginal (as opposed to total) external benefit declines as GM output increases, as is typically the case.

In Figure 3.5, the initial equilibrium prior to the introduction of the GM product is at *n* where the demand curve, D intersects the initial supply curve S°. The introduction of the GM product displaces the supply curve to S' and leads to a new equilibrium at *g*. This lowers the price from P0 to P1, and raises the quantity from Q0 to Q1. Since the total surplus rises to *c-h-g-d* dollars from *a-n-b*, the introduction of a cost-saving GM product is beneficial to society if it confers a positive externality.

The market equilibrium is inefficient, however, because the prevailing marginal social benefit, MSB1, exceeds the price, P1, due to the presence of external benefits. The efficient output in the presence of the GM product is Q1*, which arises at the intersection of the MSB' and S' curves. At Q1* the total surplus is maximised and equal to *c-e-d* dollars. Since Q1* exceeds Q1, the GM product would be under-produced in the absence of intervention. In the absence of transaction costs, the government could

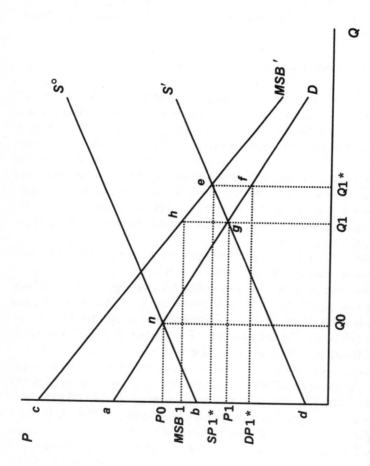

Figure 3.5 – Social benefit of a GM product exceeds the private benefit

impose a Pigouvian subsidy equal to the difference between SP1* and DP1* to correct the externality. In such a case, SP1* would represent the supply price facing producers and DP1* would represent the demand price facing consumers.

3.3.2 The GM Product has Smaller External Environmental Costs than the Non-GM

While there may be a few instances where GM products give rise to true external benefits by improving the environment, there are likely to be many important cases where GM crop production has environmental benefits relative to non-GM production. For example, consider the case where a GM crop requires less chemical use. In addition to the direct benefit to farmers there is an additional external relative benefit arising from less contamination of surface and groundwater than with a non-GM crop.

Suppose that a non-GM crop remains in production after the introduction of a GM counterpart and examine the proportions of the two types of output that comprise the production of any given aggregate quantity. As it was in Figure 3.4, the aggregate output is held fixed at Q' in Figure 3.6. Again, the quantity of the GM product is measured from *Og*, while the quantity of the non-GM product is measured from *On*. The MPCg and MPCn curves show the marginal private costs of the GM and non-GM product, respectively, for the full range of possible proportions of the two product types. Likewise, the MSCg and MSCn curves show the marginal social costs of the GM and non-GM product inclusive of external costs relating to, for example, water pollution.

If Q' units were supplied prior to the introduction of the GM crop, the market price would have been P0, the marginal social cost would have been MSC0n and a Pigouvian tax equal to the difference would have been needed to restore efficiency. After the introduction of the GM crop, the market equilibrium for the total production Q' units is at *j* where the marginal private cost curves intersect. Consequently, the output of the GM crop is Q1g while that of the non-GM crop is Q1n. The price is P1 for both types of product because they are perfect substitutes for consumers. Nevertheless, the marginal social cost for the GM product, MSC1g, is less than that of the non-GM product, MSC1n, because it causes less water pollution. Since the external costs of the GM product are less than those of

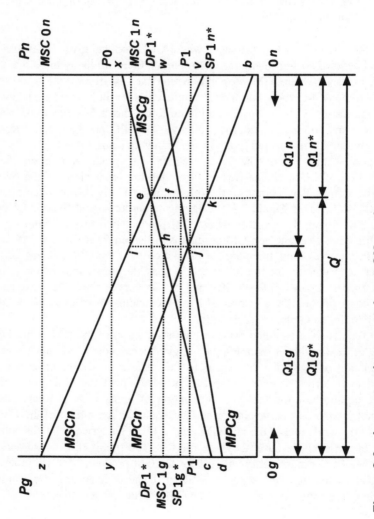

Figure 3.6 – Lower environmental-cost GM products

78

the non-GM product, there is an unambiguous social resource saving of z-i-h-c dollars arising from the introduction of the GM product. Even so, the market underproduces the GM product relative to the non-GM product.

When Q' units of the product are supplied in total, the efficient composition is at point e in Figure 3.6 where the two marginal social cost curves intersect. Thus, the efficient output of the GM product is Q1g* and that of the non-GM is Q1n*. The efficient composition of production leads to an additional social resource saving of i-e-h over that arising with the market equilibrium. The Pigouvian tax applicable to the non-GM product is equal to the difference between DP1* and SP1n* whereas the tax applicable to the GM product is DP1* minus SP1g*. The corrective tax levied on the non-GM exceeds that on the GM product because the marginal external cost associated with environmental damage is larger for the non-GM product. Relative to the non-GM, the GM product merits a subsidy!

Circumstances could easily arise where the efficient provision of Q' units of the product would require exclusively GM production even though some non-GM production persists in the market equilibrium. For example, consider an alternative construction of Figure 3.6 where on the Pn axis the intercept of the marginal social cost curve for the non-GM product at v lies above the intercept of the marginal social cost curve for GM product at x. In such a case, efficiency would require no non-GM production due to its much higher external costs. If the intercept of the marginal private cost curve for the non-GM product at b remains below the intercept of the marginal private cost curve for the GM-product at w, however, some of the non-GM product continues to be produced in the market equilibrium. A more extreme situation would arise if the intercept of the marginal private cost curve for the non-GM at y on the Pg axis happened to be below the intercept of the marginal private cost curve for GM product at d. In this case, only the non-GM crop would be produced in equilibrium even though efficiency would dictate that only the GM crop should be produced.

3.3.3 GMO Inputs are Overpriced due to Imperfect Competition

To this point we have assumed that GM firms supply GMO inputs to farm-level producers on a competitive basis. In reality, this is clearly not the case. Since biotechnology companies have large sunk costs related to R&D that they wish to recoup once the GMO reaches the marketing stage, they are often in natural monopoly situations where overall average costs are declining over relevant output levels. Since overall average costs, thus, exceed marginal costs, biotechnology firms would make losses were they to engage in efficient marginal cost pricing. Of course, if they anticipated such losses, they would not invest at all at the R&D stage. As suggested in Chapter 2, the upshot is that the biotechnology firms cannot be competitive.

The biotechnology industry can be loosely characterised as an oligopoly with differentiated products and open entry. Entry at the R&D stage should drive expected overall profit to zero on 'marginal' R&D projects (that is, the least promising projects actually undertaken) and indeed on marginal biotechnology firms. Intra-marginal projects and firms, however, would expect positive overall profits. Due to the uncertainty over R&D outcomes and future market conditions at the time when innovative activity is undertaken, some products of biotechnology will in fact realise higher profits over their life cycles than were expected, others will earn negative overall profits despite reaching the marketing stage and covering their production costs, and still others will die before leaving the laboratory and without recouping any R&D costs. This industrial structure will be explored in more depth in Chapter 6. For the moment, the important implication is that biotechnology companies intend to, and will typically in practice, sell GMO inputs to farm-level producers at prices in excess of marginal cost.

When farm-level producers buy their GMO inputs at prices in excess of marginal costs, they will supply less than the efficient level of output at any product price. This situation is shown in Figure 3.7. For simplicity, we consider a GM food that is perceived as a new higher-quality product, say because of an output trait such as a health benefit. If the GMO input had been sold to farms at marginal cost, the competitive supply curve for the GM product would have been given by S''. Since the new GMO is, once again, assumed to give rise to external environmental costs, the marginal social cost would have been MSC'' if the GMO input had been priced at marginal cost. Consequently, the efficient outcome is at e where GM production is equal to $Q2^{**}$. Given that the GMO input is actually sold to farms at a price in excess of marginal cost, the actual supply curve for the GM product is given by S'. This yields an equilibrium at g where the output is $Q1$. The GM product, therefore, is underproduced relative to the fully efficient level.

In a frictionless world where transaction costs are absent, a first-best policy solution that results in full efficiency would require two distinct interventions. First, a subsidy on utilisation of the GMO inputs would be required so as to equate price and marginal cost. This would make S'' the

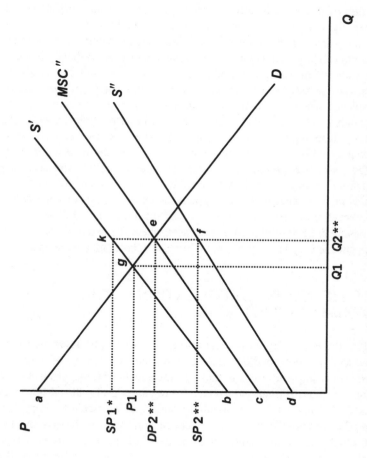

Figure 3.7 – Imperfect competition in the GMO input market

relevant supply curve for the GM output in Figure 3.7. Second, a Pigouvian tax equal to DP2** minus SP2** would have to be imposed to address the external cost of environmental damage. Suppose, however, that a subsidy on utilisation of the GMO inputs cannot be implemented. A second-best solution would be to subsidise the production of the GM crop and, thereby, stimulate some additional use of GMO input. Unless the inputs are used in technologically fixed proportions, however, the GMO input will still be underutilised relative to other inputs. Due to the persistence and indeed aggravation of this input distortion, the second-best subsidy on GM output will be smaller than the difference between SP1* and DP2**.

The analysis of environmental externalities suggests that there are many forces at play. GM products may be introduced when on efficiency grounds they should not be, or not introduced when they should be. Non-GM products may be fully displaced when they should not be or may not be fully displaced when they should be. The sum of market forces is that GM products may be overproduced or underproduced relative to efficient levels. The policy responses to environmental externalities are, consequently, complex and highly case- and time-sensitive. Further, the transaction costs associated with designing, implementing, administering and revising environmental policy towards GM products may in many cases be so onerous as to be counterproductive. When the external costs or benefits are large, however, corrective Pigouvian taxes or subsidies, though fraught with difficulties, may be advisable. In some cases where the external costs to the environment are very large, prohibitive Pigouvian taxes may be needed.

3.4   INTERNATIONAL REGULATION IN THE BIOSAFETY PROTOCOL

Given that there is a degree of environmental uncertainty associated with the products of biotechnology along with the possibility of negative externalities arising from trans-boundary movements of those products, the need for an international agreement to regulate trade in GMOs was recognised. Having an international agreement is particularly important because of differences in both the content of domestic regulations and the pace at which they were being put in place in different countries. These differences in domestic regulatory regimes were bound to arise given the complexity surrounding the design of appropriate environmental policies discussed in the previous sections and differences in the weightings given environmental benefits among societies. It was recognised that international regulation was required to protect the environment, but equally important to prevent environmental regulations from being used as technical barriers to international trade. It was important to find the correct balance between environmental and trade concerns (Phillips and Kerr, 2000).

Normally, the World Trade Organisation (WTO) would be the venue for devising rules for trade but it has consistently insisted that it does not have the expertise required to deal with sensitive environmental issues (Kerr, 2001). As a result, separate multilateral environment agreements (MEAs) have become the vehicle for dealing with the complex issues relating to international environmental management. This approach can lead to difficulties when MEAs develop rules for international trade that are not consistent with countries' trade obligations under the WTO. It is not clear, as yet, which organisation will have jurisdiction if there is a conflict between WTO commitments and MEA procedures. The WTO Committee on the Environment has been studying the issue but has yet to arrive at a determination. The relationship among international agreements continues to be a subject of debate in the international law literature (for example see Mavroidis, 2000; Palmeter and Mavroidis, 1998; Trachtman, 1999). The Biosafety Protocol negotiated in 2000 to regulate international movements of some products of biotechnology has elements that appear to conflict with WTO commitments, thus, there is little transparency for those who wish to engage in international commercial transactions in GMOs or for those charged with regulating their import.

The Biosafety Protocol (or Cartagena Protocol) was negotiated under the auspices of the Convention on Biological Diversity (CBD). In June 1992, the CBD was concluded after 10 years of negotiation as Agenda 21 of the United Nations Conference on Environment and Development (UNCED) in Rio de Janeiro (the 'Earth Summit'). The Convention entered into force on 29 December 1993, 90 days after the 30th ratification. The USA did not ratify the CBD. Under Article 32.1 of the CBD; 'a State or a regional economic integration organisation may not become a Party to a protocol unless it is, or becomes at the same time, a Contracting Party to this Convention'. Hence, the USA, the largest commercial producer of GMOs, was relegated to observer status in the negotiations for the Biosafety Protocol (BSP) and is not formally bound by the terms of the Protocol.

The Biosafety Protocol is an MEA that is charged with devising a comprehensive international regulatory approach to the protection of biodiversity. The Protocol establishes rules to manage the environmental risks of trans-boundary movements of genetically modified living organisms. Falkner (2000) argues that the Protocol fails to clarify the relationship between the BSP and other international organisations and agreements such as the WTO. The Preamble to the Protocol states:

Recognizing that trade and environmental agreements should be mutually supportive with a view to achieving sustainable development,

Emphasizing that this Protocol shall not be interpreted as implying a change in the rights and obligations of a Party under any existing international agreement,

Understanding that the above recital is not intended to subordinate this Protocol to other international agreements.

The first paragraph cited above provides no guidance if trade and environmental agreements are not *mutually supportive*. The second and third paragraphs of the Preamble would seem to be in direct contradiction. The *Emphasizing* paragraph seems to imply that a country can refer to existing WTO obligations regarding rules for international trade in GMOs. On the other hand, the *Understanding* paragraph suggests that any rules that the BSP makes regarding GMOs do not have to defer to WTO rules.

The BSP was negotiated by 138 countries over a four-year period. The agreement, which must be ratified by at least 50 countries before it comes into force, provides rules for trans-boundary movements of GM organisms intended for environmental release and for those destined for the food chain.

For living GM organisms (for example, seeds for propagation, seedlings, fish for release), exporters will be required to obtain approval from importing countries. Within 15 days of domestic regulatory approval having been granted for a new GM variety, a country would notify a Biosafety Clearing House with information about the traits and evaluations. The first time that a new GM variety is exported as seed, the exporting country would notify the importing country. The importing country then decides whether to approve the shipment or decline the shipment because of risks identified through a science-based risk assessment. This process is called 'advanced informed agreement' (AIA). Although this seems straightforward, the Protocol includes features that may be the source of conflicts in coming years (Phillips and Kerr, 2000). The most important of these is found in the Preamble where the 'precautionary principle' is formally recognised in the Protocol. As suggested earlier in this chapter, this will allow countries to block imports of a GMO by simply claiming they suspected it might be harmful to biodiversity. This is likely to be in conflict with WTO commitments, which require a scientific basis for trade barriers and a risk assessment to be undertaken (Kerr, 1999).

The framers of the Protocol have attempted to focus it tightly on environmental risks. To that end, trans-boundary movements of genetically modified organisms intended for food, feed and processing (for example, commodities) will be exempt from the AIA provisions. Nevertheless, exporters must label shipments with GM varieties as 'may contain' GMOs and countries can decide whether to import those commodities based on a scientific risk assessment. Furthermore, GMOs intended for 'contained use' (for example, national breeding programmes and research) and GMOs in transit through other countries will not require AIAs.

Successful completion of the Protocol has the potential to influence positively international trade in three significant ways. First, increased trade transparency according to the use of the AIA principle should remove friction in the market. Second, the Protocol should overcome the lack of domestic regulations in those countries with little or no experience with regulating GMOs (Mulongoy, 1997). Third, the scientific risk assessment procedures should increase trade fairness by ensuring that risks to biodiversity from GMOs, whether domestic or foreign, are assessed consistently using credible scientific risk assessment procedures. The effectiveness of this provision, however, is problematic due to the inclusion of the 'precautionary principle'.

The successful negotiation of the BSP can be interpreted as a potential win-win outcome. The global benefit, shared by all countries, is the overall conservation and protection of biodiversity. From the perspective of the biotechnology industry, successful completion of the BSP has potential benefits for further research on and development, adoption and commercial use of GM products because it would potentially increase predictability of market access.

After the agreement was reached, almost all those with an interest in the talks – developed and developing country governments, agricultural producers, biotechnology companies and public interest groups – expressed optimism that the protocol will protect the environment without unduly impeding international trade. Representatives from the 'Miami Group' of agricultural exporting countries – Canada, the USA, Australia, Argentina, Chile and Uruguay – applauded the agreement as providing sustained market access and protecting WTO rights and obligations. The EU and the

Third World Network point to the 'precautionary principle' as a key innovation. Producers and biotechnology companies cautiously support the narrow focus on varieties for intended release. Public interest groups are pleased with the 'precautionary principle' and provisions for socio-economic factors being taken into account in the decisions.

Despite this apparent widespread approval of the Protocol, it will not resolve all the concerns in the marketplace. First, as suggested above, the USA, which is the single largest producer of GM crops, will not be a party to it. Second, most developing countries have little or no experience with domestic biosafety regulation and the Biosafety Protocol provides only limited protection against any adverse impact of agricultural biotechnology. The Protocol does not cover R&D, transfer, handling, testing, use and disposal of GM products; those responsibilities will continue to fall on national governments. Third, the Protocol has not handled all the socio-economic, ethical and consumer concerns as many hoped. Those concerns remain unanswered in any existing international agreement. Finally, there are likely to be disputes that arise from the agreement but it is not clear from the information available how the Protocol will resolve them.

The economic and trade impact of the Protocol depends on how it is implemented. A recent study of the potential impact of the BSP (Isaac and Phillips, 1999) concluded that the trade impact for canola (rapeseed) could be as small as 0.5 per cent of total Canadian exports, equal to an estimated US$6 million annually (with the scope limited to first time shipments of GMOs intended for deliberate release). This impact would rise if countries designate some commodity shipments as seed for potential release. As well, the impact could rise depending on how the mandatory labelling of commodity shipments influences market access. It is possible that some countries may not reject shipments based on scientific assessments but there may be delays because of the large volume of new varieties to consider (Phillips and Kerr, 2000).

The pace of biotechnological innovation is increasing with licensing proceeding apace in North America. For example, Isaac and Phillips (1999) suggest that as many as 408 new GM varieties of canola, involving 54 novel traits, could be introduced in Canada in the near future. Many countries with limited regulatory capacity may be swamped.

The BSP also seems to have provisions that have little to do with environmental biosafety but rather appear to be an attempt to pre-empt broader issues of trade regulations for the products of biotechnology. For example, the provisions in the BSP which extend the mandate of the

Protocol beyond those strictly relating to protecting biodiversity to areas of human health are inarticulately worded and do not clarify how they fit within the BSP's mandate. Article 4 deals with the scope of the Protocol:

> This Protocol shall apply to the transboundary movement, transit, handling and use of all living modified organisms that may have adverse effects on the conservation and sustainable use of biological diversity, taking also into account risks to human health.

All other references to the risks to human health in the BSP are tacked on to the provisions in a similar manner. These provisions might be interpreted as an attempt by those opposed to biotechnology to obtain the ability to inhibit international trade in GMOs through the back door when they have been unsuccessful in obtaining it at the WTO. The potential for conflict with WTO conventions makes it imperative that the question of which organisation take precedent over the other be decided quickly (Hobbs, 2001). Consumer issues and more general trade issues are covered in Chapters 4 and 7, respectively.

While the BSP may be reasonably well designed to deal with issues related to trade in GMOs that will enter agronomic or aquaculture production, they seem poorly designed for regulating trade in GM products that will not directly enter the environment through agricultural production. While the biodiversity mandate of the BSP makes it the appropriate forum for the regulation of the former, it is not even clear that it should have jurisdiction over the latter. Regulations in these areas would appear to relate primarily to trade in goods and food safety, which have customarily been within the mandate of the WTO. The BSP is inconsistent with the WTO in a number of areas. While it is a well-established principle that a country can voluntarily give up its recourse to WTO disciplines, one suspects that this will not always be the case for the issue of trade in GM products. Hence, it is imperative that jurisdictional issues be sorted out quickly because there are many interested parties that have a large stake in the outcome.

NOTES

1. Even with butterflies, information could remain incomplete after laboratory experiments, say with respect to the relative demerits of *Bt* corn versus over spraying with chemicals in the case of conventional corn.
2. There may be further indirect net benefits on markets for substitute and complementary goods. In markets for substitutes, where prices fall, there is an indirect net benefit

because the consumer gains outweigh the producer losses, while in markets for complements, where prices increase, a net benefit arises because producer gains outweigh consumer losses. For clarity we will abstract from these indirect effects throughout much of the subsequent discussion.

3. It is worth emphasising that the supply-side curves drawn in Figures 3.2 and 3.3 are not identical to those in Figure 3.4. The supply and marginal social cost curves drawn in Figures 3.2 and 3.3 are drawn allowing total output to vary but conditional on the initial output being entirely non-GM and the final output being entirely GM. The marginal private and social cost curves drawn in Figures 3.4 are drawn conditional on a given total output but allowing the composition of that output between the GM product and non-GM product to vary.

4. Consumer issues

4.1 WHY DO CONSUMERS CARE?

4.1.1 Evidence of Consumer Concerns

The biotechnology revolution has brought with it growing unease among some consumers. This unease is by no means uniform either between or within countries. The absence of a uniform consumer attitude reflects both consumer heterogeneity and the different forces affecting consumer attitudes in various countries. Broadly speaking, consumers in Europe and Japan have responded to biotechnology more quickly and more negatively than have consumers in North America. An Angus Reid (2000) poll found that consumers in Germany, France and Japan expressed stronger preferences about being less likely to buy a product that they knew contained genetically modified ingredients.[1] Relative to the other countries surveyed by Angus Reid, a larger proportion of consumers in the USA, Canada and the UK indicated that the knowledge that a product contained GM ingredients would not affect their purchase decision. Even in these countries, however, the majority of consumers indicated that they would be less likely to purchase GM products.

Consumer attitudes towards a new technology are constantly changing. Although, initially, consumers in North America appeared to be less concerned about biotechnology, the gap between consumer opinions appears to have narrowed. Einsiedel (2000) found that 72 per cent of Canadians surveyed in 1997 felt that biotechnology would improve their way of life in the next 20 years but this dropped to 63 per cent by 2000. The proportion of respondents feeling that biotechnology would make things worse rose from 9 per cent to 16 per cent over the same three-year period. Interestingly, the term 'genetic engineering' elicited a more negative response. Only 41 per cent of Canadian respondents in 2000 felt that genetic engineering would improve their way of life compared with 54 per cent in 1997, while 33 per cent of respondents in 2000 felt that genetic engineering would make things worse, up from 26 per cent in 1997.

These survey results reflect overall attitudes towards biotechnology and genetic engineering, rather than specific consumption concerns. In the same survey, while the general topic of 'food safety' elicited a high degree of concern among Canadians, concerns about genetic engineering were low relative to other food safety concerns such as the use of chemical pesticides, diseases from animals and bacterial contamination (Einsiedel, 2000). Similarly, in the USA and Japan, concerns over chemical residues have tended to be the more important food safety concerns among consumers than biotechnology *per se* (Hoban, 1999).

4.1.2 What are the Consumer Concerns?

Consumer concerns can be split into four broad groups: specific food safety concerns, fear of the 'unknown', ethical concerns and environmental concerns. Ethical concerns arise among consumers who believe that genetic engineering is unnatural. The patenting of genes also raises ethical concerns over the 'right to own life'. These concerns are discussed in Chapter 5. Environmental concerns were discussed in Chapter 3.

Instead, this chapter focuses on consumer concerns regarding food consumption. As alluded to in Chapter 1, two 'specific food safety' concerns arising from biotechnology involve allergens and the use of antibiotic-resistant marker genes. Some consumer groups fear that, through transgenics, a gene with allergenic properties could be introduced to other food products, for example, the use of a peanut gene in soybeans. A wide range of foods could be affected since soy protein is present in approximately 60 per cent of processed food products. Regulatory systems have recognised this risk and the use of allergenic genes is strictly regulated. In the USA, firms are not exploring the use of genetic material from foods commonly associated with allergies due to extensive safety and testing requirements and other regulatory hurdles. Furthermore, food labelling regulations in many countries require food manufacturers to label the presence of allergens. This is the case, for example in the USA.

Marker genes are used to track the presence of a modified gene. The use of antibiotic-resistant marker genes raised the fear that this would contribute to the growth of antibiotic resistance in humans and in animals (House of Lords, 1998).

While these specific food safety concerns should not be dismissed, by and large, they represent known practices and known risks and are being dealt with by the regulatory systems already in place. More important is the second of consumer fears regarding the 'unknown long-run consequences' of consuming GM food. This concern revolves around the perceived inability of scientists to predict the cumulative effects of consuming GM foods over a long period of time. Essentially, this is a fear of the unknown (Hobbs and Plunkett, 2000).

The fear of the unknown is important, both in terms of consumer opinion, and in terms of the challenge this poses for regulators and the food industry. It is difficult to respond to these concerns with the standard risk analysis approach, which is a three-stage process consisting of risk assessment, risk management and risk communication, since the problem is one of uncertainty, rather than risk. As pointed out in Chapter 3, the economic definition of risk implies that statistical probabilities can be attached to different potential outcomes. Uncertainty exists when there is insufficient information to establish probabilities (Knight, 1921). In the case of GM foods, probabilities cannot be attached to the likelihood of something completely unknown and totally unforeseen becoming a problem in the future – yet, this lies at the heart of consumer food safety concerns (Hobbs and Plunkett, 1999). In Isaac's (2001) terms, the risks are largely speculative.

4.1.3 The Origins of Consumer Concerns

The origins of consumer concerns over GM food are complex, but five interrelated threads are apparent: a lack of understanding of the technology; a proliferation of food safety scares; lack of trust in regulatory authorities and in the assurances of science; technology being producer rather than consumer-focused; and the influence of interest groups and the media.

Consumer opinion surveys reveal confusion over the meaning of terms such as 'biotechnology', 'genetic engineering' and 'genetically modified'. In a survey of Canadian consumer opinion in 2000, Einsiedel (2000) found that 19 per cent of those surveyed agreed that the statement 'Ordinary tomatoes do not contain genes while genetically modified tomatoes do' was true, with a further 37 per cent unsure. In an earlier survey in response to the same question, researchers found that 44 per cent of respondents in Germany and Austria felt this was true, with over a quarter of respondents in Sweden, Finland, Ireland, France and Spain also believing this statement to be true (Baylor Anderson, 2000). While these percentages can be expected to change over time as regulatory authorities and the food industry undertake consumer education and activities to improve information flows, misperceptions of this type serve to fuel consumer unease and distrust when new technologies are first introduced.

The fear of the unknown and consumer distrust over new technology has been fuelled by the proliferation of food safety scares in some countries. These events have weakened consumer confidence in the food industry. These fears have been compounded by the perceived failure of food safety regulatory systems to protect consumers. The most prominent food safety scare is the Bovine Spongiform Encephalopathy (BSE) crisis in the UK and other European beef industries. Well-publicised cases of *E. coli*, salmonella and lysteria poisoning in Europe, the USA and Japan, together with the dioxin-contamination scandal in Belgium in 1999 have served to heighten consumer concerns.

Contributing to these concerns are a reduced trust in the regulatory authorities and falling confidence in the ability of science to determine a product's long-run safety among some consumers. Again, this is inextricably linked with the BSE crisis. In the UK, a public inquiry into the BSE crisis severely criticised government ministers and civil servants for failing to react quickly as the crisis unfolded and for repeatedly assuring the British public of the safety of British beef when the available scientific evidence did not warrant such unequivocal safety assurances. Responsibility for food safety in the UK had lain primarily with the Ministry of Agriculture, Fisheries and Food. This was seen as a conflict of interest since the Ministry also represents the interests of the agricultural industry. As a result, a new, independent UK Food Standards Agency was established in April 2000. In other countries government agriculture departments remain closely involved in the regulation of food safety, leading to potential conflicts of interest and fuelling consumer unease and suspicion.

The 'first-wave' of GM products were those which primarily provided benefits to agricultural producers rather than food consumers. The reduced use of agricultural chemicals with some of the input-trait crops should, however, benefit consumers through reducing the potential for chemical residues in food. Arguably, technological change that lowers input costs for producers should also benefit consumers through lower prices; however, the extent to which this is the case depends on whether downstream food processing and retailing sectors are competitive, as was discussed in

Chapter 1. By and large, however, these potential benefits have not been well communicated to, or accepted by, consumers. Consequently, consumers in developed countries are faced with a technological change that appears to offer them little if any benefit while presenting uncertainties over long-run safety. It is not surprising, therefore, that some consumers have reacted negatively to the biotechnology revolution.

As pointed out in Chapter 1, the biotechnology debate has formed a lightning rod for a powerful coalition of interest groups, including those with environmental concerns, food safety concerns and concerns over the influence of a small number of multinational life science firms. The influence of activist lobby groups opposed to biotechnology has been stronger in Europe than in North America. Intense media interest in biotechnology and the negative tone of much coverage may also have fuelled consumer unease. Kalaitzandonakes and Marks (1999) report the results of a 'content analysis' of media coverage of agrobiotechnology in the UK and the USA from 1995 to 1998. They find that media coverage became more negative in the UK whereas reporting in the USA had not changed.[2]

4.1.4 Regulatory Responses

Policies governing the approval and regulation of GM foods differ between countries. One of the most striking differences is that between the EU and the USA and Canada. Both the USA and Canada take a 'product-based' approach to regulating GM foods. Products are assessed on the basis of their safety, regardless of whether or not they are genetically modified. GM foods have to pass a rigorous set of safety tests, just as would a new conventional food product. Existing laws are adapted to accommodate GM foods only if the food is significantly different from anything currently commercially available. The principle of 'substantial equivalence' is applied to GM versions of a conventional product. This principle means that, for example, a GM canola product must be shown to be substantively equivalent to its conventional counterpart in terms of its effect on human health (Hobbs and Plunkett, 1999).

In contrast, EU policy is 'process-based'. GM foods are regulated separately from conventional foods under the 1997 Novel Food Regulation, implying that the risks are perceived to be different. The 'precautionary principle' has become a cornerstone of EU policy towards GM foods. The application of this principle to a new technology is fraught with difficulty since it implies that all the potential risks must be known and quantifiable prior to approval. By definition, a new technology is pushing the boundaries of knowledge, delving into hitherto unknown territory. Had the precautionary principle been applied to the introduction of the motor car, this technological advance would likely have been rejected.

Policies also diverge with respect to whether the presence of GM material in a food should be labelled. While a number of countries have introduced mandatory labelling policies (for example, the EU, Japan, Australia and New Zealand), others rely on voluntary labelling to inform consumers of the presence of GMOs (for example, the USA, Canada). Further discussion of the economic implications of different labelling policies is made in section 4.5.

4.1.5 Imperfect Information

An economic analysis of consumer concerns over GM foods must begin by relaxing the perfect information assumption of traditional neoclassical economics. 'Information asymmetry' arises when one party to a transaction has more information than the other party. It can manifest itself in the form of 'adverse selection' where there is hidden information *ex ante* to the transaction, or in the form of 'moral hazard' where the actions of one party cannot be observed by the other party *ex post* to the transaction. 'Incomplete information' arises when neither party has full information. Both of these forms of imperfect information are relevant for GM foods.

Adverse selection is particularly relevant to the consumer's information problem. For some consumers, the presence (or absence) of GMOs has become an important product characteristic, yet it is not possible for consumers to detect the presence of GMOs in a food either prior to purchase or after consumption. For this reason GMOs are a 'credence' characteristic.

'Search characteristics' are those that consumers can detect and evaluate prior to purchase, for example, the colour of a shirt. 'Experience characteristics' are those that consumers cannot evaluate accurately prior to purchase but can after consumption, for example, the tenderness of a steak. In contrast, consumers are not able to detect or evaluate a credence characteristic even after consumption in the absence of some form of signalling (Nelson, 1970). In addition to GMOs, other examples of credence characteristics include BSE in beef and the production methods under which food was produced, such as animal welfare-friendly or environmentally-friendly production practices.

Information asymmetry exists because the seller has more information about the true quality characteristics of a product than the buyer, where the presence or absence of GMOs is a dimension of product quality. At some point in the food supply chain, this may become a situation of incomplete information, where neither buyer nor seller have full information about a product's GM content. A seed company, for example, would know which of their products are genetically modified when selling them to farmers. There is a strong commercial incentive to inform farmers of this since the GM traits confer a production cost or yield advantage for the farmer or may have value-enhanced output traits. Clearly, this means that farmers should know which of their crops are GM when selling them to processors but, without monitoring and testing, processors have no way of knowing. This is information asymmetry. At downstream stages of the food supply chain, such as the retailer–consumer interface, for example, the situation may be more accurately characterised as one of incomplete information. In the absence of regulatory or industry-driven solutions to the information problem, such as labelling, neither party will have full information about the presence or absence of GMOs. The implications of imperfect information with respect to hidden quality attributes and potential labelling solutions are explored in subsequent sections of this chapter.

Given information asymmetry, there may be complex interactions between demand and supply in the market for food that could contain GMOs. These interactions arise from consumers' expectations regarding the probability of consuming GMOs. These expectations will affect the shape of the demand curve for a food product that could contain GMOs, for example, potatoes, soy, corn (maize) or canola (rapeseed) products. Presumably, consumers' expectations will be influenced by the percentage of the crop that is GM. If 90 per cent of a crop is planted to GM varieties, for example, consumers would have a much higher probability of consuming GM food than if only 1 per cent of the crop were GM. The percentage planted to GM varieties depends on farmers' adoption rates. Adoption is influenced by a variety of agronomic and economic factors, including whether the technology is production-cost-reducing. This sequence of arguments suggests rather unconventional interactions between demand and supply. The shape of producers' marginal cost curves (therefore, an aggregated industry supply curve) may become a determinant of consumer demand through the effect on consumers' expectations regarding the probability of consuming GM food (Fulton and Giannakas, 2000). This theoretical puzzle suggests that there are limits to comparative statics analysis of consumer issues in the economics of biotechnology and a more dynamic approach may provide a productive avenue for future research.

4.2   HIDDEN QUALITY AND LONG TERM FOOD SAFETY

We have seen that over the supply chain as a whole, information is likely to be asymmetric, particularly in the case of an input-trait GMO. While farm-level producers, as well as the biotechnology firms, have full information on whether particular crops are or are not genetically modified, final consumers will often be unable to determine whether a particular batch of a final product contains GM material. Whether or not consumers care, product characteristics involving genetic modification will be hidden in the absence of an effective identity preservation system (IPS) involving labelling and certification. Further, without an IPS, extensive co-mingling is likely as product moves downstream through the supply chain from farms to processors and on to distributors and retailers.

In the absence of an IPS, the available information will only sustain a single blended market and a 'pooling equilibrium'. It is well known that such hidden-type or adverse selection problems tend to generate markets that are dominated by an inefficient proportion of low-quality products or 'lemons' (Akerlof, 1970). As we will see, this proposition can be extended to pooling equilibria involving GMOs and non-GMOs (Plunkett, 2000; Plunkett and Gaisford, 2000). Consumer issues relating to hidden quality problems also have profound trade implications (Gaisford and Lau, 2000; Kerr, 1999), which are examined in Chapter 7.

The asymmetric information problem posed by the advent of alternative GM products potentially could be addressed by an IPS (Hadfield and Thomson, 1998; Hobbs and Plunkett, 1999). A fully effective IPS would lead to separate markets for GM foods and non-GM foods and, thus, to a 'separating equilibrium'. We will investigate the implications of mandatory and voluntary IPSs later in this chapter. We will also consider the incentives to cheat or misrepresent GM products.

To focus on the essential elements of the hidden quality problem, we assume a highly stylised supply chain in which farm-level producers sell directly to final consumers. In other words, we abstract from other stages of production chains such as processors, distributors and retailers, or equivalently we assume perfect pass-through. We relax this assumption in Chapter 6 when we investigate who captures the economic rents from biotechnology.

We will also temporarily impose two additional simplifying assumptions concerning the supply chain that help focus our initial attention on the hidden quality issue pertaining to consumers. First, we will temporarily assume that there is a single biotechnology firm. While this temporary single-firm assumption is clearly a dramatic overstatement, as pointed out in Chapter 1 the sales of the biotechnology industry as a whole are highly concentrated in a few very large firms in spite of there being numerous small suppliers. Second, we will assume for the moment that the single biotechnology firm uses contracts, in effect, to integrate forward and control all farm-level production that uses its GMO input. Although this too is undoubtedly an exaggeration, as will be discussed in Chapter 6, detailed contracts between biotechnology firms and users of their products are common. Of course, if there is a single biotechnology firm, it is effectively a monopolist. Nevertheless, it may follow a variety of pricing strategies that include accommodating a fringe of competitive farmers using non-GM inputs or just pre-empting output by fringe farms. In addition, it may engage in more standard monopoly pricing. As we will see, each of these strategies will be profit-maximising in particular circumstances.

There are three categories of economic agents that need to be analysed in detail. First, and most crucial, there are consumers who themselves cannot tell, but potentially care, whether the product is genetically modified. Second, there are independent farm-level producers who initially produce a non-GM product and who may persist as a competitive fringe after the advent of the GM alternative. Third, there is the biotechnology firm with its forward linkages into GM production. Only after examining consumers, non-GM farms and the biotechnology firm separately and in detail, is it possible to construct a cogent analysis of biotechnology innovation in the presence of asymmetric information.

4.2.1 Consumers

Consumers are diverse. Some consumers have grave concerns regarding transgenics while others are unconcerned. Further, these differences in attitudes arise in spite of the fact that current scientific evidence often points to the 'substantial equivalence' between a GM product and its corresponding non-GM product. The issue from the consumer standpoint, however, is not what is known, but what is unknown. Any anxiety about particular long-term health implications of consuming a GM food or more broadly-based fears of the unknown develops in the context of incomplete information. Incomplete information gives rise to at least two well-founded reasons for differences in attitudes across individuals and countries. First, people have different attitudes towards, and thus costs of risk. Second, in the absence of complete knowledge about the objective probabilities of long-term health outcomes, people may formulate dramatically different subjective probabilities. Gradually as new information becomes available, we might expect these subjective probabilities to be updated by *Bayes' Rule* to converge on the underlying objective probabilities, whatever they happen to be, and thus become more uniform across individuals. In the short term, however, wide differences should not be surprising.

Consider the following example. In the summer of 1998, Arpad Pusztai, an expert on plant proteins found, while working at the Rowatt Institute in Aberdeen, Scotland, that GM potatoes can damage rats' vital organs and weaken their immune systems. A review by Stanley Ewen, a pathologist at Aberdeen University's Medical School, supported Pusztai's conclusions (Western Producer, 1999a). However, in May 1999, a new review by The Royal Society, which is an independent academy of British scientists, indicated that Pusztai's research was flawed in its design, execution and analysis. Therefore, the second review concluded his results were irrelevant (Western Producer, 1999b). In the wake of such scientific controversy, there certainly seems room for a wide spectrum of 'reasonable' consumer reactions toward GM foods in general and GM potatoes in particular.

We will adopt a classification system where group A consumers perceive a GM product to be of lower quality than the corresponding non-GM product at least to some degree, while group B consumers regard the GM and non-GM as perfect substitutes on a one-for-one basis. Notice that group B is homogeneous, whereas Group A need not be. Neither type, however, can distinguish between the GM and non-GM food even after consumption because, as pointed out in the previous section, genetic modification is a 'credence' characteristic. We accept the legitimacy of the different consumer attitudes and avoid the alternative of paternalism (Hadfield and Thomson, 1998; Hobbs and Plunkett, 1999; Plunkett, 2000). For simplicity, we also assume that preferences are not open to manipulation although it is clear that advocacy groups on both sides of the biotechnology issue are attempting to affect the preferences of individuals.

The two-group classification system for consumers is adequate to deal with the asymmetric information problems that arise for input-trait GM products. Output-trait GM products would give rise to complications in quality perceptions because people would have to make quality assessments by weighing costs relating to fears of possible detrimental long-term health effects against known benefits such as longer shelf life or health advantages. On balance, significant numbers of consumers would undoubtedly perceive the GM foods to be of higher quality than the corresponding non-GM foods. Output-trait GM foods, however, are likely to pose far fewer informational issues since they will either be directly verifiable to consumers or be credibly revealed to them through IPSs paid for by suppliers.

For group A consumers, the marginal benefit or marginal utility of consuming an additional unit of the non-GM always exceeds the marginal utility of the (input-trait) GM food although the latter will often be positive. As we have seen, however, the product type is not observable. Consequently, utility and demand will depend on expected (or weighted average) quality. There will be a single market with a 'pooling equilibrium' where both groups of consumers will expect a weighted-average blend of quality. Further, the probability of consuming the non-GM food, which is equal to the expected proportion of non-GM food in any batch of the product, may typically be inferred on the basis of the acreage of non-GM and GM crops planted. For any given quantity of the pooled product, group B consumers are unaffected as the proportion consisting of the non-GM falls, but group A consumers are made worse off and they are willing to pay less. Thus, the demand curve for any single group A consumer shifts downward, reflecting this reduced willingness to pay.

In any population consisting of some group A consumers, market demand will be reduced as perceived quality declines, as shown in Figure 4.1. In this diagram, P denotes the pooled price, Q denotes the pooled market quantity, and θ represents the proportion (or probability) of non-GMs. The demand curve labelled D1 applies when only the non-GM product, which group A perceives to be high quality, is produced (i.e., θ = 100%). By contrast, the demand curve D2 applies if only the 'low-quality' GM food is produced (that is, θ = 0%). Finally, the $D(\theta j)$ curve is applicable when a mix of the two products is produced with θj representing

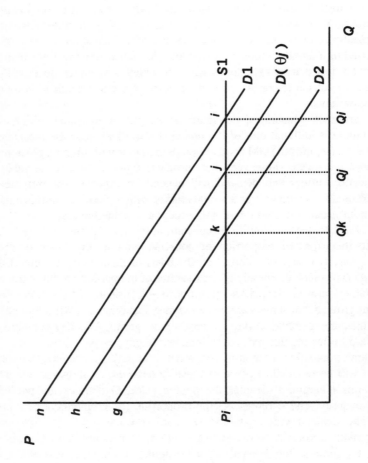

Figure 4.1 – Quality effects in consumer demand

100

the particular proportion of non-GM product (that is, 0% < θ < 100%). The closer is the proportion of non-GM product to zero (100) per cent, the closer a D(θj) curve would lie to the D2 (D1) demand curve.

Consider the impact of a decline in the proportion of non-GM product from θ = 100% to θj given that the prevailing pooled price remains at Pi. Such a decline in the proportion of non-GM product would cause a loss of market-wide consumer surplus equal to area *n-i-j-h* dollars because of the adverse effect on group A consumers. A larger decline in the proportion of non-GM product from θ = 100% to θ = 0 would cause a larger decline in consumer surplus equal to *n-i-k-g* dollars. We call such declines in consumer surplus that stem from perceived declines in product quality among group A consumers, 'adverse quality effects'. These adverse quality effects are modelled more formally in the Appendix to this chapter.

We emphasise that adverse quality effects are asymmetric across consumers since group B consumers are unaffected. If the society consisted of only type B individuals there would be no such adverse quality effects because the D1 and D2 demand curves would be contemporaneous. Further, the magnitudes of these perceived quality effects are likely to be subject to considerable (downwards or upwards) revision over time as all consumers learn more about the GM food and revise the subjective probabilities that they attach to possible adverse long-term health outcomes.

4.2.2 Non-GM Farms: a Competitive Fringe

Producers of non-GM crops are assumed to be perfectly competitive, and we take a long-run perspective that allows for free entry and exit. For simplicity, it will also be assumed that non-GM production is subject to constant costs so that as aggregate output expands or contracts the costs of individual farms do not vary. Consequently, the competitive industry supply curve for the non-GM product is perfectly elastic as shown by the S1 curve in Figure 4.1. Increasing costs and upward-sloping competitive supply curves would entail only minor modifications (Plunkett, 2000). Indeed, we will introduce such supply curves in our discussion of international trade issues in Chapter 7.

It is necessary to comment further on the demand and supply interactions that are implicit in Figure 4.1. Since the D1 demand curve prevails when there are only non-GM products present, there is an initial equilibrium at i prior to the advent of the GM product. Both the quantity demanded and the quantity supplied are equal to Qi in this initial equilibrium, and the price is Pi. If it were the case that θj per cent of the total output continued to be non-GM after the introduction of the GM product, then the relevant demand curve would be $D(\theta j)$, the quantity demanded would be Qj and the quantity of the non-GM product supplied would be θj multiplied by Qj (that is, less than Qj). The remainder of the output would consist of the GM product and be produced by farms integrated directly with the biotechnology firm. On the other hand, if the biotechnology firm undercut Pi by an infinitesimal amount, then non-GM output would be completely pre-empted, the demand curve would be D2, and the entire quantity demanded, Qk, would be provided by farms tied to the biotechnology firm. That is to say, no output would be provided by fringe, non-GM farms.

4.2.3   The Single Biotechnology Firm

The single biotechnology firm faces a two-stage problem. At the initial R&D stage, it must decide whether to invest to create the biotechnology for a new GM product. As an extreme simplification, it will be assumed that the magnitude of the required investment is fixed and the innovation arises with certainty if the investment is made. While these investment assumptions could easily be relaxed, they are sufficient to shed light on the essential aspects of the hidden quality issue relating to biotechnology. If the investment is made, the biotechnology firm will enter the second marketing stage in which it integrates forward to the farm level, produces the GM food and sells it to consumers. Thus, the biotechnology firm chooses whether or not to invest at stage one and how much GM output to produce at stage two.

The biotechnology firm's problem is solved backwards as in all problems of this type. The biotechnology firm solves the stage two output choice problem first, conditional on the investment having been made, and then it can determine whether the stage one activity of investing is worth while. In stage two, the previously made R&D expenses have become sunk costs that do not directly affect the profit-maximising output choice. Since the investment costs are sunk, the biotechnology firm is effectively maximising its net revenue from production or what we could view as its stage two producer surplus.

The maximisation of net production revenue requires that GM output be chosen so as to equate marginal revenue and marginal cost. This implies that it is necessary to examine closely the marginal revenue curve and, thus, the demand curve facing the biotechnology firm. Figure 4.2 shows the price, P2, and quantity, Q2, choices for the biotechnology firm (as indicated by the axes labels). Due to the potential presence of a competitive fringe of non-GM producers, the biotechnology firm will not have any sales at prices above Pi in Figure 4.2. If the biotechnology firm sells at a price equal to Pi it can sell any output up to Qk in Figure 4.1. Consequently, the demand curve facing the biotechnology firm and its marginal revenue curve are perfectly elastic over this set of outputs as shown in Figure 4.2. For prices below Pi in Figure 4.1, there will be no non-GM output. Consequently, over this range of prices, the Db demand curve facing the biotechnology firm shown in Figure 4.2 corresponds exactly with the D2 demand curve in Figure 4.1. Thus, at GM outputs above Qk, increases in output serve to reduce price. Since each increment in output reduces the price earned on all intra-marginal sales, marginal revenue is less than price. As a result, the biotechnology firm's marginal revenue curve, MRb, lies below the demand curve it faces, Db, for GM outputs above Qk. Now consider the situation at the kink in the demand curve, where the price is Pi and the GM output is Qk. In this situation, an infinitesimal increase in output causes a discrete drop in marginal revenue giving rise to the vertical segment of the marginal revenue curve MRb shown in Figure 4.2.

Figure 4.2 shows the case where the biotechnology firm's marginal costs are low and its marginal cost curve, MCb, intersects the downward sloping segment of the marginal revenue curve. In this low marginal cost scenario, the optimising behaviour of the biotechnology firm involves 'standard monopoly pricing'. The output chosen is Qm. The price, Pm, which is set above marginal cost, is not constrained by potential competition by the fringe non-GM farms. Even if the price were raised a little, non-GM farms would not participate. Since the reduction in marginal cost stemming from innovation is sufficient to cause the price to fall below the pre-innovation price of Pi, we will say that this is a case where the innovation has been 'drastic'.

Alternative scenarios are shown in Figure 4.3. Panel (a) shows a situation where the biotechnology firm's marginal costs lie in an intermediate range, and its marginal cost curve intersects the vertical segment of the marginal revenue curve. In this intermediate marginal cost scenario, the biotechnology firm's optimising behaviour involves 'pre-emptive pricing'. Price is set at (or just below) Pi and the biotechnology firm produces Qk units of output so as to just displace the fringe producers. While the price remains above marginal cost, it is clearly constrained by

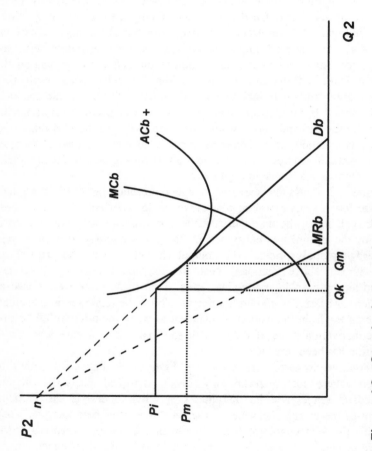

Figure 4.2 – Standard monopoly pricing

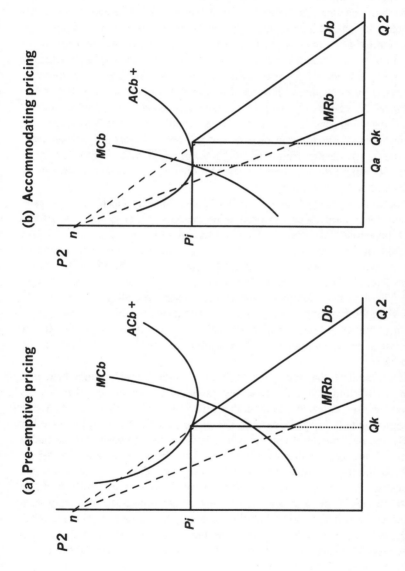

Figure 4.3 – *Pre-emptive and accommodating pricing*

105

potential competition from the non-GM fringe. Finally, panel (b) of Figure 4.3 shows a case where the biotechnology firm's marginal costs are in a high range such that the marginal cost curve intersects the horizontal segment of the marginal revenue curve where price is equal to marginal revenue. In this high marginal cost scenario, the firm engages in accommodating pricing when it maximises its net production revenue at stage two. In particular, it sets price equal to Pi, produces an output of Qa and, thus, allows fringe producers to produce the remaining quantity demanded by consumers.[3] Further, because the supply curve of the fringe producers has been assumed to be perfectly elastic, the biotechnology firm's marginal cost is equal to price when the fringe producers are accommodated. Since the price does not fall below its pre-innovation level with perfectly elastic fringe non-GM supply and either pre-emptive or accommodating pricing, these are cases where the biotechnology innovation can be said to be 'non-drastic'[4].

The biotechnology firm will invest at stage one, if and only if its stage two producer surplus or net production revenue exceeds the cost of the R&D investment in present value terms. In other words, overall profit inclusive of the R&D costs incurred at stage one must be greater than or equal to zero. In Figures 4.2 and the two panels of Figure 4.3, the ACb+ curves include both the production and R&D costs of the biotechnology firm. The diagrams, therefore, show cases where overall profit is equal to zero when the biotechnology firm invests and produces the optimum output. The investment at stage one, therefore, is just worth while. If the firm's R&D costs had been higher, the firm would not have invested in any of the three cases.

If we assume that the situation with a single biotechnology firm is a Nash equilibrium where the next best potential biotechnology firm has no regrets over not entering, the incumbent firm's overall profits would have to be approximately equal to zero as shown in Figures 4.2 and 4.3. In other words, the best potential entrant would have earned negative profits had it entered. This suggests that we place special emphasis on the situation where the biotechnology firm's overall profits are negligible. Then later we can generalise the model and consider equilibria that arise with multiple biotechnology firms and where all but a single marginal firm may earn significant positive profits. For the moment, the situation where overall profits are equal to zero also sharpens the focus on consumer issues. An innovation in biotechnology will be beneficial, if and only if there is a positive net benefit to consumers.

4.3 A SINGLE MARKET WITH HIDDEN QUALITY – WHEN MARKET SEGMENTATION IS NOT POSSIBLE

The analysis of the impact of an innovation in biotechnology when asymmetric information is present requires that we integrate consumers, non-GM farms and the innovating biotechnology firm into an overall framework. If the innovation is to be adopted at all, it must at least partially displace the non-GM product. To accomplish this, the biotechnology firm's marginal cost curve for the GM product must fall below the pre-existing non-GM competitive supply curve for at least some range of outputs. Three different outcomes are possible in the aftermath of an innovation in biotechnology, and the one that will prevail in any given situation depends on the extent of cost saving in production offered by the new technology. If the cost savings are large and the marginal costs of producing the GM product are low enough, the biotechnology firm will entirely displace non-GM farms and engage in standard monopoly pricing. If the cost saving is less pronounced and marginal costs fall in an intermediate range, the biotechnology firm will engage in pre-emptive pricing which just suffices to displace fringe non-GM output. Finally, when the cost saving is small and the marginal costs of producing the GM product are higher, the biotechnology firm will practise accommodating pricing and a fringe of competitive non-GM farms will remain in existence. We now examine the implications of biotechnology innovation when each of these three strategies is the profit-maximising outcome.

4.3.1 Standard Monopoly Pricing

If there is a large cost saving from transgenic innovation and the stage two marginal production costs of the biotechnology firm are sufficiently low, the marginal cost curve of the biotechnology firm will intersect the negatively sloped segment of the marginal revenue curve as shown in Figure 4.2. The biotechnology firm will maximise its stage two net production revenue, and thus its overall profit, by engaging in standard monopoly pricing. Further, the biotechnology innovation can be said to be drastic in that there will be a perceptible price reduction. In Figure 4.2, the price charged by the biotechnology firm is *Pm*, which is below the competitive price of Pi at which the non-GM was initially available. This price reduction from Pi to Pm is also shown in Figure 4.4. As a result of the reduction in price below the minimum long-run average cost for non-GM production, all non-GM farms are ultimately driven from the market.

Since consumers will realise that the market is dominated entirely by the GM product, members of group A, who value GM products less, will perceive a decline in quality. Consequently, the market-wide demand curve in Figure 4.4 will shift from D1 all the way to D2. The introduction of the GM product gives rise to two opposing effects on consumers. On the one hand, area Pi-k-m-Pm dollars is a gain in consumer surplus from the decrease in price. Both groups of consumers benefit from this price reduction. On the other hand, n-i-k-g dollars is a loss of consumer surplus from the deterioration in quality. This is an adverse quality effect on society as a whole that is borne entirely by group A consumers.

If other potential biotechnology firms do not regret their decisions to stay out of the market, the overall economic profit of the biotechnology firm will be negligible. Indeed in Figure 4.2, the overall profit of the biotechnology firm is shown to be equal to zero. In such no-regrets or Nash equilibrium situations, society will be better off in the wake of the introduction of the GM if and only if the beneficial price effect exceeds the adverse quality effect. In Figure 4.4, however, the adverse quality effect is larger than the beneficial price effect because area n-i-k-g exceeds area Pi-k-m-Pm. Thus, the society represented in Figure 4.4 is made worse off.

The biotechnology firm could conceivably be earning positive overall profits in disequilibrium situations where other potential biotechnology firms regret their decisions to stay out of the market. In such situations, however, society could still be worse off after the introduction of the GM product. In particular, society would be worse off if the adverse quality effect outweighs the beneficial effects of the reduction in price and the presence of overall profit. Of course, if the reverse were true, society would be better off.

Regardless of whether society as a whole is better off or worse off, the two groups of consumers are affected differently. Group B consumers, those who perceive no quality difference, are all unambiguously better off after the introduction of the GM product because they do not care whether the product is genetically modified and they benefit from the reduction in price. Indeed, if the society consisted entirely of group B consumers, the D1

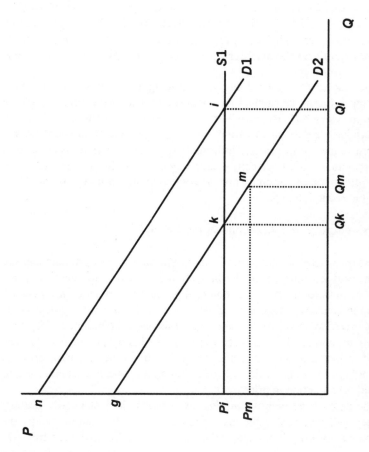

Figure 4.4 – A drastic innovation in biotechnology

and D2 demand curves in Figure 4.4 would coincide, the adverse quality effect would not exist and society would be unambiguously better off after the introduction of the GM innovation.

Group A consumers will generally differ in the degree to which they perceive the GM product to be lower quality than the non-GM. Consequently, some members of group A are likely to be worse off after the introduction of the GM product while others are likely to be better off. Some group A consumers may not be willing to consume any of the product after the GM comes onto the market. Such consumers would be unambiguously worse off because they would experience a large adverse quality effect and no beneficial price effect. Among those less extreme group A consumers who still purchase the product, the adverse quality effect may dominate the beneficial price effect for some, while the reverse will be true for others.

In the case where standard monopoly pricing arises, group B consumers gain, some group A consumers gain while others lose and society may be better off or worse off. The possibility of benefits to individuals and society hinges critically on the fact that the biotechnology innovation is drastic and leads to a reduction in prices. Unfortunately, these beneficial price effects are not inevitable. With perfectly elastic non-GM supply, we have seen that neither pre-emptive pricing nor accommodating pricing leads to a perceptible reduction in price.

4.3.2 Pre-emptive and Accommodating Pricing

In situations where the reduction in marginal cost is less pronounced, the profit-maximising strategy of the biotechnology firm is to select its price and output so as to just pre-empt non-GM production. In panel (a) of Figure 4.3, the biotechnology firm's marginal cost cuts the vertical segment of its marginal revenue curve. As we have seen, this leads the biotechnology firm to choose an output of Qk and set a price at (or barely just below) *Pi*. The non-GM is just displaced from the market. In this case, the innovation in biotechnology can be said to be non-drastic because there is no (perceptible) reduction in price.

In the case of pre-emptive pricing, as with standard monopoly pricing, consumers will realise that the market is now completely dominated by the GM product. As a result, the market demand curve shifts to the left from D1 to D2 as shown in both Figures 4.1 and 4.4. The adverse quality effect remains as before. In both figures, the market-wide adverse quality effect is equal to the loss of *n-i-k-g* dollars. Since the price remains at *Pi*, there is no beneficial price effect. Consequently, the introduction of the GM product is unambiguously harmful to society in the equilibrium situation where the incumbent biotechnology firm's overall profit is negligible and potential rival firms do not regret their decisions not to enter. In panel (a) of Figure 4.3, the biotechnology firm's overall profit is equal to zero. With pre-emptive pricing, society would only gain from the introduction of the new biotechnology if disequilibrium profits accruing to the biotechnology firm were large enough to outweigh the adverse quality effect.

The introduction of the GM innovation, once again, affects different consumers differently. Group A consumers who, *ceteris paribus*, prefer the non-GM product are all adversely affected. Of course, among members of group A, the degree of damage will depend on the degree of distaste for the GM product and, thus, the size of the individual adverse quality effect. By contrast, all group-B consumers who treat the GM and non-GM as identical products are unaffected by the introduction of the GM product. Consequently, if society consisted only of group B consumers and the D1 and D2 demand curves in Figures 4.1 and 4.4 coincided, society as a whole would be unaffected by the introduction of the GM product. In the presence of some group A consumers, however, society stands to be worse off when the introduction of the GM product leads to pre-emptive pricing.

Similar results are obtained with accommodating pricing. Suppose the reduction in marginal cost associated with the introduction of the GM product is even less dramatic, so that the marginal cost curve of the biotechnology firm intersects the horizontal segment of its marginal revenue curve as shown in panel (b) of Figure 4.3. The profit-maximising biotechnology firm selects an output of Qa and charges a price of *Pi*. This choice accommodates the presence of a fringe of competitive non-GM farms that provide for the remaining market demand at the price of *Pi*. For example, suppose that the total output of the biotechnology firm and all non-GM farms is Qj as shown in Figure 4.1. With the biotechnology firm producing Qa as shown in Figure 4.3, this would leave a total of Qj minus Qa to be produced by non-GM farms. If the proportion of non-GM output happens to be θj (that is, the difference between Qj and Qa divided by Qj is equal to θj), then the quality-adjusted market demand curve in Figure 4.1 would be D(θj) and exactly Qj would be demanded at the price of *Pi*.

The introduction of the GM product does not generate a beneficial price effect for consumers when there is accommodating pricing. The decline in the proportion of the GM product from 100 per cent say to θj, shifts the market demand curve from D1 to be D(θj) in Figure 4.1. Since some non-GM production remains in the market, the demand curve does not shift all the way to D2 as it did with standard monopoly pricing or pre-emptive pricing. There is, nevertheless, a market-wide adverse quality effect. *Ceteris paribus*, the adverse quality effect is smaller when there is accommodating pricing and some non-GM production remains in the market than when there is either pre-emptive or standard monopoly pricing and the non-GM production is entirely displaced. In both of the latter cases, the adverse quality effect in Figure 4.1 was equal to a loss of *n-i-k-g*. This is larger in magnitude than the loss of *n-i-j-h* dollars that arises with accommodating pricing.

Even though accommodating pricing and pre-emptive pricing lead to quantitatively different adverse quality effects, the qualitative impact is similar. The presence of an adverse quality effect and the absence of a beneficial price effect imply that the introduction of the GM innovation will make society unambiguously worse off in equilibrium situations where the biotechnology firm's overall profit is negligible. Society would only be better off if there were sufficiently large disequilibrium profits to outweigh the adverse quality effect on consumption. Group A consumers are all worse off, albeit to a lesser degree than with pre-emptive pricing. Members of group B are, again, unaffected.

4.3.3   Biotechnology, Agriculture and the 'Lemons Problem'

The forgoing analysis of hidden quality relating to biotechnology is closely related to Akerlof's (1970) classic analysis of the so-called 'lemons problem' on used car markets. Akerlof assumed that consumers were unable to differentiate between low-quality used cars or 'lemons' and high-quality used cars, which could be described as a 'plums'. For convenience assume that with full information equal quantities of potential lemons and plums would be traded, but the plums would sell for a higher price. Now, when information is asymmetric, assume that consumers are willing to pay the average of the two prices provided that the pooled mix of cars continues to contain an equal number of lemons and plums. The average price, however, will induce an increase in the supply of lemons and a reduction in the supply of plums. Since the proportion of lemons in the markets rises above 50 per cent, consumers will revise the price for the pooled product downwards. The lower price will then induce an even greater proportion of lemons and so on. The general result is that the market is dominated by an inefficiently large proportion of lemons, and it may even be dominated entirely by lemons. In the current context, the introduction of a GM innovation induces a reduction in willingness to pay among group A consumers that is analogous to the consumer response to the increase in the proportion of low-quality used cars.

While breakthroughs in genetics are making hidden quality or lemons problems much more common in agriculture, there are some important agricultural precedents as well. The use of growth hormones in beef production provides one such precedent (Kerr and Hobbs, 2000). There is a hidden quality problem because consumers cannot detect the presence of hormones in beef, except by very costly methods. It is apparent that there were initially, and likely remain, large differences in the proportions of group A and B consumers between North America and Europe. It also seems likely that there are further differences in the intensity of quality effects among members of group A on the two continents. The forgoing analysis makes it easier to understand why bans were implemented on the use and importation of beef produced with the use of hormones and why such may have been warranted in Europe but not in North America. At present, with the information built up through prolonged consumption in North America, long-term food safety concerns may be fading, even in Europe. There remain, however, ongoing ethical issues and issues relating to animal welfare of a similar nature. Ethical issues are addressed in Chapter 5.

The Bovine Spongiform Encephalopathy (BSE) case is another instructive agricultural example of the 'lemons problem' (Loader and Hobbs, 1996). Once again, consumers cannot tell whether or not the beef that they are consuming is from cattle affected by BSE. The initial evidence, which suggested substantive equivalence between beef from normal and BSE-affected cattle, is now being revised and reconsidered. Links with a new variant of Creutzfeldt-Jacob Disease (CJD) in humans, while not firmly established, now appear more likely. Consequently, many people, both in the UK and elsewhere, have revised their subjective probabilities concerning long-term health risks upwards dramatically. Thus, the size of the adverse quality effect associated with the presence of BSE-affected meat is now significantly larger. This, not surprisingly, has led to policy reversals in the UK, throughout the EU and in the rest of the world. Further, the changes in the sizes of adverse quality effects suggest that, broadly speaking, these policy changes have been warranted. Finally, while there are few if any parallels between BSE and biotechnology in terms of the underlying science, the BSE case does highlight the fact that fears of possible long-term health consequences are neither irrational nor unreasonable when there is unknown information. Further, subjective probabilities and the fears that underlie them do not always decline over time.

With respect to the lemons problem in biotechnology, the possibility of adverse quality effects stemming from the introduction of the GM product has far-reaching potential. Whenever the adverse effect from hidden quality borne by group A consumers outweighs any beneficial effect on price, we have seen that society will be worse off. In a more general setting this result will require modification because society may experience beneficial effects of an innovation in biotechnology on the producer side. To clarify how such producer benefits arise, we will introduce heterogeneity in both farms and biotechnology firms in the next section. Despite the possibility of producer benefits, however, the central point will remain unchanged. If the adverse quality effect among members of group A on the consumption side are large enough, a biotechnology innovation will leave society worse off.

4.4   A GENERAL MODEL WITHOUT MARKET SEGMENTATION

It is useful to generalise the production side of the model to allow for additional biotechnology firms and a separation between biotechnology firms and farm-level producers. Thus, there are two important changes. First, we will assume competitive farm-level production for both GM and non-GM products. To produce a GM output, firms have to purchase the corresponding GMO input. Farms, however, will be heterogeneous with respect to their ability to adopt and utilise GMO inputs. Further, some GMO inputs will be better suited to particular farms than other GMOs. Second, we will model the industry that develops and sell GMOs as an open-entry, differentiated-products oligopoly that is akin to monopolistic competition in overall structure (Plunkett and Gaisford, 2000). This industry will be denoted the biotechnology industry.

We continue to assume a highly stylised supply chain in which there is perfect pass-through at downstream stages such as processing, distribution and retail so that it is as if farm-level producers sell directly to final consumers. While each biotechnology firm makes its own particular GMO input, we will assume that all the resulting GM outputs are viewed as perfect substitutes with each other in the eyes of all final consumers. Group A consumers perceive a quality difference between GM and non-GM product even though the GM products themselves are treated as perfect substitutes with each other. The hidden quality problem also continues to exist in that consumers are unable to differentiate between GM and non-GM foods. Consequently, the information structure is such that a pooling equilibrium continues to be the only possible outcome. Before we investigate the ramifications of such a pooling equilibrium, it is necessary to provide a comprehensive treatment of both the farm sector and the biotechnology industry.[5]

4.4.1 The Farm Sector

Since we will continue to take a long-run perspective and allow the entry of biotechnology firms, we also assume that there is free entry into the farm-level production of either the non-GM product or any of the varieties of the GM product. Of course, production of a particular variety of GM product requires the farm to purchase the corresponding GMO. There are constant costs in farming in the sense that the input costs of all non-GMO inputs facing individual farms do not depend on aggregate farm output. We assume that all farms are competitive on both input and output markets. This means that a sufficient number of farms that elect to purchase any particular GMO input exist and that none of them have any monopsony power. Since a pooled product market with a single pooled price will prevail for the non-GM and all varieties of GM outputs, farms will make the decision on which product to produce solely on the basis of differences in costs.

Technology, and thus costs, are uniform across all farms in the production of the long-established non-GM output. Profit-maximisation implies that each non-GM farm produces where price is equal to marginal cost. The zero profit, free entry and exit condition implies that price is equal to average cost. Seen together, these requirements imply that the price earned by any farm producing the non-GM product must be equal to the minimum average cost. Since the minimum average cost does not vary across farms or with industry size, the supply function for the non-GM output is perfectly elastic. In Figure 4.5, the supply curve for the non-GM output is S1 where the price Pi is equal to the minimum average cost.

Farms are not uniform in ability to adopt and use GMO inputs and thus

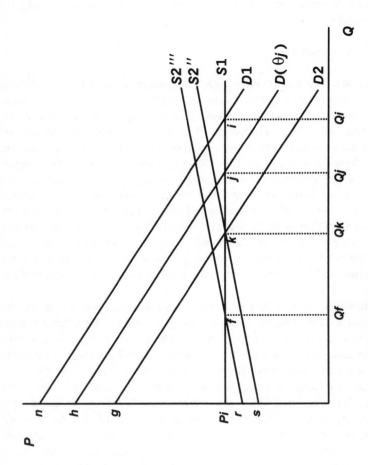

Figure 4.5 – A general model with a constant price

produce GM outputs. In practice, differences in the ability of farms to successfully adopt new technologies are frequently observed. With respect to the current model, differences in costs across farms using a new biotechnology may arise because the GMO is complementary with specific characteristics of human capital, soil, climate, pest infestation and so on. Further, as we will see subsequently, product differentiation across GMOs will mean that particular GMO inputs will be better suited to particular farms.

Each farm that produces a particular GM output will choose its quantity to produce where the pooled price is equal to its marginal cost. At any given pooled product price, intra-marginal GM producing farms will be profitable, but the last farm to enter into the production of each GM output will earn zero profits. As the product price rises, new farms will be able to enter into GM production and those already producing will expand and become more profitable. Hence aggregate GM output will expand, which gives rise to the upward sloping GM supply curves, $S2'$, $S2''$ and $S2'''$ shown in Figures 4.5 and 4.6. Suppose that in Figure 4.5 the introduction of GMOs leaves the pooled price unchanged at Pi but leads to $S2''$ for aggregate GM output by farms. A beneficial producer surplus of area Pi-k-s dollars is introduced by the advent of GM outputs because of the profits earned by intra-marginal farms.

Suppose that all biotechnology firms increase the prices for their GMOs above those that gave rise to the supply curve $S2''$ and the producer surplus Pi-k-s in Figure 4.5. For convenience suppose that biotechnology firms were all initially charging the same price and they all raise their prices by the same amount. As a result of the input price increase, fewer farms will be competitive in the production of GM outputs and those that remain competitive will produce less output. Consequently, aggregate GM output will be lower at each possible pooled price for the product and the GM supply curve will shift to the left, say to $S2'''$ in Figure 4.5. The producer surplus associated with the pooled price of Pi also declines to Pi-f-r dollars.

Before turning to the biotechnology industry, it is useful to probe more deeply into the question of changes in GMO prices by examining the impact on the derived demands for GMO inputs by the farm sector. An increase in the price of all GMOs will certainly cause a decline in quantity demanded for each GMO. Individual biotechnology firms, however, cannot force their industry to act in concert. Consider the two-firm biotechnology industry represented in Figure 4.7. For biotechnology firm 1 (denoted the

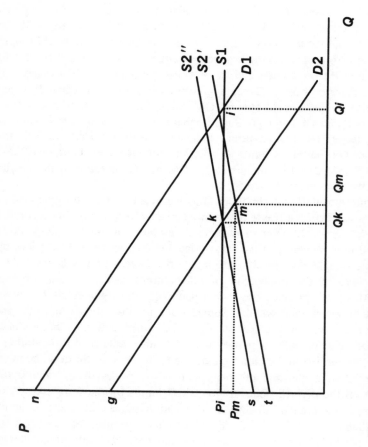

Figure 4.6 – A general model with a price decline

118

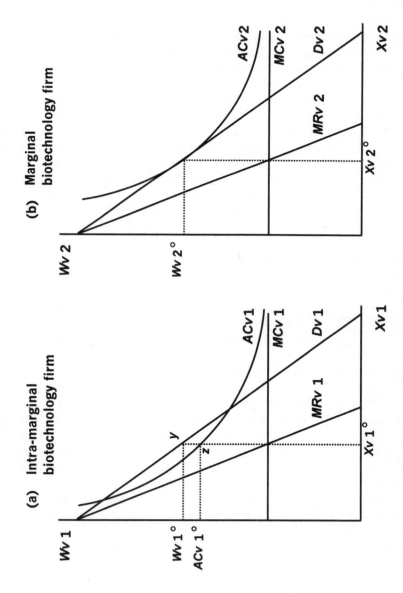

Figure 4.7 - A biotechnology industry with two firms

119

intra-marginal firm) in panel (a), Xv1 represents the quantity of its particular variety of GMO and Wv1 represents the price. Similarly, the quantity and price for firm 2 (the marginal firm) in panel (b) are Xv2 and Wv2 respectively.[6] Now suppose that firm 1 raises the price of its GMO variety, while the price of firm 2's variety remains constant. If only GM outputs are being produced by the farm sector, the magnitude of the decline in the quantity demanded for biotechnology firm 1's variety will clearly be larger when its price is raised alone rather than in concert with firm 2's GMO prices. Nonetheless, the derived demand curve facing firm 1, contingent on a constant price from firm 2, will be negatively sloped, as shown by Dv1, rather than perfectly elastic. This is because GMO inputs are not perfect substitutes for the farms that use them. While marginal farms will move into substitute GMO inputs or perhaps into non-GM production, intra-marginal farms will continue to use the GMO input albeit at somewhat reduced levels. Thus, if a biotechnology firm raises the price of its GMO, the quantity that is demanded declines, but it does not suddenly disappear altogether.

4.4.2 The Biotechnology Industry

Since there can be more than one player in the biotechnology industry, profit maximisation will now involve 'strategic interaction' among potential biotechnology firms. That is to say, the best decisions and strategies of any one firm will depend on the decisions of the others. When economic agents interact strategically, they are involved in what is called a 'game'. In our model, the biotechnology firms will be engaged in a three-stage game. Stage one is an entry stage, which requires an irreversible investment from each potential biotechnology firm that wants to participate in the GMO market. Each biotechnology firm has to decide whether or not to commit itself fully to a costly R&D program to develop a GMO. When a firm invests, then research begins. Stage two occurs at the point in the research process where each of the biotechnology firms that entered must select the particular characteristics that will ultimately distinguish its GMO. Each active biotechnology firm ultimately develops a single firm-specific variety of GMO based on its stage two decision. Stage two, therefore, is seen as the product differentiation stage. At stage three, the biotechnology firms participate in a differentiated-products oligopoly selling their GMOs.

It is necessary to solve the game by considering optimisation at stage three conditional on the entry and product differentiation decisions of all the parties. Knowing how stage three will be played, we can work backwards to determine the product differentiation choices at stage two and, thereafter, the entry decisions at stage one.

From the stage three perspective, the previous outlays on R&D of the active biotechnology firms, which have chosen to enter, have become sunk costs that no longer influence optimal decision-making. We assume that the active biotechnology firms constitute a Bertrand, price-setting oligopoly. Each active biotechnology firm chooses the profit-maximising price for its GMO conditional on any given prices chosen by its rivals. In a Nash equilibrium, no firm will regret the price that it has chosen. Since the GMOs are differentiated across biotechnology firms, the qualitative differences between a Bertrand price-setting and a Cournot quantity-setting oligopoly are minimal.[7] Consequently, we could equally well have chosen to model the stage two as a Cournot oligopoly.

For simplicity, we will assume that there is a high degree of symmetry across biotechnology firms. On the cost side at stage three, all biotechnology firms will be assumed to have the same stage two production cost functions and, thus, the same marginal costs. Further, we will assume that these marginal costs are constant in our diagrammatic exposition. On the demand side, suppose that the participating biotechnology firms happen to have chosen to differentiate their products such that they face symmetric derived demands for their varieties of GMOs and thus have symmetric marginal revenue functions. The resulting symmetry in demands and costs will then lead to a symmetric Nash equilibrium in which each active biotechnology firm produces the same output and charges the same price for its GMO variety. Since it will soon become apparent that such a pattern of product differentiation is an equilibrium outcome at stage two, we examine symmetric stage three equilibria in more depth.

Figure 4.7 is constructed such that the two-firm biotechnology industry is symmetric. For firm 1, the marginal cost curve, MCv1, intersects the marginal revenue curve, MRv1, at the output of Xv1° as required for the maximisation of net production revenue and, thus, overall profits. Since the demand curve for the firm's variety of the GMO is Dv1, the firm will choose a price of Wv1°. Analogously, firm 2 chooses an output of Xv2° and a price of Wv2° for its variety. Given the underlying symmetry, each firm sets the same prices and quantities so that Wv1° = Wv2° and Xv1° = Xv2°.[8] As analysed previously, the demand curve facing any biotechnology firm is negatively sloped because GMO inputs are not perfect substitutes for individual farms. Consequently, marginal revenue is always less than price.[9] While the symmetry of the Nash equilibrium in prices is such that both biotechnology firms will earn the same net production revenue or stage two producer surplus, the overall profitability of each firm will also be influenced by the R&D costs that it experienced at stage one.

When more than one biotechnology firm enters, there will be more than one variety of GMO available. Consequently, each biotechnology firm will have to choose the particular characteristics for its GMO with an eye to the choices made by its rivals. Each firm, in effect, must strategically choose a location in 'product space' for its GMO. While in reality some locations in product space are likely to be more attractive than other locations, we will assume for simplicity that the product space has no inherently favoured locations. A circle arrangement of possible product varieties with one potential farm having a most preferred variety at each point on its circumference is an example of such a product space.[10] If other things such as prices are constant, each farm will be drawn most strongly to the available variety of the GMO that is closest to its most preferred variety.[11]

The nature of the product differentiation equilibrium will depend on whether the non-GM technology remains competitive after the introduction of GM products. If the non-GM output is still produced, the only requirement for a Nash equilibrium in product space locations is that the chosen varieties of the GMO are a sufficient distance apart that each biotechnology firm only competes for buyers with the non-GM technology. If the non-GM technology is entirely displaced, then each biotechnology firm will choose a location that is equidistant from its closest rivals with which it is in direct competition. Consequently, the Nash equilibrium for the sub-game starting at the product differentiation stage will involve symmetric locations in product space. In either of these two cases, the biotechnology firms will face symmetric demands at stage three.

To participate at stages two and three, a potential biotechnology firm must invest a firm-specific amount in R&D at stage one. For each firm, investment is a yes or no decision involving a fixed outlay that will yield a successful biotechnology innovation. The amount that has to be invested in R&D for successful innovation, however, varies across potential biotechnology firms. We will number potential biotechnology firms in sequence from lowest to highest R&D costs. Given the symmetry of stage three net production revenue, this means that overall profitability will always be lower for active biotechnology firms with higher numbers.

Biotechnology firm 1 will have the greatest incentive to enter and it will do so provided its profit as a monopoly would be greater than or equal to zero. Biotechnology firm 2 will also enter if its overall profit after the product differentiation and duopoly sub-game would be greater than or equal to zero. If biotechnology firm 2 would be profitable, firm 1 will remain profitable since firm 1 is always more profitable than firm 2. Similarly, biotechnology firm 3 will enter provided that its profit would be non-negative after the three-firm product differentiation and oligopoly sub-game. Consequently, biotechnology firms will enter in sequence until the last firm, or marginal firm, would earn negligible profit. Potential biotechnology firms with higher entry costs would end up with negative profits and, thus, will stay out of the market. This entry situation is a Nash equilibrium for the overall game, since no firm will regret its entry, product differentiation or pricing decision.

In Figure 4.7, the ACv1 and ACv2 curves show the average costs, inclusive of stage one R&D costs, for firms 1 and 2. Consequently, biotechnology firm 1 is an intra-marginal firm, which is earning positive profit, while firm 2 is a marginal firm, which is earning zero (or normal) profit. Further, the dollar value of firm 1's profit is equal to area $Wv1°$- y-z-$ACv1°$. The overall structure of the biotechnology industry where the marginal biotechnology firm earns zero profit can correctly be seen as an adaptation of Chamberlain's classic model of monopolistic competition (Eaton et al., 1999, chapter 16).

4.4.3 The Hidden Quality Problem Revisited

We can now examine the full impact of the introduction of a variety of input-trait biotechnologies for a particular food product. Depending on the level of aggregate GM production by the farm sector, the non-GM output may or may not still be produced. In the previous single-integrated-firm model, the aggregate output of the GM product simply depended on the magnitude of the firm's marginal cost in integrated production through to the final output. In the current more general model, however, GM output depends on a complex array of forces.[12] Nevertheless, the equilibrium strategies of the firms in the biotechnology industry may lead to any one of three results, which are roughly parallel with the cases of standard monopoly pricing, pre-emptive pricing and accommodating pricing in the single-integrated-firm model. Firstly, the aggregate GM output may be large enough to displace all non-GM output and cause a price reduction for consumers. Second, aggregate GM output could displace non-GM output without causing a price reduction. Third, the GM output could be sufficiently low that the non-GM output remains in production at the initial price. We will examine each of these scenarios in turn.

First, we consider the situation where the GM output entirely displaces the non-GM outputs and causes a reduction in the pooled price of the final product. This situation can be analysed by referring to the supply curve, S2' in Figure 4.6. The initial equilibrium is at point i where the price is Pi and the quantity is Qi. Given that the introduction of GM innovation leads to the complete displacement of the non-GM output, the demand curve shifts from D1 to D2 as a result of the perceived decline in quality among group A consumers. A comparison of the positions of the D2 demand curve and the S2' supply curve at the initial price of Pi, reveals that there is excess supply of the product. Consequently, the product market equilibrates at point m where the price has fallen to Pm and the quantity is Qm, which is entirely comprised of GM products.

In the case of complete product displacement and price reduction, there is once again an adverse quality effect and a beneficial price effect on the consumer side on the product market. In other words, in Figure 4.6 there is a loss in consumer surplus of area n-i-k-g dollars that is attributable to the decline in quality and a gain in consumer surplus of Pi-k-m-Pm dollars from the reduction in price. Now, however there are additional producer side benefits both on the product market and the GMO input market. Intra-marginal farmers gain a producer surplus of Pm-m-t from being able to utilise the new biotechnologies. In addition, intra-marginal biotechnology firms earn positive profits on the GMO input market. For example, biotechnology firm 1 in panel (a) of Figure 4.7 earns a positive profit of $Wv1°$-y-z-$ACv1°$ dollars. Notwithstanding the gains on the production side and the favourable price effect, society could lose as a result of the introduction of GMOs. As it happens in Figure 4.6, there is a net loss on the product market because the gain of area Pi-k-m-t is smaller than the loss of area n-i-k-g. Unless the aggregate profit of the intra-marginal biotechnology oligopolists is large enough to offset this net loss on the product market, society will be adversely affected.

There are several groups of clear winners in the case of complete product displacement and price reduction, and also some losers. On the production side, the intra-marginal farms and biotechnology firms are more profitable while on the consumption side group B consumers are all better off, because they perceive the GM product to be a perfect substitute for the non-GM product. Among the group A consumers, those with individual adverse quality effects that are sufficiently small will also gain. By contrast, those members of group A with larger adverse quality effects will lose. Further, those who no longer consume the product at all, and thus receive no benefits from the reduction in price, will be especially hard hit.

Now consider the second scenario where the non-GM output is completely displaced but the product price does not change. Such a situation arises when the post-innovation GM supply curve is S2″, which is in Figures 4.5 and 4.6. In this case, the product market equilibrium moves from point *i* to *k* because the biotechnology innovation leads to the advent of the supply curve S2″, while the replacement of the non-GM with the GM product shifts the demand curve from D1 to D2. The price remains at *Pi*, but the quantity drops from Qi to Qk because group A consumers will no longer purchase as much of the product. On the consumption side, the adverse quality effect of *n-i-k-g* dollars lost still prevails, but there is no longer a beneficial price effect. Group A consumers lose from the introduction of GM products while members of Group B are unaffected. On the production side, there is a gain of *Pi-k-s* in producer surplus to intra-marginal farms on the product market. Intra-marginal biotechnology firms also earn positive profits. Nevertheless, if the adverse quality effect outweighs the favourable producer effects, society as a whole will be worse off. In Figures 4.5 and 4.6, the gain of area *Pi-k-s* is smaller than the loss of area *n-i-k-g* so that there is a net loss on the product market. Society, therefore, will be adversely affected unless the aggregate profit of the intra-marginal biotechnology oligopolists is large enough to offset this net loss on the product market.

The third scenario, where the non-GM output remains in production, is qualitatively similar to the second scenario but *ceteris paribus* both the magnitude of the adverse quality effect and the magnitude of the gain in producer surplus by intra-marginal farms is smaller. Suppose that biotechnology innovation leads to the GM supply curve, S_2''' in Figure 4.5. Further, consistent with partial displacement of the non-GM output, the smaller decline in perceived quality among group A consumers now shifts the demand curve to an intermediate position such as that shown by D(θj). As a result, the post-innovation equilibrium involves an aggregate GM output of Qf, a non-GM output of Qj minus Qf, and a consumption level of Qj. The adverse quality effect on group A consumers is now *n-i-j-h* and the gain in producer surplus to GM farmers is *Pi-f-r*.

In all three scenarios, the presence of hidden information leads to an adverse quality effect for group A consumers that has the potential to make society as a whole worse off in spite of the existence of producer benefits.

One way to address the lemons problem in the used car market might be to certify or guarantee used cars. Analogously, the lemons problem related to biotechnology could be alleviated through the implementation of an identity preservation system in conjunction with product labelling.

4.5 SOLUTIONS TO HIDDEN QUALITY – LABELLING OPTIONS

The hidden quality problem, which arises because there is unknown information on the scientific front, suggests a possible role for reliable labelling (Hadfield and Thomson, 1998). With labelling as a signal for quality, the market failure caused by asymmetric information can potentially be corrected or at least mitigated, perhaps with little direct government involvement. Reliable labels would transform credence characteristics into search attributes making it possible for consumers to judge quality where they previously could not (Caswell, 1997).[13] To provide meaningful quality information in support of product labels, however, it is necessary to have an effective identity preservation system (IPS) where the supply chains for the GM and non-GM products are separated to prevent co-mingling.

4.5.1 Overview of Identity Preservation Systems

While a fully effective IPS would completely solve the hidden quality problem, such a system would be prohibitively costly. There are two types of cost associated with an IPS. First, inherent separation costs may arise from the loss of economies of scale in operating dual supply chains and from monitoring to prevent inadvertent co-mingling between GM, non-GM and other related products. Second and more important, there are transaction costs associated with monitoring and enforcement efforts to prevent deliberate deception by GM food producers and handlers. An effective IPS will generate a price premium for non-GM products whenever there are group A consumers that prefer the non-GM product. This, in turn, provides an incentive for deception or cheating on the part of GM food producers, which in the absence of some form of control or policing mechanism, would undermine the effectiveness of the IPS.[14]

Labelling schemes may potentially be voluntary or mandatory and they may identify either the presence or absence of GMOs in food products.

GM-producing firms will have an incentive to mislead consumers either by not complying with labelling guidelines or requirements to identify the presence of GMOs, or by misrepresenting their products when the labelling seeks to identify non-GM products. Nevertheless, the extent and especially the incidence of the transaction costs associated with maintaining effectiveness will be markedly different for alternative systems.

A voluntary or mandatory IPS that identifies the presence of GMOs would operate on a disclosure basis. Supply chains would be divided and two separate markets would face consumers. On the one hand, there would be a directly identified GM food market consisting entirely of complying GM foods. On the other hand, there would be a residual market consisting of both non-GM foods and non-complying GM foods. Compliance may well be a problem, but the burden of transaction costs on GM firms is relatively light.

Since non-compliance is legal with a voluntary IPS that identifies GM foods, such a system is likely to leave significant quantities of non-compliant GM-products pooled with non-GM foods. Group A consumers, however, wish to either directly or indirectly identify non-GM foods. Consequently, voluntary GM identification systems of the types under discussion in North America are likely to be largely ineffective from a consumer standpoint and mainly cosmetic from a public policy standpoint.

A mandatory IPS for GM foods would officially require disclosure and would likely reduce non-compliance making the system more effective. Fewer non-compliant GM foods would be pooled with non-GM foods, and the benefits of the IPS to group A consumers would be greater. In effect, non-GM foods would be indirectly identified. While a mandatory IPS would likely entail significantly higher monitoring and enforcement costs, many of these additional transaction costs would typically be borne by the government rather than private parties.

Market incentives could possibly lead to the voluntary identification of non-GM foods because group A consumers are willing to pay a premium for non-GM foods. Since group A consumers wish to identify GM foods, rather than non-GM foods, such a market-based system appears to be promising. In practice, however, the division of the supply chain would not be perfectly effective. On the one hand, there would be an identified but impure non-GM market consisting of participating non-GM foods and misrepresented GM foods. On the other hand, there would be a residual market comprised of (non-misrepresented) GM foods and any non-participating non-GM foods.[15] A non-GM food IPS, therefore, must operate on a documentation basis to control the problem of misrepresentation of GM foods as their non-GM counterparts. In particular, documentation may be required to prove that all ingredients used in production were not genetically modified and that the product did not come into contact with any GMO. In some cases, testing of food products to determine the absence of GMOs may be scientifically possible and commercially practical, but often it will be necessary to identify upstream firms throughout the supply chain that use non-GMO inputs, and carefully monitor all their production practices. Consequently, much higher private costs will be borne by firms to substantiate the absence rather than the presence of GMOs (Hobbs and Plunkett, 1999).

Ultimately, it will be necessary to analyse the economic implications of identity preservation systems that are both costly and subject to deception or cheating. Nevertheless, it is useful to proceed in steps. First we will consider a completely frictionless IPS, then we will introduce costs and thereafter we will consider cheating.

4.5.2   Perfect Identity Preservation

We examine a perfect or frictionless IPS that accurately and costlessly identifies non-GM and GM foods for two important reasons. First, this analysis is a useful benchmark to aid in the assessment of more realistic IPSs. Second, it is possible to show that in the absence of hidden quality, the introduction of GM foods would be unambiguously beneficial if only consumer concerns were at issue.

We continue to work within the general production-side framework consisting of a competitive farm sector and an open-entry, differentiated-products biotechnology oligopoly. We also continue to assume that consumers in group A prefer non-GM to GM foods, but that they treat all varieties of GM foods as perfect substitutes. Since consumers are now assumed to be able to distinguish accurately and costlessly between non-GM and GM foods there will now be two separate product markets and a 'separating equilibrium'.

The separating equilibrium can be analysed using Figure 4.8 where the non-GM market is shown in panel (a) and the GM market is shown in panel (b). The initial demand curve for the non-GM food, which prevails prior to the introduction of the GM innovation, is D1i. The farm sector's supply curve for non-GM food, S1, continues to be perfectly elastic. This supply

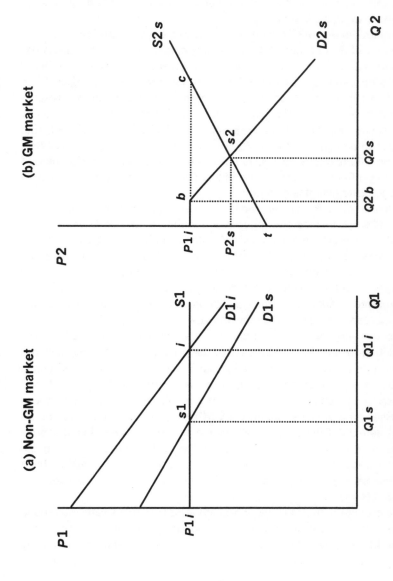

Figure 4.8 – Perfect product identification

curve reflects free entry, uniform technologies and constant costs (that is, input costs which are independent of aggregate output). Consequently, the initial equilibrium is at i where the price is $P1i$ and the quantity is Q1i. This is the same initial equilibrium as in Figures 4.5 and 4.6 since only the non-GM food is available in all cases.

The introduction of GM foods gives rise to the S2s supply curve for GM foods in panel (b) of Figure 4.8. This supply curve, like those for GM foods in Figures 4.5 and 4.6, is positively sloped because some farms are better able to adopt and make use of the features of the new biotechnologies. Farm sector GM supply, however, is subject to open entry and constant costs at the industry level. The D2s demand curve, which arises for GM foods, is drawn conditional on a final price for the substitute non-GM food that continues to be equal to $P1i$. If $P2$ were equal to $P1i$, group B consumers would be willing to buy up to Q2b units of the GM food. For them, the GM and non-GM foods are perfect substitutes. Thus, demand for the GM food is perfectly elastic over this interval.

At lower prices for the GM food, members of group B are willing to buy more, and some members of group A are willing to switch. Given that the price of the non-GM food remains at $P1i$, the equilibrium in the GM market is at $s2$ where the quantity is Q2s and the price is $P2s$. It should be observed that the GM price would have been equal to $P1i$, rather than below it, if the supply curve had intersected the demand curve to the left of point b. Due to the perceived quality differences by group A consumers, the price of the GM food cannot be greater than the non-GM price.

The demand for the substitute non-GM product is affected by the introduction of the GM food. In effect the price of the GM food declines from an infinite level to $P2s$. As all group B and some group A consumers move to the substitute GM product, the demand curve for the non-GM food shifts inward to D1s. This demand curve for the non-GM food is drawn conditional on a price of $P2s$ for the GM food. Thus, the final equilibrium for the non-GM food is at $s1$ where the quantity is Q1s, but the price remains at $P1i$. It is very important to emphasise that the shift in the demand curve is not a quality effect arising on a single pooled market, but a substitute price effect due to the general equilibrium interaction between the two markets.

The economic impact of the introduction of GM foods can be analysed by considering the markets sequentially. Our assessment begins on the non-GM market with the GM price held at its initial level, which is effectively infinite. There is no change in producer or consumer surplus on the non-

GM market since the price of the non-GM food does not change from $P1i$ and the price of the GM food is held constant. This result is highly intuitive. The only consumers that remain on the non-GM market are some of the members of group A. They pay the same price and are neither worse off nor better off.

Now, with the price of the non-GM food at its final level, which happens to still be $P1i$, we shift our analysis to the GM market. On the GM market, there is a gain from the creation of new consumer surplus equal to area $P1i$-b-$s2$-$P2s$ dollars. This consumer gain on the GM market aggregates the benefits of all group B consumers and those members of group A with a weak aversion to the GM food who are better off switching in response to the lower price. It should be observed that this consumer gain is predicated on a final GM price that is below rather than equal to $P1i$. While consumers would not have been hurt if the GM price had been equal to $P1i$, they would not have benefited either. In addition to the possible consumer benefit, there is a gain of new producer surplus equal to $P2s$-$s2$-t dollars. This benefit accrues as profits for intra-marginal GM farms. Finally, there is also a gain behind the scenes on the GMO input markets, because intra-marginal biotechnology firms, such as firm 1 in Figure 4.7, earn positive overall profits. In the case of a frictionless and costless IPS where only consumer concerns are at issue, society as a whole would be unambiguously better off after the introduction of the GM foods and, further, no consumers would be hurt.

4.5.3 Costly Identity Preservation

The next step is to examine cases where identity preservation systems are costly to operate, but completely effective in identifying the non-GM food. We begin by briefly considering a mandatory IPS for GM food where costly monitoring and enforcement by the government or its agencies results in complete compliance by GM producers. Except for the inclusion of the government's transaction costs attributable to the operation of the IPS, the market analysis shown in Figure 4.8 will generally remain applicable. When the introduction of GM food is accompanied by a mandatory GM food IPS, no consumers will be worse off, group B consumers are likely to be better off, and both intra-marginal GM farms and intra-marginal biotechnology firms will be better off by merit of positive overall profits. Given the costs associated with monitoring, however, society need not be better off. Society will be worse off whenever the transaction costs of the IPS borne by the government outweigh the gains to private parties.[16]

A voluntary, non-GM food IPS offers an alternative to a mandatory GM food IPS. The non-GM food system is somewhat more complex for two reasons. First, in addition to the pure non-GM food market, there will be a residual market where varieties of GM foods will be sold and where non-participating non-GM food may be sold. The pure non-GM market is shown in panel (a) of Figure 4.9, while the residual market is shown in panel (b). Second, the transaction costs of the IPS are borne by participating non-GM firms, leading to important alterations in the analysis of the non-GM market. We continue to abstract from deception by assuming that the costly IPS completely precludes the misrepresentation of GM foods as non-GM foods.

In Figure 4.9(a), there is an initial equilibrium prior to the introduction of GM foods at i where the price is $P1i$ and the quantity is $Q1i$. As GM foods are introduced, a voluntary non-GM IPS arises spontaneously because consumers in group A are willing to pay more for non-GM food. The IPS, however, involves significant separation and transaction costs. For simplicity, we assume that the per-unit costs associated with the IPS are constant and shift the non-GM supply curve from $S1i$ to $S1s$ in panel (a) of Figure 4.9. Thus, the per-unit costs of the IPS are equal to the difference between $P1s$ and $P1i$.

The $S2r$ demand curve in Figure 4.9(b) shows the supply of GM foods to the residual market while $S1r$ represents the supply of non-GM food to that market. The $D2r$ demand curve is constructed for the case where the residual market happens to be dominated entirely by GM foods and it is drawn conditional on a price of $P1s$ for the non-GM food. At a price for GM food equal to $P1s$, up to QRb' units can be sold to group B consumers.[17] At prices below $P1s$, the demand curve for the residual market is negatively sloped because consumers in group B are willing to buy more at lower prices and some members of group A will be induced to switch to the GM food. Given that the price of the non-GM food is $P1s$, the residual market is in equilibrium at r. The price is PRr and the quantity is QRr, which consists entirely of GM food. The demand curve for non-GM food shifts to $D1s$ due to the introduction of the substitute GM foods at a price of PRr. This leads to an equilibrium on the pure non-GM food market at $s1$ where the price is $P1s$ and the quantity is $Q1s$.

Two special equilibrium situations could potentially arise. First there

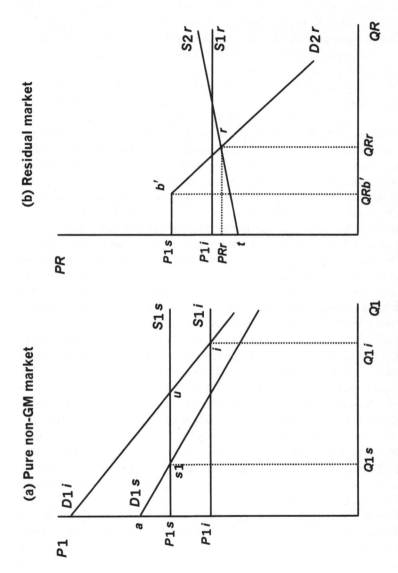

Figure 4.9 – Costly non-GM food identification with no cheating

will be a pooling equilibrium with positive quantities of the non-GM present in the residual market if the S2r GM supply curve intersects the D2r GM demand curve above the S1r non-GM supply curve. In such a situation, the demand curve applicable to the residual market will lie somewhat to the right of D2r reflecting the somewhat higher expected product quality. Second, the IPS may be too expensive for separate trade in the pure non-GM food. This would occur if point *a*, the intercept of the D1s demand function shown in panel (a), is below P1s indicating that no consumers are willing to pay the costs of this IPS. When the pure non-GM market does not arise there may be some non GM-foods supplied to the residual market, but this does not have to be the case. As discussed in the previous two sections, it is possible for only one (residual) market to operate and for it to be entirely dominated by GM foods. Indeed, the previous analysis of a single pooled market can be properly reinterpreted as a situation in which a voluntary non-GM food situation is too costly to arise spontaneously.

To assess the impact of the introduction of the GM innovation with a costly non-GM IPS in Figure 4.9, we begin on the non-GM market and hold the GM price at its initial infinite level. Since the relevant demand curve remains D1i, there is a loss of consumer surplus of *P1s-u-i-P1i* dollars caused by the increase in the price of the non-GM food. This indicates the loss to all consumers 'before' all the group B and some of the group A consumers depart for the GM market. Having adjusted the price of the non-GM food to *P1s*, we now turn to the residual market. Here there is a gain in consumer surplus of *P1s-b'-r-PRr* dollars. This gain on the residual market is shared by all group B consumers and those in group A who switch.

Overall, group B consumers will typically be at least as well off and they will be strictly better off in situations such as that depicted in Figure 4.9 where the residual market is completely dominated by GM food and the price falls below *P1i*. In Figure 4.9, some of the group A consumers who switch will also be better off due to the price decrease while others will be worse off due to the quality loss. Group A consumers who do not switch are necessarily worse off because of the increase in the price of non-GM food brought about by the IPS.[18]

There is a also a gain in producer surplus of *PRr-r-t* dollars accruing to intra-marginal GM farms on the residual market in Figure 4.9, and a further gain on input markets due to the overall profits of intra-marginal biotechnology firms. In principle, society could be worse off after the introduction of biotechnology in spite of the spontaneous development of a voluntary non-GM IPS. Society as a whole will only gain if the combination of the producer and consumer gains on the new GM food market and the gains on the GMO input market are sufficient to outweigh the losses caused by the costs of the IPS on the non-GM market. Further, IPSs are not likely to be completely deception-free, as we have so far assumed, unless they are prohibitively costly.

4.6 CHEATING AND ITS CONTROL

In the absence of a price premium for non-GM food, the deception of consumers or cheating would not be a problem for an identity preservation system. In Figure 4.8, suppose that the aggregate quantity of GM food that the farm sector had wished to supply at a price of $P1i$ had been less than the quantity Q2b, which group B consumers wished to purchase. In this case, compliance would have been costless for non-GM farms since the same price, $P1i$, would have been available in both markets. Thus, for situations where there is a low level of desired GM supply and/or societies with a high proportion of group B consumers, something approaching perfect identification might be achieved voluntarily. In the case of a voluntary GM food IPS, there would be no forgone benefit from non-compliance; GM-producing farms would lose nothing from truthful disclosure. In the case of a voluntary non-GM IPS, there would be no forgone benefit to GM-producing farms from misrepresenting their product so minimal documentation requirements from non-GM-producing farms would be satisfactory.

In reality, however, there will frequently be the potential for a price premium for the non-GM food. Given either a voluntary GM food IPS where there are negligible penalties for non-compliance by GM firms or a voluntary non-GM IPS with minimal documentation requirements, deception would become pervasive in the presence of such a potential price premium. In the situation shown in Figure 4.8, desired supply of the GM food exceeds the quantity Q2b that group B consumers would purchase at a price of $P1i$. In the absence of deception, there is a price premium of $P1i$ minus $P2s$ for the non-GM food. GM-producing farms would conduct arbitrage across the markets and eliminate the price differential. That is to say, they would simply sell the excess supply of GM food which is equal to the distance b-c in panel (b) as non-complying or misrepresented GM foods into the now impure non-GM market. The total surplus on the GM market would be greater by b-$s2$-c dollars, but this would be more than offset by an adverse quality effect on the impure non-GM market.

Relative to a single pooled market, there may be a minimal gain to group A consumers from having a voluntary IPS in spite of rampant cheating. Suppose that non-GM output is not completely displaced by non-complying GM food on the impure non-GM market. In this case there is a somewhat higher concentration of non-GM foods, and thus somewhat higher quality for members of group A than would prevail on a single pooled market. This is because those consumers in group B who are served by the identified GM market purchase 100 per cent GM food. In economic terms, this would seem to be the only positive result available from a voluntary GM food IPS.

In an attempt to control widespread non-compliance by GM-producing farms, a voluntary GM food IPS could be made mandatory and government expenditures could be made to monitor and enforce the programme. Likewise, in the context of a voluntary non-GM food IPS, documentation requirements could be increased in an attempt to control misrepresentation by GM-producing farms. While we have seen that controlling cheating will be costly, it is now necessary to show that typically cheating cannot be completely eliminated. Consequently, it is necessary to reconsider both a mandatory GM IPS and a voluntary non-GM IPS in a context that allows for cheating and its control.

4.6.1 Non-compliance in a Mandatory GM Food IPS

A mandatory GM IPS directly identifies GM food, but only indirectly identifies non-GM food. Further the degree to which the non-GM food can be identified depends on the effectiveness of the IPS. In reality, there will be an impure non-GM market where non-GM foods are pooled with non-complying GM foods as well as the directly identified GM market consisting of complying GM food. In Figure 4.10, the impure non-GM market is shown in panel (a) and the GM market is shown in panel (b). The initial equilibrium is at i where the price is $P1i$ and the quantity is $Q1i$.

Now consider the introduction of GM food in conjunction with a mandatory GM food IPS. Suppose that the government sets its expenditure level on enforcement and monitoring at a non-prohibitive level that ultimately allows a positive proportion of fraudulent sales to go undetected. As is typically the case with policing of all kinds, some illicit or criminal

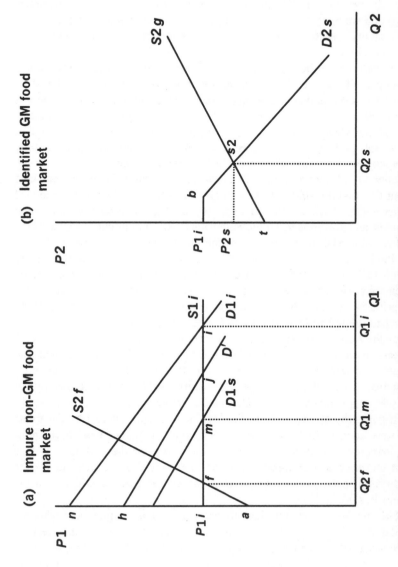

Figure 4.10 – Non-compliance with a mandatory GM food IPS

activity goes undetected. If GM-producing farms simply maximise their expected profits, they will choose to cheat and sell some of their output fraudulently whenever the pooled price in the impure non-GM market is above the price in the GM market. This remains true even when penalties go beyond simple confiscation of output that is discovered to be fraudulent. Undoubtedly, some farms will resist the temptation not to comply, but others will not.[19]

In addition to being beneficial to individual GM-producing farms, cheating is likely to be beneficial to the biotechnology industry. Since the impure non-GM market acts as an additional outlet for GM product, there is a net increase in demand for GM food. This, in turn, gives rise to a greater demand for GMO inputs. *Ceteris paribus*, GMO prices will be higher, biotechnology firms will be more profitable and additional biotechnology firms may enter because of cheating at downstream stages.

In panel (a) of Figure 4.10, S2f is the supply curve for fraudulent GM output successfully sold into the non-GM market when the price in the GM market is *P2s*. Thus, the S2f curve shows the fraudulent output net of what is caught and confiscated by the authorities. The supply curve for non-GM food remains S1i. In the absence of the separate alternative market for the GM food, the demand curve in the impure non-GM market would shift to the left to D' due to the drop in quality perceived by group A consumers. Given the presence of the separate substitute market for the GM food where the price settles at *P2s*, the demand curve for the non-GM food shifts further to the left to D1s. All group B and some group A consumers move out of the impure non-GM market in response to lower prices on the GM market. Given the price of *P2s* in the GM market, the equilibrium in the impure non-GM market is at *m* where the pooled or mixed quantity consumed is Qm, the fraudulent GM quantity sold is Q2f, the quantity of non-GM supplied is Qm minus Q2f, and the price is *P1i*.

In panel (b) of Figure 4.10, the legitimate supply curve for GM foods sold into the identified GM market is S2g when the pooled price in the non-GM market is *P1i*. Similarly, the demand curve for the GM food is D2s when the price in the impure non-GM market is *P1i*.[20] Consequently the equilibrium in the GM market is at *s2* where the quantity is Q2s and the price is P2s.

The impact of the introduction of GM food in conjunction with the mandatory GM food IPS is analysed by considering the markets in sequence. First we consider the impure non-GM market holding the price on the identified GM market at its initial effectively infinite level. Since the demand curve shifts from D1i to D′ prior to the movement of consumers to the GM market, there is an adverse quality effect on group A consumers of *n-i-j-h* dollars. Further, on the impure non-GM market, there is a gain in producer surplus from fraudulent sales equal to *P*1*i-f-a* dollars. Given the final price on the impure market, which remains at *P*1*i*, we move to the identified GM market. Here, there is a gain of producer surplus of *P*2*s-s*2*-t* dollars and a gain in consumer surplus of *P*1*i-b-s*2*-P*2*s* dollars. In addition, intra-marginal biotechnology firms gain on the GMO input market.

Overall, all group B consumers gain due to the lower price for the new GM food, but all those group A consumers who continue to buy exclusively on the impure non-GM market lose due to the adverse quality effect. Some of the members of group A who switch will be better off because their individual adverse quality effects are offset by their favourable price effects. Others will be worse off because the reverse is true.

Given any particular level of government expenditure on monitoring and enforcement, society as a whole may be better off or worse off with the introduction of GM food in conjunction with a mandatory GM food IPS. Society will lose if the adverse quality effect on the impure non-GM market plus the government loss from outlays on monitoring and enforcement outweighs the producer gains on all markets and the consumers gains on the GM market. A mandatory GM food IPS does have the advantage that the level of monitoring and enforcement is a policy variable. Monitoring and enforcement can be chosen by the government so as to maximise net social welfare. In particular, the optimum level of monitoring and enforcement would serve to equate the marginal benefit (that is, the 'increase' in the total surplus across the impure non-GM market, the identified GM market and the GMO input market) with the marginal cost (that is, the increase in monitoring and enforcement costs).[21]

4.6.2 Misrepresentation in a Voluntary Non-GM Food IPS

A voluntary non-GM food IPS has the potential to confront GM producers and handlers that are discovered to have misrepresented GM food as non-GM with significant costs and penalties. Offenders can be sued for damages and may often be open to criminal charges such as fraud. The system operates, however, by imposing documentation requirements on all firms that wish to participate in the identified non-GM market and monitoring that documentation. In principle, the monitoring function could be conducted by an industry body at the expense of participating firms, or it could be adopted by the government at the expense of taxpayers. Since monitoring and enforcement activities have public goods' aspects some participation by the government in this aspect of a voluntary IPS may be warranted. As documentation requirements and monitoring are increased, on the one hand, less misrepresentation will be attempted and less will succeed. This will tend to keep the non-GM market purer. On the other hand, costs to participating firms, and thus consumers, will increase.

Consider the operation of a voluntary non-GM food IPS where the documentation requirements and monitoring level have been set at a given level. There will be an identified but impure non-GM market as shown in panel (a) of Figure 4.11, and a residual market as shown in panel (b). Participating non-GM and successfully misrepresented GM foods are pooled on the impure non-GM market. Genuinely represented GM food and any non-participating non-GM food is sold on the residual market. Consequently, pooling may occur on the residual market as well as the impure non-GM market, but the concentration of the non-GM foods will be higher on the impure non-GM markets or group A consumers will not pay the price premium.

In Figure 4.11, the initial equilibrium is at i where the price is $P1i$ and the quantity is $Q1i$. When GM foods are introduced in conjunction with the voluntary non-GM food IPS, the supply curve for successfully misrepresented GM food sold on the impure non-GM market is $S2f$, which is drawn conditional on a price of PRr in the residual market. The demand curve for the residual market, $D2r$, reflects the situation when only the GM food is available on that market. The perfectly elastic segment of this demand curve arises because all group B consumers are willing to shift markets at a price of $P1u$, given that price prevails in the impure non-GM market. Consequently, an equilibrium situation for the residual market is shown at r where the equilibrium quantity, QRr, is comprised entirely of GM food, and the equilibrium price is PRr.

The voluntary non-GM food IPS imposes documentation requirements that lead to additional transaction costs on each unit sold. We assume that these per-unit transaction costs are constant and equal to the difference between $P1u$ and $P1i$ in panel (a) of Figure 4.11.

Thus, the supply curve for non-GM food to the identified but impure non-GM market is $S1u$. While fraudulent GM sales are also subject to similar transaction costs, there remains a net premium of $P1i$ minus PRr that provides the incentive for cheating that leads to the $S2f$ curve. The

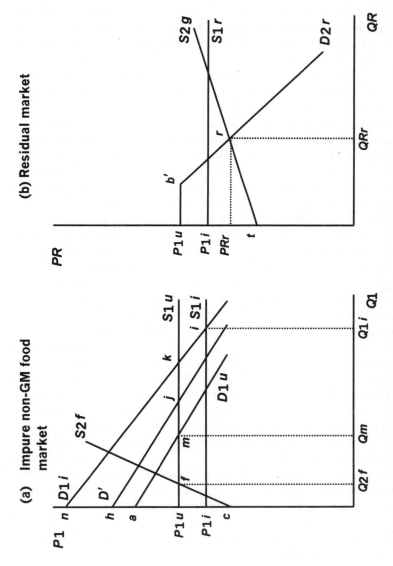

(a) Impure non-GM food market

(b) Residual market

Figure 4.11 – Misrepresentation with a voluntary non-GM food IPS

141

adulteration of the non-GM market would shift demand from D1i to D′ in the absence of consumers moving to the residual market. This reflects the adverse quality effect experienced by group A consumers. Given that substitute product does become available at a price of *PRr* on the residual market, all group B and some group A consumers vacate the impure non-GM market and the demand curve shifts further to the left to D1u. This leads to an equilibrium on the impure non-GM market at *m* where the price is *P1u*, the quantity consumed is Qm, fraudulent GM sales are Qf, and non-GM sales are equal to Qm minus Qf.

Starting in the impure non-GM market and holding the price in the residual market at its original infinite level, there is an adverse price effect on all consumers of *P1u-k-i-P1i* dollars, and a further adverse quality effect on group A consumers of *n-k-j-h* dollars. There is, however, a gain of *P1u-f-c* dollars in producer surplus from fraudulent sales on the impure non-GM market. Moving to the residual market, having changed the price on the impure non-GM market to *P1u*, there is a gain in consumer surplus of *P1u-b′-r-PRr* dollars. Since *PRr* is less than or equal to *P1i*, there is an unambiguous overall gain to group B consumers. Some, but not all, members of group A who switch markets will be better off as well. Those members of group A who choose to remain on the now impure non-GM market must be worse off because they experience both an adverse price effect and an adverse quality effect. On the residual market, intra-marginal GM-producing farmers experience a gain in producer surplus of *PRr-r-t* dollars, and on the GMO input market intra-marginal biotechnology firms will generate positive profit. Society as a whole may gain or lose from the introduction of GM food in conjunction with the voluntary non-GM food IPS. Society will be worse off whenever the adverse price and quality effects on the impure non-GM market outweigh the sum of the consumer gains on the residual market and the producer gains on all markets.

By contrast with a mandatory GM food IPS, most if not all of the costs of a voluntary non-GM food IPS are borne by commercial interests. Further, at least the documentation requirements and often the monitoring levels will be set on the basis of private commercial goals rather than to maximise societal welfare. This, too, is unlike the mandatory GM food IPS where the policing mechanism could be set to maximise social welfare. Of course, the commercial goals associated with a voluntary non-GM food IPS may often be quite benign. The IPS, for example, could be designed to maximise the volume of non-GM sales in the impure non-GM market. Finally, it should be observed, once again, that market forces will not permit spontaneous development of a voluntary non-GM food IPS if there is insufficient demand. If the intercept of the final pooled demand curve for the impure non-GM market given by point *a* in panel (a) of Figure 4.11 falls below *Plu* for all possible settings of documentation procedures, a voluntary non-GM food IPS is not sustainable.

4.6.3 Consumer Conundrums and Policy

The hidden quality or lemons problem, which was examined by Akerlof (1970) in relation to the used car market, poses complex consumer problems with respect to the introduction of biotechnology. As a result of adverse quality effects, society as a whole may be worse off when the introduction of GM foods leads to a simple, single-market pooling equilibrium.

A market-driven voluntary non-GM food IPS may or may not develop spontaneously. Such a development, if it occurs, does not necessarily imply an improvement relative to either the initial situation or a simple pooling equilibrium. Relative to the initial situation, a voluntary non-GM food IPS causes higher non-GM prices and there continues to be an adverse quality effect due to cheating. Relative to a simple pooling equilibrium, the adverse quality effect is diminished, but an adverse price effect is introduced.

A mandatory IPS for GM food may or may not represent an improvement over the initial situation, a simple pooling equilibrium or a voluntary non-GM food IPS. With a mandatory IPS for GM food, adverse quality effects persist because of cheating but are diminished relative to a pooling equilibrium. In comparison with a voluntary non-GM food IPS, the mandatory IPS for GM food shifts the burden of transaction costs relating to monitoring and enforcement to the government. While much of the adverse effect on non-GM prices that is associated with a voluntary non-GM food IPS is avoided, a new tax burden is created. The mandatory GM food IPS does have the advantage that it can be designed with an eye to maximising societal welfare.

We emphasise that a general ranking of the various alternative market arrangements and potential policy interventions simply does not exist. As a practical matter, the hidden quality issues that biotechnology poses for consumers require careful empirical analysis on a case-by-case basis. When, how and even whether, to proceed with a particular new GMO is essentially a difficult, but not intractable, empirical question. In certain cases, introduction of GMOs should proceed apace whether or not a

144   *The Economics of Biotechnology*

voluntary non-GM food IPS arises spontaneously. In other cases a mandatory GM food IPS should be implemented regardless of whether a voluntary non-GM food IPS would have developed in its absence. Sometimes more extensive testing and more prolonged field trials would be useful to reduce the extent of unknown information. Occasionally, outright bans may be indicated. Further, in conjunction with the environmental issues discussed in the previous chapter and the ethical issues treated in the next chapter, consumer issues connected with hidden quality pose some serious new issues for international trade which will be addressed in Chapter 7 (Gaisford and Lau, 2000).

NOTES

1. The poll, carried out in November and December 1999, covered 5171 consumers in Germany, the UK, France, Japan, Australia, the USA, Canada and Brazil.
2. The authors note an important caveat to their findings – content analysis cannot distinguish causality, that is, whether media messages are a reflection of public opinion or whether they create public opinion.
3. The residual quantity produced by fringe non-GM farms exceeds the difference between Qk in Figure 4.1 and Qa in Figure 4.3 panel (b). When some non-GM product is marketed, consumers will purchase more than Qk at the price of Pi. For example suppose that the proportion of non-GMs corresponds with θj in Figure 4.1. Then, total consumption is at Qj, and non-GM producers will provide Qj minus Qa, which is larger than Qk minus Qa.
4. Plunkett (2000) shows that if the fringe supply curve were upward sloping, say due to increasing costs, the biotechnology firm's price would still be above marginal cost with accommodating pricing. Further, in such a setting, the innovation would be drastic or price-reducing even in cases of pre-emptive or accommodating pricing.
5. The authors gratefully acknowledge discussions with T. Folkins and C. Lau on the structure of the farm sector and the biotechnology industry. The authors, however, are responsible for any shortcomings in the formulations that follow.
6. The rationale for calling biotechnology firm 1 an intra-marginal firm in Figure 4.7 and firm 2 a marginal firm will be discussed later.
7. In the Cournot quantity-setting model with either differentiated or homogeneous products and in the Bertrand price-setting model with differentiated products, price remains above marginal cost (Gravelle and Rees, 1992, pp. 300–308).
8. In Figure 4.7, the demand curve and thus the marginal revenue curve facing either one of the firms depends on the price set by the other firm. This means that biotechnology firm 1 will not regret its choice of a price of Wv1° provided that the Dv1 demand curve for firm 1 is drawn conditional on a price of Wv2° from firm 2. Similarly, firm 2 will not regret its choice of a price of Wv2° provided that the Dv2 curve for firm 2 is drawn contingent on a price of Wv1° from firm 1. Given these circumstances, the situation shown in Figure 4.7 is a Nash equilibrium in prices.

9. The elasticity of demand facing each firm depends on whether the non-GM technology is in use. *Ceteris paribus*, a biotechnology firm will face more elastic demand if it faces indirect competition from the alternative non-GM technology as well as its GMO-producing rivals. There will be a critical value for the symmetric price of GMOs above which the non-GM and GM products coexist and below which only GM products will be able to compete. If this critical symmetric price for GMOs happens to be the Nash equilibrium symmetric price, each biotechnology firm will be producing and pricing at a kinked point on the demand curve for its GMO. For reductions in output, demand will be more elastic than for increases in output. Further, in this case where the profit-maximising output, which equates marginal cost and marginal revenue, occurs at the kink, the marginal revenue curve has a vertical segment.

10. In the classic Hotelling model where the product space is a line segment (Eaton et al., 1999, 28–38), locations in the middle, where there are buyers on both sides, are more attractive than locations at the extremes where there are only buyers on one side. The circle, however, removes this problem.

11. The circle could be thought of as physical locations around a city with locations varying in terms of soil, temperature, rainfall and pest infestation. The measure of desirability of all four locational characteristics varies from a maximum of one to a minimum of zero. Locations on the circle can be indexed using a compass. Suppose that soil quality peaks in the north and varies linearly either way round the circle to a minimum in the south. Analogously, assume that temperature is best in the east and worst in the west, rainfall is best in the south and worst in the north and the freedom from pest infestation is best in the west and worst in the east. At all locations on the circle, the blend of characteristics differs but the aggregation of the quality measures is always equal to two. Given that non-GM production depends only on the aggregate of the four quality numbers, the productivity of each location for non-GM outputs is the same. Now suppose that there is a potential GMO that achieves its peak productivity with the exogenous blend of characteristics that prevails at each point on the circle. Finally, suppose that potential GMOs are equivalent in all respects except their optimum location.

12. Farm sector production decisions for GM products depend positively on the magnitude of cost reductions associated with each GMO's use and the number of varieties of GMOs, but negatively on the prices of GMO inputs. The prices of GMOs (farm inputs) depend positively on the marginal production costs for GMOs and the demand for GMOs. In turn, the demand for GMOs depends positively on the productivity of GMOs at the farm level, but negatively on the number of rival varieties. The number of varieties of the GMO depends negatively on R&D costs but positively on stage three net production revenue. Finally, stage three net production revenue depends negatively on marginal cost and positively on demand.

13. There has been considerable discussion and analysis of other signals of quality such as investing in a reputation (Klein and Leffler, 1981; Shapiro, 1983), advertising (Nelson, 1974; Milgrom and Roberts, 1986) and pricing (Bagwell and Riordan, 1991; Shieh, 1993). While these signalling methods can be appropriate for experience goods where quality is evident or discernible at low cost upon consumption, they are highly problematic for credence goods like non-GM products (Plunkett, 2000).

14. For another context in which deception arises with credence goods, see Darby and Karni (1973).

15. Making a non-GM food IPS mandatory would offer consumers the additional feature of indirectly identifying the presence of GM foods. Since this information is not desired by either group A or group B consumers, such a mandatory system has little additional to offer.

16. If the costs of lost economies of scale associated with the separation of supply chains are significant, there would be an upward shift in the S1 curve in panel (a) of Figure 4.8. This would lead to higher prices and, thus, welfare losses for group A consumers who remain on the non-GM market. This is qualitatively similar to what occurs with a voluntary non-GM IPS, which is considered subsequently.

17. Since P1s is greater than P1i, the quantity QRb' that consumers in group B are willing to switch from the non-GM to GM food in Figure 4.9 is less than the quantity Q2b in Figure 4.8.

18. It is possible to conceive of a situation where the final price on the residual market is higher than $P1i$ making group B consumers, and thus all consumers, worse off. Such a situation could occur if the residual market was encumbered with significant additional separation costs arising from the loss of economies of scale in supply chains. In this case, the intercept for the S1r supply curve for non-GM food to the residual market would lie above $P1i$ and open the possibility for a final price above $P1i$.

19. In a study on cheating that is in progress, Folkins (2000) shows that marginal GM producing farms, which could just earn zero profit, must either cheat or revert to non-GM production. Further, such a marginal GM-producing farm will sell cheating output above its minimum average cost and legitimate output below its minimum average cost. This may leave the farm sector open to charges of dumping on any legitimate sales that are exported.

20. Technically, the D1s and D2s demand curves are also drawn conditional on the proportion of non-GM food that ultimately prevails in the pooled market which is (Qm – Q2f)/Qm.

21. The level of penalties for non-compliance can also be chosen optimally. As is typically the case, penalties are subject to credibility or time consistency constraints. This rules out very large penalties that would have very large deterrence value. This is because it would not be optimal to enforce such penalties if a violation were detected.

APPENDIX

It is useful to provide a somewhat more formal treatment of the quality effects associated with the introduction of biotechnology. The utility function of a sample household that happens to be in group A can be written as:

$$u_h = u_h\left(q_{h1}, q_{h2}, q_{h0}\right) \quad \text{where: } \frac{\partial u_h}{\partial q_{h1}} > \frac{\partial u_h}{\partial q_{h2}} \text{ for all } h \text{ in } \{A\}.$$

Here, q_{h1} denotes household h's consumption of the non-GM food, q_{h2} is the consumption of the GM food and q_{h0} is the consumption of a composite numeraire good. The defining feature for membership in group A is that a household perceives the non-GM food to be of higher quality so that its marginal utility from consuming an additional unit of the non-GM food is always greater than that from consuming the GM food. The latter, however, may be positive.

Recall that genetic modification is a credence characteristic, which is not detected even after consumption, and that any batch of the product may be a blend of the GM food and the non-GM food. A simple method of handling these issues is to assume that the utility function can be rewritten based on expected consumption of the non-GM food, θq_{h1}, and the GM food, $(1-\theta)q_{h2}$.

$$u_h = u_h\left(\theta q_h,\, (1-\theta)q_h,\, q_{h0}\right) = u_h\left(q_h, \theta, q_{h0}\right) \quad \text{for all } h \text{ in } \{A\}$$

The probability or the expected proportion of the non-GM food is $\theta = q_1/(q_1+q_2)$ where q_1, and q_2 represent the total production levels of non-GM foods and GM foods. This probability, we assume, is known by all consumers on the basis of observed production data, but beyond the control of any consumer. The probability parameter θ acts as a measure of perceived product quality while $q_h \equiv q_{h1} + q_{h2}$ is a measure of the pooled quantity consumed in the utility function of members of group A.

For members of group B, the GM food and non-GM food are perfect substitutes. Thus, their utility functions have the form:

$$u_h = u_h\left(q_{h1} + q_{h2}, q_{h0}\right) = u_h\left(q_h, q_{h0}\right) \quad \text{for all } h \text{ in } \{B\},$$

which is independent of the proportion of non-GM foods.

For any household in group A, the minimisation of spending subject to a utility constraint yields an expenditure function of the form:

$$y_h = e_h\left(p, \theta, u_h\right) \quad \text{for all } h \text{ in } \{A\},$$

$$\text{where: } \frac{\partial e_h\left(p, \theta, u_h\right)}{\partial p} = D_h^c\left(p, \theta, u_h\right).$$

Here p represents the price of the pooled product. The price of the numeraire, which is always $p_0 = 1$, is omitted for notational brevity. Income, of course, must be equal to expenditure and, further, Shepard's lemma indicates that the derivative of the expenditure function with respect to price is the Hicksian or compensated demand function.

The compensating variation (CV) provides a money-metric measure of consumer welfare change. We adopt the convention that positive changes in consumer welfare are associated with positive values of the CV. In the current context, the compensating variation, thus, is defined as the negative of the amount of money that would have to be given to a household to compensate it for changes in the pooled price, income and/or product quality parameters (Boadway and Bruce, 1984, pp. 39–43).

$$CV_h \equiv e_h\left(p^f,\theta^f,u_h^f\right) - e_h\left(p^f,\theta^f,u_h^i\right)$$

Here i denotes the initial circumstances and f denotes the final circumstances. This definition can be usefully rewritten as:

$$CV_h = e_h\left(p^f,\theta^f,u_h^f\right) - e_h\left(p^i,\theta^i,u_h^i\right) - e_h\left(p^f,\theta^f,u_h^i\right) + e_h\left(p^f,\theta^i,u_h^i\right)$$
$$- e_h\left(p^f,\theta^i,u_h^i\right) + e_h\left(p^i,\theta^i,u_h^i\right)$$

Given that expenditure is equal to income, and using the fundamental theorem of calculus, we obtain:

$$CV_h = y_h^f - y_h^i + e_h\left(p^f,\theta^f,u_h^i\right) - e_h\left(p^f,\theta^i,u_h^i\right) + \int_{p^h}^{p^i} D_h^c\left(p,\theta^i,u_h^i\right)dp$$

As the price of the pooled product, p, approaches infinity, none of the product will be consumed and the expenditure required to attain any particular utility level such as u_h^i (through consuming the numeraire alone) will be independent of product quality given by θ.

$$\lim_{p\to\infty} q_h = 0, \qquad e_h\left(p,\theta^i,u_h^i\right) = e_h\left(p,\theta^f,u_h^i\right)$$

Given this equality, the CV becomes:

$$CV_h = y_h^f - y_h^i + e_h\left(p^f,\theta^i,u_h^i\right) - e_h\left(\infty,\theta^i,u_h^i\right) + e_h\left(\infty,\theta^f,u_h^i\right)$$
$$- e_h\left(p^f,\theta^f,u_h^i\right) + \int_{p^h}^{p^i} D_h^c\left(p,\theta^i,u_h^i\right)dp$$

Using the fundamental theorem of calculus once again, this can be rewritten as:

$$CV_h = y_h^f - y_h^i + \int_{p^f}^{\infty} \left\{ D_h^c\left(p,\theta^f,u_h^i\right) - D_h^c\left(p,\theta^i,u_h^i\right) \right\} dp$$

$$+ \int_{p^h}^{p^i} D_h^c\left(p,\theta^i,u_h^i\right) dp$$

Thus, the dollar value measure of welfare change given by the compensating variation can be decomposed into an income change, a quality effect and a price effect. The underlying changes in profits would give rise to endogenous income changes in a full general equilibrium approach. In the chapter text we adopted a partial equilibrium consumer and producer surplus approach where consumer incomes are parametric. Given a quasi-linear utility function, $U = U(q_1, q_2) + q_0$, the change in consumer surplus is an exact measure of welfare change and it is equal to the compensating variation.

$$\Delta CS_h = CV_h = y_h^f - y_h^i + \int_{p^f}^{\infty} \left\{ D_h\left(p,\theta^f\right) - D_h\left(p,\theta^i\right) \right\} dp$$

$$+ \int_{p^h}^{p^i} D_h\left(p,\theta^i\right) dp$$

In the applications in the chapter text, the income change was always equal to zero, but price and quality effects arose frequently.

5. Ethical concerns

5.1 ETHICAL OBJECTIONS TO BIOTECHNOLOGY

5.1.1 Biotechnology and Ethics

The ethical dimension is a very important one in discussions regarding biotechnology. Consumers do not just buy products. They buy the bundle of characteristics that are encompassed by the product. The acceptability of a product in ethical and moral terms, by both individuals and society, can be very important in shaping its demand. What are the ethical dimensions that are relevant in this discussion and how do they impinge on consumption, production and regulation of biotechnological products? For some individuals, the debate over ethical issues can be summed up by the slogan: 'Should man play God?'. In other words, they perceive that there is something unnatural and unethical regarding the transfer of genes from one species to another. The apparent difference in consumer attitudes when comparing the use of genetic engineering in medicine and medical treatment, on the one hand, and the use of the technology in food production does raise some interesting questions regarding this simple view of ethics. The 'playing with God's work' view of biotechnology, however, fundamentally holds that genetic modification is unethical *per se* and should not be allowed to take place at all. Another view suggests that in itself genetic modification is, in principle, neither ethical nor unethical but carrying out genetic modification does have ethical consequences and concerns. These concerns can be summarised as follows:

1. issues of safety for consumers and the environment. These have been raised elsewhere in this book but under a different guise;
2. ownership and issues of competition;
3. respect for autonomy – particularly with regard to traditional farming practices;

4. consumer choice;
5. implications for social and cultural direction and norms.

5.1.2   Religious Attitudes Towards Genetic Modification and Biotechnology

There are a number of religious dimensions to ethical concerns regarding biotechnology that need to be examined carefully. The report of the UK Committee on the Ethics of Genetic Modification and Food Use summarised religious views on biotechnology (MAFF, 1996). One particular issue arises from the perceived unnaturalness of genetic modification and whether products derived from this process become 'tainted' in some way.

The Committee found that each of the major religions had a view on this issue and these views differed to some degree. Islamic objections to genetic modification stem from the belief that God created all life forms in the best design which should not be altered by humans unless they were correcting deviations back to the original form. The products of biotechnology not used in this way can be viewed as tainted. In particular, Muslims see the preservation of a species as paramount and that genetic modification may disturb the balance. Muslims see a distinct difference between 'natural' cross-breeding and genetic modification. There is a concern not to interfere with the world as created.

Hindus and Buddhists also share some of the Muslims' concerns. In these two religions there is a reverence for the natural world. Evolution is held in high esteem. Natural selective breeding is consistent with this view. Any adverse impact that it may have on the natural world can be reversed. This may not be the case with genetic modification whose impact may be instantaneous and non-reversible.

Opposite views are held by other religions, albeit with various reservations. For example the Baha'i faith welcomes genetic modification as the fruit of intellectual endeavour. This is especially so in areas that are aimed at relieving hunger and ill health.

Christians in the main have little concern with genetic modification *per se*. The view is largely held that 'man' has been given power over nature in order to improve welfare. The relationship between man and nature should not, however, be exploitative. In other words, as long as safeguards exist to ensure food and environmental safety as well as animal welfare, genetic modification is acceptable.

The Jewish faith also broadly agrees with the Christian view on genetic modification. Nature is there to benefit humankind. If its manipulation is necessary to promote or prolong life, then intervention is justified. In common with Christians, the Jewish faith believes that man has a duty to protect and nurture the natural world.

Sikhs also accept these views regarding man's intervention in the natural world. Scientific advance is there to be exploited for the benefit of humanity.

While Judaism and the Sikh faith do not have any problems with genetic modification and the use of biotechnology in general, dietary issues do arise that raise problems for followers of these faiths.

5.1.3 Specific Religious Objections

One major concern expressed by members of the Jewish, Muslim, Sikh and Hindu faiths is the possibility that their followers may consume forbidden foods. In the future, it is possible that genetic modification may introduce pig or beef genes into animals that otherwise would have been considered acceptable to eat according to the particular faith's doctrine. The introduction of a gene from a prohibited species would make such a food product unacceptable for consumption by members of the particular religious community.

The transfer of genes of human origin to other organisms also raises concerns for some religions. All major religions prohibit cannibalism, but views vary regarding the nature and status of organisms containing introduced genes of human origin. For Muslims, the transgene retains its human nature and, therefore, retains its taboo. For Jews, as long as the host or recipient organism retains its own character, then there is no objection. Hindu and Sikh views come near to Muslim views on this issue while Christian attitudes approach those of the Jewish faith.

Attitudes to the transfer of genes of animal origin to plants by the major religions reflected those associated with the transfer of genes of animal origin to other animals. Some vegetarians also have doubts regarding the acceptability of animal to plant genetic transfers. Vegetarian attitudes do, however, vary. In particular, if the animal gene were to be synthetic, some vegetarians suggest that the GM organisms would be acceptable in their diets. For example, chymosin enzymes, which are used in cheese production and mimic those of rennet obtained from calves' stomachs, have gained a measure of acceptability. Few ethical concerns seem to have been raised regarding the transfer of genes of plant origin to other organisms.

 Objections are raised by some religious groups regarding the transfer of genes of what can be called non-food animals to other organisms such as food animals and plants. Muslims, who are forbidden to eat the meat of meat-eating animals, have expressed particular concerns in this area. Other non-religious groups might also have objections. As the Committee on the Ethics of Genetic Modification and Food Use put it, there may well be objections to the consumption of food containing genes of animals that cause human revulsion (rats, scorpions, and so on) and those to which there is a great deal of human attachment (for example, horses, dogs, cats and so on) (MAFF, 1996).

5.1.4 Issues of Safety

If the use of biotechnology is not banned *per se*, its applications do raise ethical concerns regarding what sort of safety measures need to be in place. The growth in the applications of biotechnology is largely driven by commercial considerations. In pursuing commercial criteria, it could be the case that the long-term interests of the users of biotechnology – both consumers and producers – are not adequately served.

 For example, while scientists are able to manipulate genetic material easily the long-term consequences of this manipulation are not so well known. Further, the emphasis on the commercial application of science rather than the pursuit of research for its own sake has shifted the emphasis of scientific enquiry and claims. It is clear that the privatisation of scientific research brings pressure to emphasise the applications of research rather than its limitations. As suggested in Chapter 2, the cost of biotechnological research has meant that much of the research will be carried out by large corporations that have access to extensive R&D funds. These firms can be vertically integrated over large segments of the supply chain and control many stages of the production process. In the area of foods this means that companies could control the development/sale of seeds through to the production and sale of the final crop or foodstuff. As a result, there is less opportunity for oversight by governments. This internalisation of research and production suggests that a system of industry self-regulation may not be appropriate for several reasons.

 First, firms take a short-term view. They have to make adequate returns from their investments to satisfy their investors, and conventional accounting systems value companies over relatively short spans of time. Many of the ethical concerns are, however, of a more long-term nature. Self-regulation may not give sufficient weight to the long-term concerns of society.

Second, the emphasis on short-run returns may prevent alternative methods and solutions from being examined. In the area of agriculture, where the adoption of biotechnology is claimed to increase yields, other mechanisms and processes which might bring about similar results would not be examined. Examples of this might be farmer education, crop rotation and the use of non-chemical fertilisers.

Third, the approach adopted by firms to keep them ahead of their rivals by continuous innovation has led them to equate change with improvement. As a result of commercial rivalry, firms may attempt to gain a 'first-mover advantage' but in the process become less prudent in their safety or testing protocols.

For these reasons, all firms cannot be relied upon to self-regulate their behaviour. This conflict between private and public interest suggests that public interests can best be served by public bodies specifically established to look after these interests. In other words, either a government department should be made responsible or a specific agency has to be set up to ensure that society's welfare is being adequately protected.

If an agency or government department is set up to regulate the biotechnology industry what principles should be applied? The Food Ethics Council in the UK, a private body established to provide an ethical input into policy-making, suggests that in general the 'precautionary principle' should be adopted (Food Ethics Council, 1999). In their view, this would place the onus of proof on producers. They would have to make sure that developments did not have any adverse effects on human or animal health or the environment before production was allowed. If benefits were demonstrated regarding, say, the application of biotechnology to food production, then it should only go ahead on the basis that the risks were known and the procedures were in place to deal with them should they become reality. The precautionary principle, however, can be regarded as very conservative. As suggested in Chapter 3, operationalising the precautionary principle as a decision-making tool has proved very difficult and alternatives need to be explored.

Those interested in the ethics of biotechnology have suggested some alternatives. 'Need' could be used as a principle of regulations. For example, before allowing a process to proceed it would have to be demonstrated that there was a need for the outcome, that is, the development of drought-resistant crops, drugs that could deal more effectively with old or new ailments, reducing inputs and hence costs and so on. Alternatives to biotechnology should also be considered. Can the outcomes envisaged from the applications of biotechnology be achieved by other more traditional means? If so, are the biotechnology products needed?

5.1.5 Ownership and Competitive Issues

Several issues have been raised. To begin with there is the issue of whether genes on which and over which modification takes place should come under private ownership. For some people, the moral imperative against ownership can be summed up as 'whatever God has created let no one own'!

Further ethical issues also arise. For example, what advantage is conferred on companies developing biotechnology products? How is the balance of power between seller and purchaser affected? If the seller is conferred an advantage, how does the seller use that advantage? Is the nature of the competition fair? For example, if by purchasing GM seeds from a particular company, a farmer is also required to purchase particular herbicides to receive the benefit of the GM seed, is the company exploiting its position? Economists and regulators tend to view these as competition policy issues and we deal with these commercial aspects in Chapter 6. For some individuals such questions are moral issues that cannot be adequately dealt with through competition policy. Their view is that biotechnology is an important technical change that has far-reaching implications for the organisation of industry, society and the sharing of wealth. Hence, its advancement should be put on hold until the ramifications are less opaque and society has had a chance to express explicitly its preferences regarding how the future should unfold.

5.1.6 Human Ethics

One of the major concerns with biotechnology relates to its use in human engineering. While these issues do not often relate directly to agricultural production there are areas of overlap such as the breeding of pigs or other domesticated animals to provide replacement organs for humans. There is, however, considerable spillover from human issues surrounding the technology to its development in the agricultural sphere. Considerable concern has been expressed regarding the use of the technology for human genetic engineering. This is a central ethical issue that cannot be dealt with here. One of the concerns is that it will not be possible to effectively monitor the use of the technology to prevent human genetic engineering and, hence, the only way to prevent abuse is to prevent the further development of the technology including its agricultural applications. This may influence domestic regulations. It may also manifest itself in consumer boycotts or resistance to products being introduced into the marketplace. It should be noted that for those individuals who have ethical concerns in this area, this is a different issue than being able to privately choose to consume a product. They may perceive that there are large externalities from the existence of the technology itself and, hence, be paternalistic in wanting to restrict the choices of others in society.

5.1.7 Ethical Decision-making and the Ethical Matrix

To aid ethical decision-making the Food Ethics Council (1999) in the UK has developed a so-called 'ethical matrix'. It identifies three ethical principles. First, respect for well-being that covers health issues and matters of welfare. The second principle deals with issues of autonomy such as freedom of choice while the third principle is concerned with social justice and fairness. These three principles encompass most people's ideas of right and wrong. By applying these principles it is possible to work out the implications for a variety of interest groups or stakeholders who are likely to be affected by the adoption of a new technology. The matrix does not make decisions but summarises the issues that need consideration in the decision-making processes. Table 5.1 summarises the main issues to be covered when considering the ethical acceptability of GM crops.

The first column consists of the major stakeholders who will be affected. The top row lists the three principles and below each heading the values attached to each stakeholder. For example, well-being for the Biota would mean conservation, while for producers it would suggest adequate incomes and working conditions. Availability of safe food would be the guiding principle for consumers.

Using this matrix and examining a GM corn (maize) variety with stacked traits offering pest resistance and herbicide tolerance as an example: How ethically acceptable is this product? In this variety, one gene

Table 5.1 The ethical matrix

Respect for	Well-being (health and welfare)	Autonomy (freedom/choice)	Justice (fairness)
The Biota*	Conservation	Biodiversity	Sustainability
Producers	Adequate income and working conditions	Freedom to adopt or not to adopt	Fair treatment in trade and law
Consumers	Availability of safe food	Respect for consumer choice (e.g. labelling)	Affordability

*Biota are 'the plants and animals of a region' (that is wildlife or the 'living environment')
Source: Food Ethics Council (1999)

provides resistance to a herbicide (glufosinate) while a second gene (*Bt*) makes the plants toxic to certain insects. The Food Ethics Council (1999) conclusions are as follows:

> For the Biota, where the principles suggest conservation with biodiversity and sustainability as being key issues, using genetically modified varieties should lead to the reduction of agrochemicals. There may, however, be a host of adverse effects such as the increased vulnerability of plants to pests as a result of pests adapting to the toxins over time. The more effective destruction of weeds may rob insects and invertebrates of vital habitats and, hence, reduce their number. This in turn may well adversely affect the number of other animals and birds for which the insects are a food source. The *Bt* toxin may also harm non-target species such as the monarch butterfly and lacewing.

Producers may gain or may lose in ethical terms as a result of the adoption of this variety of GM corn. While producers in developed countries would gain financially from reduced inputs of agrochemicals (an income gain), the possibility that GM crops might outcross with weedy relatives and result in increased herbicide resistance in weeds, could lead to adverse income effects. Cross-pollination might well damage the livelihood of organic farmers who want to have a non-GM organic crop to sell at the current premiums. Further, as they are only allowed to use *Bt* sprays, the development of *Bt*-resistant insects could also harm their incomes. While some producers will gain, it is likely that others will lose out in terms of autonomy (freedom of choice). If producers are also required to adopt or purchase complementary products from the companies producing GM seeds, then their autonomy will be eroded further.

How will consumers fare under this matrix of ethics? There may be benefits from increased output, expanded choice, lower prices, reduced chemical residues and improved nutrition. There may be issues of food safety, reduced choice (no organic food), increased likelihood of allergies and increased antibiotic resistance. So while food availability may be positive, there may be negative aspects regarding autonomy, freedom and choice. Finally there is the issue of affordability of food. If food is plentiful, then prices should be low. If the producers of biotechnology, however, have sufficient market power or the downstream food processing and retailing sectors are oligopolistic, then they will be able to prevent, to some degree, the fall in price and capture the benefits from the technology.

Looked at through this ethical matrix and subscribing to the implicit values inherent in it, GM corn can be viewed as giving a mixed image. On the one hand, there are ethical benefits to all the stakeholders, but on the other there are ethical costs. In one sense the ethical matrix does its job well; it highlights the issues involved. In this way it mirrors the economist's cost-benefit analysis. Like cost-benefit analysis it also suffers from the fact that what goes into the matrix reflects society's or the analyst's values. While in the case of the ethical matrix the values encompassed by and in it can be said to reflect those of society at large, the weights used when trying to come to a judgement can vary. The result of this would be different ethical outcomes depending on who makes use of the matrix.

Ethical issues are very important in any discussion of biotechnology and genetic modification. The implications are enormous whether a product is acceptable to the market or not. Currently, in Europe there is a backlash against GM foods and a swing in favour of organic produce. The scare over BSE, while not directly associated with biotechnology, has certainly undermined the public's faith in the application of science and technology in the food sector. There is also a feeling regarding the unnaturalness of genetic modification. To some extent, this is a natural response when change is rapid and new ideas difficult to grasp. Conservatism on behalf of the public is not, however, the only factor here. Ethical issues are real. Some of the world's major religions have problems in accepting genetic modification *per se*. Even those that do not have such a difficulty have reservations. Even if these are set aside, the use of biotechnology and genetic modification in food products does have ethical consequences that need to be dealt with. Maybe science will be able, in the future, to eliminate some of these concerns (for example cross-pollination, allergies and so on) but many will remain. Economic analysis may shed some light on this complex issue.

5.2 AN APPROACH TO FORMALLY MODELLING ETHICAL CONCERNS

A person's ethical judgements go beyond matters of self-interest such as personal pleasure and pain, and take a broader view by addressing the common good. Ethical precepts may be applicable to personal life or to relationships with other humans, the environment, broader nature and/or God. On some questions there is a remarkable degree of ethical consensus across individuals from widely different social, cultural and economic backgrounds, religious traditions and so on. Most people, after all, are comfortable speaking of fundamental human rights and there is little disagreement over the basic elements of legal systems. On other issues, there is a lack of ethical consensus. Biotechnology is likely to be one of these latter issues.

Where there is a high degree of ethical consensus, there are often nearly universal answers to position-reversing tests. If I were in anyone else's shoes, I would still contend that it is wrong to steal. This, of course, does not mean that theft will not occur, but it does mean that there will be broad agreement that theft is 'wrong'. For similar reasons, there is likely to be widespread agreement that improvements in economic efficiency are good in most cases. With biotechnology, position-reversing tests of ethical judgements fail to generate unambiguous results. Consider the following question: if I were to switch positions with a person in a future generation, would I advocate the release of GMOs into the environment today? Largely because of the presence of incomplete information concerning the future effects of biotechnology, completely opposing answers to this question will be forthcoming from different individuals. This will be true even if the individuals concerned are fully up to date on the currently available information pertaining to the technology. Where biotechnology is concerned, therefore, we should expect widely divergent ethical judgements from different individuals and groups.

Given the breadth of the ethical domain, the potential for controversy and the important potential effects on economic behaviour, it is useful to provide a framework for systematically incorporating ethical concerns into our discussion of biotechnology. There are some ethical issues relating to biotechnology that are directly bound up with environmental and consumer food safety concerns but other ethical issues go beyond these concerns. We begin with the former ethical issues, which are directly related to our discussion in previous chapters, and then move to the latter issues.

5.2.1 Ethical Dimensions of Food Safety and Environmental Concerns

Figures 5.1 and 5.2 provide overviews of the consumer and environmental issues examined thus far. In Figure 5.1, an individual makes a personal consumption decision. If the non-GM food is chosen for consumption, there are known immediate net benefits, which provide the rationale for purchasing the product, and generally no long-term adverse health effects. If the GM food is consumed, there are once again immediate net benefits. Due to incomplete information, however, the long-term health consequences of consuming the GM food are uncertain. Individuals will attach their own subjective probabilities to potential adverse (and/or favourable) health outcomes. Indeed, the GM and non-GM foods may turn out to have equivalent long-term health effects. Since individuals differ with respect to their subjective probabilities and their degrees of risk aversion, they will make different relative quality assessments between GM and non-GM foods. Thus, there are solid economic grounds upon which some individuals may deem GM foods to be of lower quality. As new relevant information becomes available, of course, product quality assessments are subject to revision one way or the other.

The introduction of GM foods frequently poses hidden quality problems for direct consumption, which were examined extensively in Chapter 4. Whenever GM food and non-GM foods are pooled together, consumers will be unable to tell whether and to what extent the product that they are consuming has been genetically modified. Even when some form of labelling and identity preservation system is in place, there remain some hidden quality issues due to accidental contamination or deliberate cheating.

The second generation (output-trait) genetic modification adds a further dimension to the quality issue in consumption. Genetic modifications may

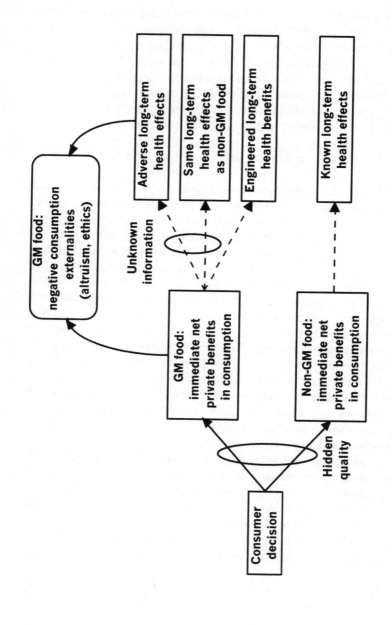

Figure 5.1 – Consumer GM food decisions

offer immediate benefits such as improved taste, enhanced food preparation properties, longer shelf life and so on. Alternatively, there may be long-term health benefits, for example, from improved nutrition as noted in Figure 5.1. In these cases, the perceived quality of the GM food for any individual may or may not be higher than for the non-GM food and long-term health concerns may persist. With output traits, unlike input traits, producers will have a clear incentive to invest in a labelling and identity preservation system that will reduce hidden quality problems. Cheating by non-GM producers, however, is still a potential complication leading to hidden quality problems.

Long-term food safety concerns can also give rise to consumption externalities in the presence of an altruism ethic as suggested by Figure 5.1. While each individual's personal consumption decision based on narrow self-interest formed the basis for our discussion, individuals may certainly be affected by the consumption decisions of others. Individuals with fears of adverse long-term health consequences may be concerned about and negatively affected by other people consuming GM foods. Consequently, there are external costs associated with any one individual's decision to consume GM foods in the presence of the altruism of others with long-term health concerns.

Production decisions pertaining to GMO versus non-GMO products give rise to the spectrum of environmental externality problems discussed in Chapter 3 and summarised by Figure 5.2. A farmer is faced with a choice between production utilising a GMO or a non-GMO. The choice depends on the private net benefits or profits from using GMO versus non-GMO inputs. The decision one way or the other generates immediate externalities or external costs (and/or benefits) for the environment. In many cases the external costs of production using GMOs may be lower than those associated with non-GMOs. Further, environmental externalities may arise because the long-term environmental effects of the release of GMOs into the environment are subject to unknown information. Different people, once again, may legitimately have different assessments of potential for long-term environmental problems associated with dangers to biodiversity and so on. While the equilibrium pattern of production depended on private profits, efficiency depends on net social benefits inclusive of external costs.

There is an ethical dimension to these environmental externalities that were discussed previously in Chapter 3. Externalities typically arise when the activities of market participants spill over and directly affect third

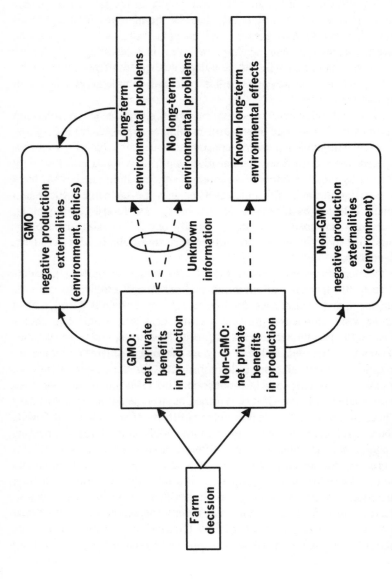

Figure 5.2 – Producer GMO decisions

parties in ways that are not mediated by markets. If reductions in local Monarch butterfly populations arose as some producers adopted *Bt* corn, this might directly and adversely affect local residents. People with a caretaker or 'stewardship ethic' towards the environment in other locales, however, may also perceive adverse indirect effects from the reduction in butterfly populations even though they do not experience the loss directly. Such a stewardship ethic or 'existence value' clearly has the potential to enlarge environmental externalities concerning biotechnology.

When people have a strongly held stewardship ethic concerning the environment, it is likely to affect their individual consumption decisions and quality perceptions. Ethical objections to GMOs based on perceived duty towards the environment, therefore, may lead back to hidden quality problems in individual consumption.

There are, of course, important ethical issues pertaining to biotechnology apart from those connected with the environment and long-term food safety. First, we will consider how additional ethical considerations can aggravate the hidden quality problem and then we will consider further externality problems.

5.2.2 Ethics and Hidden Quality

With input-trait genetic modifications at least, we could reasonably assume that the immediate consumer benefit of consuming the GM food and non-GM food were the same so long as the focus was on consumers and long-term health and food safety issues. When ethical issues become the focus, however, there are numerous reasons why this is not the case. To begin with, consider the possible implications of GMOs for the food consumption rituals and restrictions that are prevalent in many cultural and religious traditions as discussed earlier in this chapter. For example, suppose that a pig gene is introduced to cattle and, for clarity, assume that no adverse long-term health effects are anticipated. Potentially, the consumption of the beef that has been subject to genetic engineering could be perceived to violate dietary prohibitions on pork consumption in the Jewish and Muslim traditions. More broadly, some have questioned whether eating food products modified by human genes might make consumers cannibals. In both cases, perceived quality differences and, thus, hidden quality issues can arise on dietary grounds even if there are no long-term health concerns.

These types of dietary concerns may, in part, be based on ignorance or misunderstanding of the underlying science. DNA is not species specific.

Human beings, for example, have genes in common with many plants and animals, which is the very reason genes can be transferred between different organisms (Grace, 1997). The details of the science, however, may not be sufficient to allay the personal dietary concerns of many individuals. The mere fact that the transferred gene came from pigs or humans may itself be sufficient to trigger an ethical response from some people.

Ethically motivated differences in perceived product quality may emanate from sources other than dietary sensitivities. Some people may object to genetic modifications on animal welfare grounds, and prefer not to consume the resulting product. Further, some people object to tampering with nature or encroaching on God's domain through genetic modification. While these broad ethical issues may go well beyond the level of personal consumption, we maintain our focus on that issue for the moment.

Whenever ethically motivated differences in perceived quality arise for some consumers, hidden quality problems of the type discussed in Chapter 4 will recur. Further, the adverse quality effects on individuals with dietary sensitivities or other ethical objections to GM foods may be quite extreme. In the presence of hidden quality and a pooling equilibrium, it is easy to imagine that many such individuals will entirely cease their consumption and thereby lose their entire consumer surplus. This may occur even if there is a reduction in price, which provides offsetting benefits to those for whom continued consumption is optimal. Consumption will always be discontinued if an individual's marginal utility from consuming the GM food is zero or negative for all possible quantities. Further, even in the context of a labelling and identity preservation system, the relatively low probability of consuming GM foods that arises from accidental contamination and cheating may sometimes precipitate this type of dramatic response. When people have dietary objections to a GM food, they may simply take the view that 'one bad apple spoils the lot'.

5.2.3 Ethics and Externalities

People who have fundamental ethical objections to genetic modification because they believe that it is unnatural or because they believe that it is 'playing God' are likely to experience a wide assortment of external effects as well as the problems noted above pertaining to individual consumption. We can say that these fundamental objections are based on an individual's world view. For many, concern with respect to the possibility of genetic

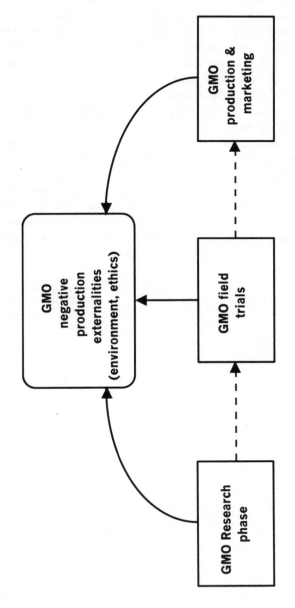

Figure 5.3 – GMO development by biotechnology firms

modification involving humans may be central and lead to overarching objections to biotechnology in general. After Pandora's box has been opened, some may fear that implementing limits pertaining to human genetic modification will prove to be impossible. With such broad ethical objections to biotechnology, individuals may experience additional adverse external effects that go beyond those relating to production and consumption that are shown in Figures 5.1 and 5.2. As Figure 5.3 indicates, adverse external effects may also arise from the full range of activities of biotechnology firms including research, field trials of GMOs, and production and marketing of GMO inputs.

Unlike long-term environmental and health fears that may subside over time provided that the information obtained through experience turns out to be favourable, some ethical issues such as dietary objections may persist. Other more pandemic ethical concerns, however, may eventually subside. When technologies, which were introduced in the past, have elicited resistance based on the broad precepts of religious traditions or broad world views, the resistance has often receded gradually over time with experience. Whether this will be true for biotechnology remains to be seen.

6. Who gets the biotechnology rents?

6.1 CAPTURING THE RENTS

Technological changes tend to increase the welfare of societies that can successfully adopt them. The question of who benefits from the increase in welfare is, however, more complex. The increase in welfare need not benefit any particular group, including the innovators. The division of the benefits arising from a technological change depends on the interplay between the means by which property rights are assigned, the ability to appropriate and protect property rights within the market and the effect of the technological change on the market. Further, in a dynamic sense, the rate at which technological change takes place may also be affected by the ability of innovators to capture the rents that arise from the innovative process. As pointed out in Chapter 2, the inability of private innovators engaging in non-biotechnological breeding to capture sufficient returns to justify their investment in R&D was one of the major reasons why this type of biologically-based research was largely carried out in the public rather than the private sector. The advent of biotechnology has allowed the private sector to undertake a considerably larger proportion of biologically-based research than in the past. The difference this change has made to the division of rents can be illustrated using Figure 6.1.

Prior to the innovation, the market is in equilibrium where $S1 = D$. Price is A and the quantity produced and consumed in the market is $Q1$. Now assume that there is a biologically based technological change provided as a public good because it is not possible for the innovators to capture any of the benefits. The supply curve shifts out to $S2$ due to the increase in efficiency. A new equilibrium is reached at price F and quantity $Q2$.

There has been an increase in welfare arising in the market equal to area H-B-C-E. It should be noted that this increase in welfare takes no account of the public investment in R&D that the new technology required. As

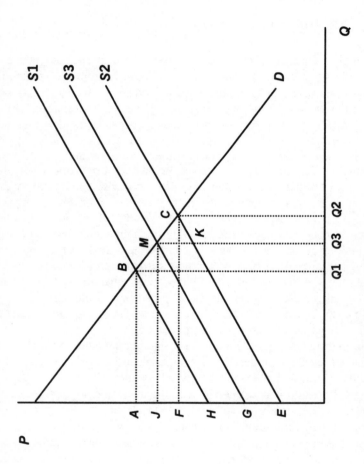

Figure 6.1 – Biotechnology rents

170

suggested in Chapter 2, studies of the rate of return to public investment in R&D in agriculture tend to show relatively high rates of return (Alston et al., 2000). In this simple model there are only consumers and producers to divide the increase in welfare as the public sector supplies the innovation as a public good. A competitive market is also assumed. Consumers win unambiguously from the technological change. As price declines from A to F consumer surplus increases by area A-B-C-F. Whether or not producers win or lose depends upon the relative size of areas A-B-H (producers surplus *ex ante* to the technological change) and F-C-E (the *ex post* producers surplus). If F-C-E > A-B-H then producers are winners as a result of the technological change.

The case when private firms that have monopoly rights to innovations can also be illustrated using Figure 6.1. In this case the private firm that owns the property rights can use its market power to raise the price to producers of inputs incorporating the innovation. If there is no difference in the unmonopolised supply price of the private and public innovation, the privately produced innovation is technically identical to a publicly produced innovation and there can be no substitution of inputs in production; this increase in cost is reflected in the wedge between *S2* and *S3*. The supply curve in the market becomes *S3* with the owner of the innovation receiving the vertical difference between *S3* and *S2* on every unit of output. Moving innovation from being a public to private good leads to a dead weight loss of welfare equal to MCK. The increase in welfare is H-B-M-K-E. Consumer surplus increases by A-B-M-J (< A-B-C-F). Producers may win or lose depending upon the relative sizes of A-B-H and J-M-G. The owner of the rights to the innovation receives G-M-K-E. As in the case of the public innovation, the changes in welfare do not take account of the costs of developing the innovation. If the strong assumption of no input substitution is relaxed, G-M-K-E will be shared among the owner of the rights to the innovation and other input suppliers. Moschini and Lapan (1997) provide a model that explicitly deals with the benefits accruing to the innovating industry.

Farmers are acutely aware that they are now having to pay for what they used to receive as a 'free' public good and there has been considerable debate surrounding this issue. The debate has been particularly acrimonious because the suppliers of the innovation tend to be large transnational corporations. Farmers in developed countries have a long tradition of resisting monopolistic players in their supply chains such as railroads or grain buyers and handlers. The purveyors of biotechnology are often painted as simply the newest manifestation of the monopolistic threat to widely dispersed farmers in competitively organised industries. The debate has not been without effect. One of the most effective methods of capturing the rents from biotechnology would be the 'terminator' gene that prevents germination in crop outputs, effectively preventing the saving of part of a crop for seed. Incorporation of the 'terminator' gene was put on hold by Monsanto (Mooney and Klein, 1999) until there has been a 'full airing of the issues' (Monsanto, 1999). Suppliers of GM seeds have attempted to improve their ability to capture the rents from their innovations by putting in place 'technology-use agreements' whereby farmers agree not to save any of their crop for seed as a condition of purchase. These contracts have also been very contentious.

In the USA, while plant breeders' rights have existed for some time, in the 1980s the US courts began to extend patent rights to a broader spectrum of life science inventions. In 1980, the US Supreme Court in *Diamond* v. *Chakrabarty* found that biological material is patentable if obtained through human intervention. Utility patents for plants are now routinely used to protect transgenic crops in the USA and other countries. Animals and other non-human multicellular organisms can also be patented (Moschini, 2001).

Moschini et al. (2000) develop a model to estimate the welfare effects of GM soybeans. Their model encompasses the welfare effects for both the country of innovation (the USA), a major area of foreign adoption (South America) and the 'Rest of the World'. Their estimates for 1999 adoption rates for GM soybeans suggest that consumers would receive 40 per cent of the economic benefits arising from the technological change, producers 16 per cent and the innovator 44 per cent. If there were to be a complete world-wide adoption of the crop, the model produces estimates that apportion the gains as follows – consumers 41 per cent, producers 22 per cent and the innovator 37 per cent.

While there may be considerable rents available for the innovator, capturing those rents is a complex process. Of course, a model with only three economic actors – consumers, producers and innovators – is too simple. A large number of other actors are involved including co-requisite technology patent holders, seed propagators, the distribution system to farmers, complementary input suppliers, the post-farm-level processing and distribution system and retailers. All will be interested in appropriating some of the economic benefits arising from the innovation. Most of the observed changes in industrial organisation in the agribusiness sector affected by GM technology can be attributed to strategic positioning to capture the available benefits.

6.2 BIOTECHNOLOGY AND THE CHANGING STRUCTURE OF INDUSTRY

The rapid pace of technological change in agricultural biotechnology, the characteristics of the technology and the strategic response of firms to these changes have altered the structure of the input supply sector and are changing vertical relationships between firms downstream in the agrifood chain. A number of economic theories shed light on what is happening, why it is happening and how the agrifood chain may evolve in the future as a result of further technological change.

6.2.1 Structural Trends: Merger, Acquisition and Alliance Activity

Three key structural trends have emerged. First, many of the large chemical and pharmaceutical companies have sold off their chemical manufacturing divisions, reinventing themselves as 'life science' companies. As part of their life science platforms, these companies invested in the seed and biotechnology sectors. This occurred either through backward vertical integration or through strategic alliances and joint venture partnerships with seed companies and biotechnology innovators. Often, the biotechnology innovators that were acquired were small start-up firms, the leading innovators in biotechnology. Monsanto, for example, purchased Calgene and Agracetus in the 1990s; Dow purchased Mycogen in 1996. Major seed merchandisers were also purchased by the life science companies, for example, DuPont purchased Pioneer Hi-Bred International.

A second major trend has been mergers between the large multinational life science companies leading to increased concentration in this sector. Marks et al. (1999) report that over US$22 billion was spent on acquisitions by biotechnology firms between 1995 and 1999, mostly in the biotechnology and seed industries.

A third trend has been closer vertical co-ordination – largely through strategic alliances and joint ventures – between life science companies and downstream feed and food processing companies (Brennan et al., 2000). The changing structure of the input supply sector will be discussed first, followed by presentation of key economic theories that help explain these changes. Changes in the structure of downstream food and feed processing sectors will then be addressed.

6.2.2 The Changing Structure of the Input Supply Sector

Concentration levels in agricultural input markets have increased and, given the rapid pace of technological change, are continuously changing. A snapshot picture provides an indication of the extent of concentration. By the late 1990s, three firms (DuPont, Monsanto and Novartis) accounted for over 60 per cent of the market share for seed corn in the USA. At the same time, two firms dominated the US soybean seed market (Monsanto and DuPont). Monsanto controlled 87 per cent of the US cotton seed market by 1998 (Kalaitzandonakes and Hayenga, 2000). Brennan et al. (2000) report a four-firm concentration ratio of 100 per cent in the US plant biotechnology market in 1998. The agricultural chemical markets in North America and Europe have also become more concentrated.

The driving forces behind these changes in industry structure include the physical characteristics of the technology, strategic choices by firms and the institutional environment in which these firms are operating. Seed proved to be the most effective 'delivery mechanism' for agricultural biotechnology. Access to superior germplasm is necessary for the commercialisation of these technologies – germplasm is an essential complementary asset for agricultural biotechnology (Kalaitzandonakes and Hayenga, 2000). As a result, there were strong incentives for closer relationships with seed companies through contracts, strategic alliances, joint ventures or vertical integration.

The vertical and horizontal mergers and acquisitions undertaken by the major agricultural chemical companies represented a 'strategic choice' to develop a life science platform. Shimoda (1998, p. 5) defines the life science business concept as including:

> pharmaceutical, agriculture-related (crop protection chemicals, agricultural biotechnology, seeds, and animal health), and nutrition/consumer businesses.

The life science companies recognised the potential for biotechnology to reduce farmers' reliance on traditional chemical inputs. Agricultural biotechnology products also offered these companies an opportunity to extract more rent from the agrifood chain by producing higher value products and building in product differentiation at the genetic level. Thus, a related strategic motivation was the ability to raise barriers to entry into the industry through product differentiation, R&D spending, patent protection and restricted access to complementary assets.

A third motivation for merger and acquisition activity has been 'institutional failures', in particular weak patent protection and incomplete contracts. The ability for firms to capture rents from the innovation process depends on their ability to protect the intellectual property inherent in their innovations. As discussed in Chapter 2, patents are an important means by which firms protect their intellectual property. A multitude of patent disputes have arisen between biotechnology firms over the control of patent rights and contractual rights to use key biotechnologies. These disputes bring into question the existence of definitive intellectual property rights to the technologies (Kalaitzandonakes and Hayenga, 2000). In this situation, it becomes extremely difficult to write complete contracts to govern the exchange of intellectual property between independent firms.

6.2.3 Insights from Economic Theory

A number of economic theories shed light on the impacts of innovation on changing industry structure in the input supply sector, including product life-cycle theory, transaction cost economics, competency theory and a collage of theories focusing on issues of market power.

'Product life-cycle theory' and the theory of dominant design suggest a parallel relationship between innovation and industry dynamics. Following a technological breakthrough, during the early phases of innovation, entry into an industry is stimulated as firms innovate. Both new entrants and existing firms compete for the dominant product design, and entry peaks during this 'fluid' phase. As the product matures and a dominant product design emerges, however, entry barriers rise and industry concentration increases. Product innovation falls off and is replaced by process innovation in a 'transitional' phase. Once the dominant design has emerged and the industry has consolidated around a few dominant firms, both product and process innovation dwindle. The remaining firms enter a 'specific' phase wherein they adopt the features of the dominant product concept and compete instead on cost, volume and capacity efficiencies (Kalaitzandonakes and Hayenga, 2000; Marks et al., 1999).

Kalaitzandonakes and Hayenga (2000) argue that innovation and industrial structure in the crop biotechnology industry have followed this pattern, with firm entry into crop biotechnology peaking in the early 1980s following a series of scientific breakthroughs. A variety of potential product forms competed for technical dominance, for example, transgenic plants and genetically engineered micro-organisms that could be applied to a seed as an innoculent. Eventually, transgenic plants emerged as the dominant design in the form of input-trait crops with built-in pest resistance. This signalled a move out of the 'fluid' phase of the innovation life cycle and was quickly followed by industry consolidation through merger and acquisition activity.

'Transaction cost economics' (TCE) offers insights into the nature of vertical co-ordination between agrobiotechnology, seed and feed and food processing companies. Vertical co-ordination refers to the means by which products move along the production, processing and distribution chain from input supplier to final consumer. There exist a spectrum of vertical co-ordination possibilities or 'governance structures', from spot markets at one extreme, to vertical integration at the other, with a range of 'hybrid' methods in between, including various types of contracts, strategic alliances and joint ventures (Hobbs, 1996). In a spot market, products move between stages (for example, production to processing) in response to price signals. In a vertically integrated firm, this movement is co-ordinated via within-firm managerial orders. The co-ordination mechanism may be more complicated in the case of hybrid governance structures. Coase (1937) was the first to pose markets and hierarchies (firms) as alternative means of organising production. He argued that there were costs to using the market mechanism and that a firm will emerge when the costs of organising a transaction within a vertically integrated firm are less than organising that transaction through the market.

The transaction cost approach recognises that there are costs to carrying out transactions and that the governance structure which emerges will be that which minimises the sum of production and transaction costs (Williamson, 1979). Transaction costs include: (1) *ex ante* search costs that arise prior to a transaction, for example in searching for information on products, prices and/or trading partners; (2) negotiation costs which arise from the physical act of the transaction, for example, the legal costs of drawing up contracts or the services of an agent; and (3) *ex post* monitoring and enforcement costs that arise after a transaction has been agreed to and include the costs of ensuring that the pre-agreed terms of the transaction are adhered to, and also the costs of seeking redress in the event these terms are reneged upon.

Williamson (1979) explains how the characteristics of a transaction, including uncertainty, frequency and asset specificity,[1] affect which governance structure is the most transaction-cost efficient. Complexity was later added as another important transaction dimension. In the presence of complexity and high levels of uncertainty and asset specificity, we expect to see vertical integration.

Uncertainty, complexity and asset specificity characterise the transaction between agrobiotechnology innovators and seed distributors. Initially, a variety of contractual, strategic alliance and joint venture relationships existed between biotechnology and seed companies. The complexity of new biotechnological products, however, meant that they often contained several potentially patentable traits. Adding to this complexity was the fact that ownership of the intellectual property in these technologies was not definitive – there were a number of overlapping patents, leading to disputes among biotechnology companies and between biotechnology and seed companies as to who owned the rights to use which technologies. Furthermore, as innovation progressed and increasingly more traits were patented, a new product might contain patentable traits owned by more than one company. Added to this complexity is a situation of uncertainty, which arises for two reasons. First, the uncertainty over the ownership of intellectual property rights and second, uncertainty born of time. There are significant time-lags between the initial genetic engineering innovation of a specific trait and the commercialisation of this technology. Contracts that co-ordinate biotechnology and seed assets are necessarily drawn up years before a product reaches the market (Kalaitzandonakes and Hayenga, 2000). Both problems mean that writing complete, fully contingent contracts is almost impossible. As a result, the transaction costs of drawing up such contracts and monitoring and enforcing the contractual agreement may become prohibitive. This creates a strong incentive for vertical integration between the biotechnology and seed companies so as to internalise this transaction cost.

The investment in a biotechnology innovation may be appropriable by a seed company because the innovation is generally specific to the germplasm through which it will be delivered. This creates a potential hold-up problem and increases monitoring and enforcement costs for the biotechnology firm. *Ceteris paribus*, vertical integration of the biotechnology and seed companies may be a more transaction-cost efficient governance outcome.

'Competency (or capabilities) theory' explains the existence, structure and boundaries of firms by individual or team competencies – the skills and tacit knowledge – within a firm. Hence, firms will form closer vertical relationships through strategic alliances, joint ventures or contractual relationships or will vertically integrate in order to access these competencies in other firms. Teece et al. (1994, p. 18) describe a firm's competencies as:

> . . . a set of differentiated technological skills, complementary assets, and organizational routines and capacities that provide the basis for a firm's competitive capacities in one or more businesses.

Knowledge is central to the competency approach. There are three types of knowledge: (1) codifiable knowledge that can be specified in formulas, designs and patents; (2) tacit knowledge that is acquired through learning-by-doing; and (3) distributed knowledge which is only valuable if used in conjunction with others, thereby requiring co-operation or use within a vertically integrated firm.

The competency theorists argue that transferring knowledge between independent firms through the market may be ineffective, whereas a vertically integrated firm as an organisation facilitates learning and the transmission of information between production stages. Firms emerge when they can co-ordinate the learning process more efficiently than is possible through open market transactions. The argument is reminiscent of Coase's (1937) explanation of the existence of a firm, which became a cornerstone of the transaction cost approach. The capabilities of a firm set limits on its boundaries and provide an incentive for merger and acquisition activity to expand that knowledge base.

Combining insights from the competency approach and TCE enhances our understanding of the changing structure of the biotechnology industry. Transferring tacit knowledge between firms is complex and subject to uncertainty, thus resulting in high transaction costs and providing a motivation for closer vertical co-ordination. Oxley (1997) argues that technology is a mixture of codified data and poorly defined tacit know-how. While it may be possible to transfer codified data between firms through fully contingent contracts, the transfer of tacit know-how is problematic. It may not be possible to specify all the pay-off relevant activities in a contractual agreement or it may be difficult to adequately monitor and enforce relevant activities. This situation leads to incomplete contracts and moral hazard risk.

Some economists have argued that a high degree of tacit know-how in a technological innovation would reduce the danger of the technology being appropriated by a partner firm since it is more difficult to appropriate the intellectual property in a patent if the partner firm also needs the knowledge that goes with the patent. A seed company, for example, would find it more difficult to appropriate the transgenic technology of a biotechnology firm if this would also require knowledge of gene splicing technology. Oxley (1997) disagrees, arguing that the inclusion of tacit know-how in a contractual relationship makes contracting more difficult as the knowledge asset cannot be precisely specified.   The rash of court cases over agrobiotechnology patent ownership and patent infringements would tend to support the latter view.

Firms are often reluctant to settle patent disputes through the court process because court proceedings are in the public record and, as such, commercially sensitive information about new technologies may be revealed to competitors. It may also be difficult for a third party to verify appropriation of tacit knowledge between contractual parties. Both the negotiation costs of attempting to draw up fully contingent contracts to govern the transfer of agrobiotechnology innovations between biotechnology firms and seed distributors, and the monitoring and enforcement costs of policing a contractual relationship, are likely to be high. More hierarchical governance structures, such as vertical integration, would lower these transaction costs.

Economic theories pertaining to 'market power' and 'efficiency' also provide useful insights.   A long-standing dilemma has been whether monopoly power increases or decreases the incentive for innovation. Arrow (1962) found that a monopolist, already extracting monopoly profit, would have less to gain from an innovation that would reduce its existing earnings than would a firm in a competitive industry earning zero economic profits. This view is reinforced by the 'X-inefficiency' literature which argues that, in the absence of competitive pressures, 'managerial slack' and X-inefficiencies arise. Particularly in situations in which there is a 'divorce' between ownership and control, managers have a reduced incentive to manage their firm efficiently, to push employees harder and so on, meaning that the firm is not operating on the boundaries of its efficiency frontier (Leibenstein, 1966). Similarly, there may be a reduced incentive to innovate.

While many economists argue that competition encourages innovation as profit-maximising firms compete for market share, Brennan et al. (2000) point to a lack of clear evidence that decreased competition leads to a reduction in innovation activity. Furthermore, Schumpeter (1942) found that large firm size and a dominant market share position encourage innovation through the ability of these firms to achieve economies of scale in R&D. The protection of intellectual property rights strengthens the incentive to invest, which provides greater opportunities for larger firms, reinforcing their dominant position (Lesser, 1998). The efficiency gains from economies of scale, it is argued, offset any losses from decreased competition.

In the case of agricultural biotechnologies, R&D and new product development are lengthy and expensive processes. There would appear to be merit in the argument that economies of scale exist in biotechnology R&D. Yet, many of the leading innovators in agrobiotechnology in the early to mid-1990s were small start-up companies. How do we reconcile the apparent contradictions within economic theory regarding the relationship between innovation and industry structure? The answer may lie in the type of innovation and the subtle, yet important, differences between radical innovations and non-radical innovations. Some economists have argued that small entrant firms have a greater incentive to introduce radical innovations thereby making obsolete existing technologies or products, while incumbent firms are more likely to be focused on variations of existing technologies (Lesser, 1998). Overall, the economics literature is divided as to whether innovation encourages or inhibits industry concentration. Of course, the causality could run the other way – does concentration encourage or inhibit innovation? What is clear is that regardless of direction, innovation and industry structure are inextricably linked.

The 'contestability' of a market may be important in determining whether firms in a highly concentrated industry behave competitively and have an incentive to innovate. A market is perfectly contestable if there are no barriers to entry or exit. If the dominant firms use their market power to make economic profits, entry will occur, competing away these profits. The nature and extent of 'barriers to entry' are central to whether a market is contestable. One of the concerns about the changing structure of the agrobiotechnology sector is the ability of incumbent firms to create barriers to entry, which inhibit competition and lead to a misallocation of resources and a loss in social welfare. Potential barriers to entry are both physical and financial.

Physical barriers to entry arise from the nature of the technology. If firms are able to patent a key genetic component or technique, it becomes an essential building block for future product innovations. Patent protection allows them to restrict or control access to this genetic material or enabling technology. Brennan et al. (2000) report that, in the USA, the top four firms held 41 per cent of the patents in corn by 1996, 53 per cent of the soybean patents by 1997, 77 per cent of tomato patents by 1997 and 38 per cent of *Bt* patents by 1998. Furthermore, in 1999, US patents on key gene transformation technologies for grains were held by two firms – DuPont and Monsanto. Concerns over the potential for restrictive use of this technology prompted the US Federal Trade Commission to force Monsanto to share the rights to their agrobacterium patent for transforming grain with the University of California at Berkeley (Brennan et al., 2000). A delicate balance is therefore required – protection of intellectual property is important for encouraging innovation – yet 'overprotection' may stifle further innovation by inhibiting competition.

Traditionally, firms have been able to create barriers to entry through tie-in sales, whereby customers purchasing one product also purchased a line of related products. This strategy makes it more difficult for a new firm to break into the market as they must offer a range of similar products, rather than competing with a single product. To some extent, this has happened with the creation of crops genetically engineered to be resistant to specific herbicides. Hayenga (1998, p. 9) discusses the technology fees that growers pay to the seed company and which are part of the technology-use agreements discussed in section 6.1:

> Seed and chemical package deals often result in discounts from these fees as Monsanto, and competitors with other herbicide resistant seed varieties, link prices paid for seed and chemicals to purchase volumes of both products. The idea is to tie the seed customer more closely to the chemical product.

Independent seed companies dealing with Monsanto received substantial financial incentives to increase the proportion of their total sales accounted for by Monsanto's herbicide-tolerant varieties (Hayenga, 1998). This strategy makes it more difficult for competing herbicide-tolerant products to enter the market. Legal disputes have arisen over whether a company selling herbicide-tolerant seed has the right to prevent other herbicide manufacturers from testing their herbicides on its seed. A number of these legal disputes came to a head at the end of the 1990s:

In 1998, Zeneca claimed that Monsanto had engaged in unfair competition by foreclosing other glyphosate producers from testing their products on Roundup Ready soybeans, and restricting seed companies licensing Roundup Ready soybean technology from selling much of a competitor's glyphosate. . . . Rhone Poulenc Agro has charged that Monsanto's contracts with Roundup Ready licensees restrict competition and prevent entry in the corn herbicide market. Rhone Poulenc Agro claims that financial incentives offered to seed companies make it highly desirable to produce only glyphosate resistant corn. Further, the tying arrangements between the farmer's Roundup Ready seed and herbicide use are a barrier to entry for other herbicide producers. Monsanto does not allow competing herbicides even to be tested on Roundup Ready corn (Hayenga, 1998, p. 10)

Financial barriers to entry are of particular relevance to agricultural biotechnology given the substantial investment in R&D necessary to develop and commercialise a new technology. Furthermore, econometric studies of the US biotechnology industry reveal a significant correlation between the number of patents that a company owns and its financial valuation in capital markets (Brennan et al., 2000). A higher market valuation position enables a firm to leverage additional financial resources to invest in R & D activities, thereby putting new entrant firms at a further financial disadvantage relative to incumbent firms holding existing patents.

A combination of the physical barrier to entry inherent in patent protection and a financial barrier to entry for smaller firms arises from the threat of legal action. The complex nature of biotechnology and the uncertainty regarding overlapping patent claims means that patent infringement litigation is extremely costly. Even the threat of litigation can be sufficient to deter small would-be entrants (Lesser, 1998).

6.2.4 Changes in Downstream Feed and Food Processing Industries

Agricultural biotechnology is also resulting in changes to industry structure in the downstream food and feed sectors. This has been slower to develop because it is driven primarily by the second generation of output-trait biotechnologies. Integration into the downstream food sector may also be an extension of the life science platform of the biotechnology companies. As the discussion in Chapter 4 indicated, input-trait technologies also have implications for segregation of GM and non-GM food chains.

Products with enhanced output traits, such as improved processing characteristics, improved taste, extended shelf life, functional food properties and so on provide a strong impetus for the formation of identity-preserved supply chains so as to capture the value of the enhanced trait. Life science companies would have little incentive to invest in the development of output-trait crops or livestock products if the resulting output was blended with conventional produce and sold through a commodity marketing channel, receiving an average commodity price. Farmers would have little incentive to produce these products for the same reason.

Under this scenario, food and feed processing companies who value the enhanced trait would be required to sort products purchased through the commodity marketing channel to discover which of them contained the enhanced trait (assuming measurement technology was available to enable this). If buyers incur higher measurement and sorting costs in ascertaining the quality of a product, the net price they are willing to pay for the product declines. Sellers have an incentive to reduce measurement costs for buyers so that buyers avoid costly sorting activities (Barzel, 1980). In the case of output-trait products, identity preservation of the product containing the desired trait, if credible, removes the need for costly sorting by buyers. Sellers are able to capture value from the trait and can appropriate more of the buyer's consumer surplus by more closely aligning the price received with the buyer's willingness to pay.

The issue of 'who gets the rents' is crucial to the manner in which vertical co-ordination between life science companies and downstream feed and food processors will evolve. Marks et al. (1999) argue that changes in industry structure can be expected if ownership and strength of intellectual property rights for quality traits is similar to that of the first generation biotechnologies. We can expect to see closer vertical co-ordination through strategic alliances, joint ventures, or forward integration by life science companies into downstream industries as they attempt to capture the rents from the downstream markets where the technologies are delivered. Examples of these changes emerged during the early stages of the commercialisation of output-trait technologies. Cargill and Monsanto, for example, formed a joint venture in 1998; Novartis owns Gerber foods; DuPont and Pioneer Hi-bred originally created Optimum Quality Grains through a joint venture (Brennan et al., 2000). Among other output-trait enhanced products, Optimum Quality Grains commercialised high oil corn (an enhanced livestock feed), a low saturated fat soybean (a functional food marketed under the name LoSatSoy) and high oleic soybean and sunflower oils (Marks et al., 1999). Farmers grow these crops under contracts co-ordinated by Optimum Quality Grains. Of course, there are also strong motivations for downstream food and feed processors to be the driving force behind closer vertical linkages with their input suppliers in order to secure access to products with specific traits.

The asset specificity of investments in output-trait products also suggest closer vertical co-ordination. This specificity can occur on both sides of the transaction.   Life science companies may invest in biotechnology to enhance a trait specific to the needs of one processor.   Relatively high levels of concentration in the feed and food processing sectors create a 'small-numbers-bargaining' situation that compounds this problem. On the other hand, processors may be dependent on one life science company for the development and supply of inputs with specific enhanced traits. A small-numbers-bargaining problem also characterises this relationship. Brand name specificity leaves the processor vulnerable to opportunistic appropriation of the quasi-rents inherent in the product's brand name. In the presence of high levels of asset specificity, we expect closer vertical co-ordination. Whether this takes the form of joint ventures, strategic alliances or vertical integration remains to be seen and may depend on other transaction characteristics such as uncertainty, complexity and frequency.

Input-trait products have additional implications for industry structure. Given the negative consumer reaction to GM crops – and the policy responses of some countries, including production and import bans and compulsory labelling requirements – segregation of GM and non-GM products may be essential if non-GM products are to maintain access to these markets. This is particularly problematic for grains in the USA and Canada because of the existing bulk grain handling system whereby farmers deliver their grain to a local elevator and it is shipped in bulk to domestic and international markets. There is disagreement over the ability of bulk grain handling systems to handle segregated grains and oilseeds. Options include designated bins at elevators, designated elevators and containerised shipment, possibly from the farm to the end-user. While it is beyond the scope of this chapter to delve into the relative costs and benefits of alternative grain handling systems, two key implications for industry structure emerge. First, who will bear the cost burden of segregation for input-trait crops? Second, how will relationships between downstream food processors and retailers change if there is a strong demand for assured non-GM food?

To some extent, the first question is the reverse of 'Who gets the rents?'. While it is a relatively simple matter to acknowledge the possible presence of GMOs, proving the absence of GMOs to the satisfaction of downstream food processors and final consumers will be more difficult. If some consumers are willing to pay a premium for 'GM-free' food, there is an incentive for producers of GM food to cheat and misrepresent their products as non-GM. Clearly, this creates credibility problems for non-GM supply chains, and it is these chains that incur the burden of proof.

Processors and retailers selling their foods under a 'GM-free' assurance may need to conduct costly testing of inputs to determine whether GMOs are present. In the absence of measurement technologies to allow this (particularly for complex further processed products) or if the costs of testing are prohibitive, this assurance can only be provided through closer monitoring of upstream suppliers. The resulting monitoring and enforcement costs imposed on downstream food processors and retailers could be reduced through closer vertical co-ordination with upstream suppliers (Hobbs and Plunkett, 1999).[2]

6.2.5 The Future Structure of the Biotechnology Industry

The rapid pace of technological change means that the structure of the biotechnology industry is in a state of constant flux. Drawing solid conclusions as to the final structure of the industry in terms of the numbers of firms is prone to inaccuracy. Economic analysis can, however, bring to light a number of important trends and their potential consequences. The future structure of the industry is inextricably linked with the institutional framework for establishing and enforcing intellectual property rights, as well as the intent and strength of competition (anti-trust) regulations.

The mergers, acquisitions and alliances prevalent in the biotechnology seed complex conform with the predictions of economic theory with respect to asset specificity, capturing the value from investments and the creation of barriers to entry. Further merger, acquisition and alliance activity between life science companies and downstream feed and food processing firms can be expected. There remain important policy implications for the effects on economic welfare of industry concentration at these levels. The potential for abuse of market power remains an important concern for competition regulators and should not be ignored. However, any regulatory investigation of changing industry structure should also consider Williamson's (1971) insight that non-standard modes of organisation may be transaction cost efficient, rather than outright evidence of an abuse of market power.

NOTES

1. Asset specificity arises when one party has made an investment in an asset which is specific to another party and which has little or no value in its next best alternative use. The party making the asset specific investment is vulnerable to the other party acting opportunistically in an attempt to capture the 'specialised appropriable quasi-rents' inherent in the specific asset (Klein et al., 1978). Vulnerability to opportunistic behaviour will deter the first party from making this investment if there is not a credible means of safeguarding the asset specific investment. This situation is known as the 'hold-up' problem.
2. See Chapter 4 for a discussion of this issue.

7. International issues

7.1 BIOTECHNOLOGY AND INTERNATIONAL TRADE

Public attitudes concerning biotechnology and genetically modified foods vary considerably across countries. Amid mounting concern in many countries, there remains much more resistance to GMOs in Europe and Japan than in North America. These differences in the degree of acceptance of GMOs across countries have profound implications for international trade that are virtually certain to give rise to trade disputes (Gaisford and Lau, 2000; Kerr, 1999). Both the hidden quality problems discussed in Chapter 4 and the externality problems examined in Chapter 3 have important international dimensions that are likely to severely test the international trading system. We begin this chapter with a simple illustrative model that clarifies the basis for such international trade controversies.[1] We consider a simple two-country world consisting of Europe and North America where free trade prevails prior to the introduction of a new GM product. We assume that a new GM product is developed in North America and that any monopoly or oligopoly rents associated with the GM product accrue entirely in North America. Meanwhile, Europe prohibits domestic production of the GM product and continues to produce only the non-GM version of the product. These two assumptions simplify the analysis by ruling out direct producer-side benefits from biotechnology in Europe.

To simplify further, we assume that Europe is small relative to North America. We make this assumption to abstract from the conventional terms of trade effects stemming from import restriction and focus entirely on quality and externality issues. Consequently, Europe can import as much as it likes without having a perceptible impact on the price. Within Europe, we assume highly stylised supply chains in which processors, distributors and retailers are perfectly competitive. For simplicity, we also assume that each of these stages is initially costless and remains so unless labelling requirements force the separation of supply chains. Thus, in the absence of labelling, it is as if farm-level producers sell to final consumers.

In principle, the welfare or utility of any individual European will depend on both the quantities of the GM and non-GM products which are directly consumed as 'private goods', and the aggregate quantities of the GM food produced, consumed and imported. We will defer the consideration of the latter negative 'public-good' feature for a moment and focus first on hidden quality issues pertaining to private consumption.

7.1.1 Hidden Quality: A GM Import Embargo versus Unlabelled Imports

In Europe, we divide consumers into two groups following the classification scheme introduced in Chapter 4. Those consumers in group A perceive the non-GM food to be of higher quality in personal consumption. This may be because of fears of long-term health problems with GM-foods, or for ethical or environmental reasons as discussed in Chapter 5. Those consumers in group B treat the GM and non-GM food as perfect substitutes in personal consumption.

In the absence of a credible labelling and identity preservation system, GM food will be pooled together with the non-GM counterpart, and Europeans in group A will face a hidden quality problem. While group A consumers are not able to determine whether a particular batch of the product has been genetically modified before or even after consumption, they can infer the probabilities of consuming a unit of the GM food versus a non-GM food by observing production and trade data. Thus, they are aware of the average or expected quality. Of course, the higher the probability of consuming a GM food, the lower the expected quality and the less that members of group A will be willing to pay for any given quantity of the pooled product.

North America, we assume, consists only of group B consumers. Since the GM food can be supplied at a lower price, the GM food completely displaces the non-GM counterpart in North America. This complete switch casts the change in Europe's trading opportunities in the most dramatic way possible. Non-GM imports are no longer available on the same terms as before and will not be available at all unless they can be certified as GM-free under a labelling regime.

Figure 7.1 can be used to analyse the impact of how the introduction of a GM food in North America affects Europe's market. Europe's supply curve is S and its demand curve is Di prior to the introduction of the GM food. Initially, North America will supply Europe unlimited quantities of the non-GM food at a world price of Pi. Since the initial pre-GM European price is then equal to Pi, European consumption is equal to DQi and European production is SQi with imports making up the difference.

As a result of the development of a new biotechnology, imports of the GM food become available at a price of Pf and non-GM imports are no longer available. Consider the case where Europe permits unlabelled imports. In this case, there is a pooled market where European production is exclusively non-GM but imports are all GM. Since group A consumers perceive a decline in average quality with the pooling or mixing of GM and non-GM foods, they will be willing to pay less as a result. Consequently, the demand curve shifts to Dm and European consumption moves to DQf. Figure 7.1 shows a case where the quantity consumed happens to have fallen because the impact of the quality reduction, which lowers consumption, outweighs the effect of the price reduction, which increases consumption. Consumption would have risen if the effect of the lower quality had been smaller than the effect of the lower price. European production falls to SQf due to the lower price. Final imports are equal to the difference between DQf and SQf.

There are two opposing effects on European welfare. On the one hand, the decline in perceived quality, and thus willingness to pay, among group A consumers reduces aggregate consumer surplus by area *a-i-j-c* Euro. This loss is an adverse quality effect of the type examined in Chapter 4. On the other hand, the price reduction from Pi to Pf is beneficial to all consumers and causes an increase in consumer surplus equal to *Pi-j-f-Pf* Euro. Meanwhile, producer surplus falls by *Pi-k-g-Pf* Euro. Thus, the net benefit from lower prices is *k-j-f-g* Euro. This net benefit from lower prices occurs because Europe is on an import basis. Since the quantity consumed exceeds the quantity produced, the consumer benefit exceeds the producer loss.

European producers are hurt by the introduction of cheap unlabelled GM imports given that they are not permitted to use the new biotechnology themselves. All group B consumers gain because the price has fallen and they perceive the GM food to be of equal quality. While some members of group A will lose, others will gain. Those members of group A for whom the individual adverse quality effect outweighs the beneficial price effect will be worse off. Nevertheless, for members of group A who perceive sufficiently small quality differences between non-GM and GM food, the benefits of the lower price will more than compensate the loss in quality.

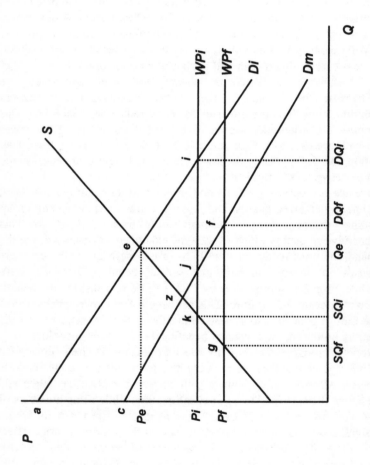

Figure 7.1 – A pooling equilibrium in international trade

Allowing unlabelled GM food imports unrestricted access to Europe leads to a positive or negative overall change in European welfare of *a-i-j-c* minus *k-j-f-g* Euro. If the beneficial net price effect outweighs the adverse quality effect, Europe gains from the new biotechnology. Unfortunately, the harmful quality effect could also dominate the beneficial price effect as shown in Figure 7.1 where area *a-i-j-c* is larger than area *k-j-f-g*. This leaves Europe worse off after the introduction of unlabelled GM food imports. We focus on this case, not because it is inevitable or even more likely, but because it poses much greater problems for policy-makers. The central issue is whether there are alternative policy responses to the advent of GM food imports that are superior to unfettered access.

We now consider the extreme case where Europe imposes an import embargo instead of allowing unlabelled GM food imports. In this case, only non-GM food remains available and the relevant demand curve remains Di. Consequently, an adverse quality effect does not arise. There is, however, a harmful price effect as Europe moves to autarky. Since non-GM imports are unavailable, the quantity produced and consumed in Europe is Qe. Thus, the price rises from Pi to the embargo price, Pe. The price increase raises producer surplus by *Pe-e-k-Pi* Euro, but reduces consumer surplus by *Pe-e-i-Pi* Euro. Since Europe is initially an importer where consumption is greater than production, the adverse effect of the price increase on consumers necessarily outweighs the beneficial effect on producers. European producers gain, but all consumers – those in groups A and B alike – lose. Europe, therefore, experiences an unambiguous loss of *e-i-k* Euro. Since Europe forfeits its previous gains from trade under an import embargo, European welfare must fall relative to the pre-GM state. From the European policy perspective, however, the overall loss relative to the pre-GM state is a moot point. Since Europe cannot prevent the development of the GM in North America, the pre-GM state cannot continue.

The key question is whether the inevitable loss from an import embargo can ever be smaller than the possible loss from permitting unlabelled access to GM imports. Europe, in fact, may lose less by prohibiting imports than by allowing unlabelled GM imports. Recall that the loss in welfare with unlabelled access is *a-i-j-c* minus *k-j-f-g* Euro while the loss in welfare with the embargo is *e-i-k* Euro. In either case area *e-i-j-z* is lost. In comparison with unlabelled GM imports, the embargo avoids the loss of area *a-e-z-c*, but it involves the loss of area *z-j-k* and forgoes the gain of *k-j-f-g*. The import embargo is superior, therefore, if area *a-e-z-c* exceeds area *z-f-g*, which happens to be the case in Figure 7.1. Of course, in other situations unlabelled imports will be superior to an embargo.

From the European perspective, the import embargo may sometimes be the lesser of two evils. Under such circumstances, import embargoes would sometimes be warranted in response to a foreign biotechnology innovation if the only two policy alternatives were an embargo or unlabelled access. The robustness of this conclusion should, of course, be evaluated by introducing other possible policy responses such as the mandatory labelling of GM imports.

7.1.2   Revealed Quality: Labelling of GM Imports versus an Embargo

Suppose that Europe requires labelling for all GM imports, while it continues to ban domestic GM production. Although North America would still be willing to export the non-GM product at the original world price, we assume that it would be prohibitively expensive for North American producers to certify that their product is GM-free and legitimately avoid the labelling requirement. From a European welfare perspective, this assumption represents a worst case scenario. It also leads to a very simple separating equilibrium in Europe. There is a high-quality non-GM market supplied exclusively by European producers and a separate low-quality GM market supplied exclusively by North American producers. For simplicity, we also suppose that Europe is able to fully and costlessly monitor and enforce the labelling requirement despite the apparent incentive for North American producers to misrepresent their GM product.

The labelling policy for GM imports can be examined using Figure 7.2. Initially the GM food is not available so that only the non-GM market shown in panel (a) is relevant. The initial European demand curve for the non GM food is D1i (which corresponds with Di in Figure 7.1), the European supply curve is S1 (which corresponds with S in Figure 7.1) and the initial world price is P1i (which corresponds with Pi in Figure 7.1). Consequently, initial domestic consumption is DQ1i (which equals DQi in Figure 7.1) and initial domestic production is SQ1i (which equals SQi in Figure 7.1). If an embargo were imposed to block the import of the new GM food, the equilibrium quantity would be Q1e (which equals Qe in Figure 7.1) and the equilibrium price would be P1e (which equals Pe in Figure 7.1). The European welfare loss from employing an embargo in response to the introduction of GM food is *e-i-k* Euro in Figure 7.2 just as it was in Figure 7.1.

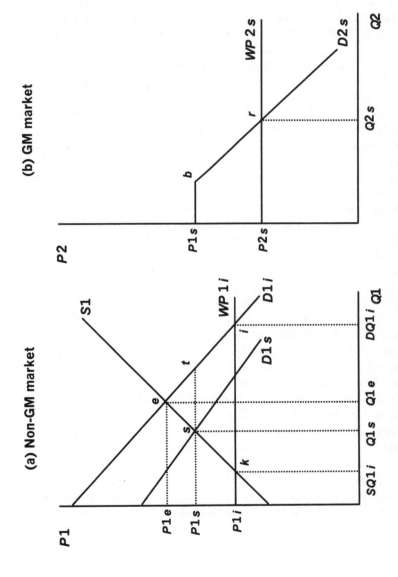

(a) Non-GM market

(b) GM market

Figure 7.2 – A separating equilibrium with labelled GM food imports

In the separating equilibrium that arises with the mandatory labelling of GM food imports, European consumers can choose to purchase from the high-quality non-GM market shown in panel (a), or they can buy from the low-quality GM market shown in panel (b). All members of group B will switch to the GM market in response to the lower price. While some group A consumers will remain in the non-GM market, others will find the attraction of lower prices on the GM market sufficiently compelling to overcome their aversion to the genetic modification. Consequently, the demand curve for the non-GM shifts to the left, to D1s given that the price of the GM food is P2s. The price of the non-GM product is subject to two opposing forces. Since non-GM imports are no longer available, there is upward pressure on the non-GM price, but since some European demand shifts to the GM food, there is opposing downward pressure as well. While we will eventually examine the case shown in Figure 7.3 where the price falls, we concentrate, for the moment, on the case shown in Figure 7.2 where the non-GM price rises. It is important to observe that even in this case where the price of the non-GM rises, it rises less with labelling than with an import embargo because some European demand shifts to the low-quality GM substitute product.

In the GM market the demand curve is D2s contingent on the non-GM price P1s. No one will purchase the GM food at a price above P1s, but all the group B consumers are willing to buy the GM food if its price is equal to P1s. This gives rise to the perfectly elastic segment of the D2s demand curve, *P1s-b*. With lower GM food prices, the quantity demanded rises because group B consumers will buy more and some members of group A will switch. In equilibrium, labelling and sorting costs will typically cause the GM food price, P2s, to be somewhat higher than the price which would have prevailed in the absence of labelling (that is, Pf in Figure 7.1). In the separating equilibrium shown in Figure 7.2, Q1s units of the non-GM food are transacted at the price of P1s, and Q2s units of the GM food are transacted at the price of P2s. Due to the perceived quality difference, P1s necessarily exceeds P2s.

We assess the impact of mandatory labelling of GM food imports on European welfare in Figure 7.2 by considering the two markets in sequence. We start on the non-GM market and raise the price from P1i to P1s while holding the price of the GM food at its initial effectively infinite level. Since the relevant curve remains D1i, the loss in consumer surplus from the higher price on the non-GM market 'before' consumers are given the opportunity to switch markets is *P1s-t-i-P1i* Euro. The gain in producer surplus from the higher price is $P1s$-s-k-$P1i$ Euro, so that there is an overall loss of s-t-i-k Euro on the non-GM market. This is an adverse net price effect. We now turn to the GM food market with the price of the non-GM food already changed to P1s. Since the relevant demand curve for the GM food is D2s, there is a gain in new consumer surplus of $P1s$-b-r-$P2s$ Euro obtained by members of group B and those members of group A who switch. This is a beneficial new-product effect.

In Figure 7.2, the overall gain to Europe from allowing GM food imports with mandatory labelling is equal to $P1s$-b-r Euro from the GM market minus s-t-i-k Euro from the non-GM market. It should be emphasised that whenever the beneficial new-product effect associated with the GM food outweighs the harmful net price effect associated with the non-GM food, European welfare rises. In Figure 7.2, however, the adverse price effect dominates and European welfare falls notwithstanding the labelling requirement.

While a labelling policy cannot guarantee gains from biotechnological imports, such a policy is typically superior to an import embargo. In Figure 7.2 we have seen that even when labelling leads to an increase in the price of the GM food, it is generally a smaller increase than that which accompanies an embargo. Consequently, there is a smaller resultant European welfare loss on the non-GM market. Whereas s-t-i-k Euro are lost with labelling, e-i-k Euro are lost with the embargo. Further, on the GM market there is a new-product gain of $P1s$-b-r-$P2s$ Euro from mandatory labelling that does not arise with the embargo. Thus, the labelling of GM food imports is unambiguously better than an import embargo by $P1s$-b-r-$P2s$ plus e-t-s Euro.

Even if Europe would be better off with a GM import embargo than with unlabelled imports, permitting labelled imports will typically yield higher welfare. There are two caveats pertaining to this conclusion. First, it should be observed that if there are only group A consumers in Europe and the perceived quality difference is sufficiently large, mandatory labelling that identifies the GM food could result in no European purchases of the GM food at the going world price. Thus, in such extreme cases, mandatory labelling will have the same effect on European welfare as the import embargo because it has the same effect on European imports.

Second, it is certainly conceivable that some of the costs of the separation of supply chains will be borne by the non-GM food market. If this is the case, the non-GM supply curve, S1, would shift upwards, opening the possibility that the GM price could rise more with labelling than with an embargo. While this suggests that cases where an import embargo was superior to mandatory labelling might be found, such situations would appear to be very remote possibilities. For one thing, it seems likely that certified non-GM imports would generally continue to enter Europe and forestall particularly sharp increases in the GM food price under the labelling regime.

The price of the non-GM food could actually fall when there is labelling. Figure 7.3 shows an alternative configuration for the final separating equilibrium where more consumers substitute the GM for the non-GM food and the demand curve for the non-GM food shifts sufficiently far to the left to $D1s'$ that the price of the non-GM food falls rather than rises. The separating equilibrium now results in a non-GM price of $P1s'$ and a quantity of $Q1s'$. On the GM food market the price, which continues to be $P2s$, now gives rise to a quantity of $Q2s'$. On the non-GM market, the lower price causes a gain in consumer surplus of $P1i$-i-t'-$P1s'$ Euro and a loss in producer surplus of $P1i$-k-s'-$P1s'$ Euro making for a beneficial net price effect of k-i-t'-s' Euro. On the GM food market the gain in consumer surplus is $P1s'$-b'-r'-$P2s$ Euro. When the non-GM price falls under mandatory labelling, there is an unambiguous increase in European welfare equal to $P1s'$-b'-r'-$P2s$ Euro from the GM market plus k-i-t'-s' Euro from the non-GM market.

While a policy of mandatory labelling of GM imports typically dominates an import embargo, allowing unlabelled GM imports may sometimes be superior to an embargo as well. This means that labelling need not always be better than no labelling. The costs of labelling GM imports, and GM output if domestic production is permitted, are likely to be significant because GM and non-GM supply chains would have to be kept separate to prevent the co-mingling of product. On the one hand, if the perceived quality difference between the GM and non-GM food is sufficiently small, the labelling and sorting costs of moving to a separating or two-market situation, rather than a pooling or one-market situation, will exceed the benefits. In such a case, labelling should not be required. On the other hand, when the perceived quality difference is large, GM labelling should be obligatory. In no cases, however, are import embargoes warranted.

It is important to examine the distributive effects of various policy alternatives towards GM imports so as to understand the political pressure to which governments are likely to be subject. When European farmers are

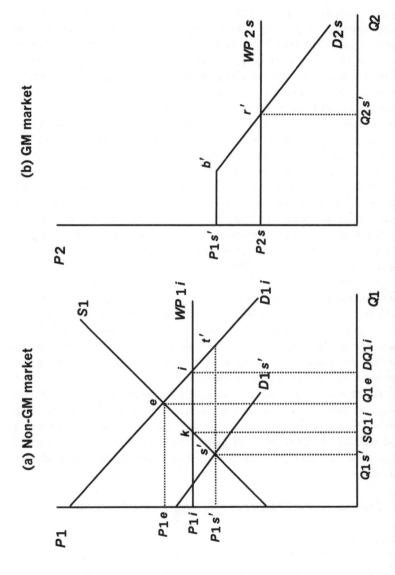

(a) Non-GM market

(b) GM market

Figure 7.3 – A possible decline in the non-GM food price

197

not permitted to adopt the GMO in production themselves, they are hurt by the introduction of unlabelled GM imports, but they are better off with an embargo. Labelled imports represent an intermediate case. Whether producers lose or gain under a labelling policy depends on whether the non-GM price rises as in Figure 7.2 or falls as in Figure 7.3. Group B consumers are made worse off by an embargo and are made better off by having either unlabelled or labelled GM food. Unlabelled GM food imports will generally be preferred so as to avoid the somewhat higher prices associated with labelling and identity preservation costs.

The group A consumers are not homogeneous in their antipathy to GM foods, but they are all made worse off by an embargo. Moreover, unless there are fears of contamination or cheating, all members of group A are better off with labelled imports rather than an embargo. Even those who do not consume any GM food with labelling will experience either a smaller adverse price effect for the non-GM as shown in Figure 7.2 or a favourable price reduction as shown in Figure 7.3. The embargo will be preferred to unlabelled imports by those members of group A with the strongest dislike for the GM food. This first sub-group certainly includes all those for whom the adverse quality effect is sufficiently strong that they cease to consume the food under pooling, but it also includes others whose preferences are such that they receive small beneficial price effects under pooling. This first sub-group, then, prefers labelling to the embargo, and the embargo to no labelling. Most of the remainder of group A prefers labelled to unlabelled imports and the latter to an embargo. Members of this second sub-group prefer the lower price and lower quality with unlabelled imports to the higher price and higher quality under the embargo. There is also a third sub-group of A who share the same ranking as those in group B. Those with the weakest preference against GM food prefer unlabelled to labelled imports and labelled imports to the embargo. This sub-group experiences a greater welfare improvement with unlabelled rather than labelled imports because the somewhat cheaper price more than counterbalances the adverse quality effect.

7.1.3 External Costs: GM Imports as Negative Public Goods

To this point, we have focused on GMOs as exclusively private goods, but the advent of GMOs pose some additional negative public-goods' issues. For example, some Europeans may be concerned over their aggregate GM food production, consumption and import levels on environmental and animal welfare grounds as well as human health and ethical grounds. Since aggregate production, consumption and import levels for GM foods may be observable, hidden quality becomes a less important issue. Externalities, however, emerge as a source of market failure. As in Chapter 3, the social costs of GM production may well exceed the private costs. This may also be true for consumption and imports. In the absence of corrective policy, overproduction, overconsumption and overimportation would be expected in such cases.

In the presence of negative GMO externalities, prohibitions on production and/or imports may sometimes improve welfare in comparison with *laissez-faire* and, occasionally, such policies may be optimal. In general, however, such prohibitions are not optimal. Rather, Pigouvian taxes on production and imports would be warranted. Such taxes are set to cover external costs and bring marginal social costs, rather than private costs, into line with marginal benefits. Suppose that only long-term, as yet unknown environmental consequences of a new biotechnology are feared by Europeans. Release of a GMO into the environment, for example, may be a threat to local indigenous species. Further, take the extreme case where these biodiversity fears warrant a prohibitive tax on domestic agricultural use of the new biotechnology in Europe. Even in this case, a prohibitive import tax on the GM import may not be efficient. While imports may pose a risk of inadvertent or opportunistic release of GMOs into the European environment, this compares with the certainty of release with European agricultural production. While there is a valid argument for permitting corrective taxes on GM imports, a blanket case for import embargoes cannot be sustained. Even the case for taxation of GM food imports depends on the degree of offshore processing. For example, products with no reproductive potential should not be subject to tax on strict biodiversity grounds.

Overall, biotechnology presents some very serious policy problems for international trade policy. Both the quality and externality problems require careful empirical analysis on a case-by-case basis. The benefits and costs of any particular biotechnology may not be uniform across countries. Even if a new biotechnology is beneficial in North America, it may be harmful in Europe. Perceived differences in GM versus non-GM product quality, for example, may be much larger in Europe. Further, due to the nullification of former trade opportunities, Europe may be worse off regardless of the policy stance that it adopts. This in itself is likely to cause tension in trade relations. Some European policy responses, however, are worse than other responses.

While a GM food import embargo may cater to the vested interests of certain European producers, environmentalists or biotechnology firms, such a policy is not in Europe's national interest. Whenever there are hidden quality issues, a mandatory labelling policy applied to GM food imports would be superior to an embargo. Whether the costly separation of GM and non-GM markets through labelling itself is warranted depends on the mix of group B and group A consumers in the population and the degree of perceived quality differences among those in group A. When group A is small or perceived quality differences are small, labelling will not be worth while. Whenever negative public-goods issues cause a difference between perceived social costs and private costs, Pigovian taxes on production and imports can be justified. Sometimes the Pigouvian taxes on domestic production may be optimally set at prohibitive levels, but prohibitive import taxes would be optimal less frequently. It should be emphasised that concrete economic studies on consumer preferences, rather than scientific evidence, should be required to document and support both labelling requirements and import restrictions on GM foods when there are public concerns.

7.2   THE WORLD TRADE ORGANISATION AND TRADE IN GENETICALLY MODIFIED PRODUCTS

The General Agreement on Tariffs and Trade (GATT), the predecessor of the World Trade Organisation (WTO), was established at the end of the Second World War. This was a period of high tariffs and other limitations on international trade. The GATT's primary mandate was the removal of the existing high tariffs and other border restrictions. A broad-based International Trade Organisation (ITO) had been negotiated as part of the New World Order that was being established by the victors (Kerr, 2000a). The ITO was to have equal status in international law to the International Monetary Fund (IMF) and the World Bank. The US Congress, however, indicated that it would not pass the necessary legislation for the USA to accede to the ITO. The ITO was stillborn (Hart, 1998). The GATT, one of the sub-agreements of the ITO, was accepted by the US Congress. It was supposed to be a temporary organisation but by default became the *de facto* institution for negotiating and administering the international rules for trade in goods. The GATT retained this role until it was rolled into the new WTO at the end of the Uruguay Round of trade negotiations in 1994. The GATT, as an organisation, ceased to exist but the agreement, which is the set of rules for trade in goods, remains in force and is administered by the Goods Council of the WTO.

The GATT's primary purpose is to provide a degree of surety for firms that wish to invest in international commercial activity. In particular, it is meant to limit the ability of domestic politicians to extend protection from foreign competition to their constituents. The capricious use of trade barriers increases the risks associated with investing in international business opportunities. This does not, however, prevent those threatened by foreign competition from asking for protection.

When the GATT was established, the high levels of tariffs were largely left over from the beggar-thy-neighbour tariff wars of the 1930s when governments, desperate to defend domestic jobs during the Great Depression, had imposed a myriad of trade barriers. The only group that was expected to lobby for protection from imports was firms – that is producers. At the time, this was probably a reasonable presumption. The GATT, and subsequently the WTO system, has been constituted in a manner that is designed to limit the ability of governments to extend protection to producers. As a result, the existing agreed rules of trade make it difficult for countries to deal with requests for protection from other groups in society – in particular consumers and environmentalists (Perdikis and Kerr, 1999). The protests by civil society groups at the Seattle Ministerial meeting of the WTO in late 1999 was largely a result of this institutional shortcoming. As developed countries have become more affluent, individuals have begun to take an increasing interest in the products available in their markets, including products of foreign origin. Various groups have been able to influence their domestic government's policy process and have been demanding protection from goods for a variety of reasons – animal welfare, beef produced using growth hormones, child labour, dolphin-unfriendly tuna, furs from leghold traps, eco-unfriendly production and so on. The WTO is increasingly being asked to deal with trade barriers imposed for these or similar reasons (Kerr, 2000b), but without much success. For the most part, the groups asking for protection from GMOs are consumers or environmentalists; producers have been largely silent.

The EU has been having the greatest difficulty dealing with consumer and environmental groups' concerns with GMOs. The domestic licensing of

GM products has been, in effect, stalled in the EU. Without domestic licensing of GM products, imports remain a contentious issue. Of course, the EU experience is diametrically opposed to that of the USA where licensing has proceeded with little difficulty. Given the long animosity between the EU and the USA over a series of trade issues, particularly for agricultural goods, the EU's more careful approach to GMOs has often been interpreted as simply another protectionist ploy in the USA (Perdikis, 2000). Hence, the stage was set for a confrontation at the WTO.

The opening salvo in the simmering dispute over GMOs was fired by the then EU agricultural commissioner, Franz Fischler, in early 1998 when he stated that the EU would like to renegotiate the WTO's Agreement on the Application of Sanitary and Phytosanitary Measures (SPS) to permit trade restrictions for reasons of 'consumer preference'. Peter Scher, special agricultural negotiator for the US Trade Representative, publicly replied that for the USA: 'There are few higher priorities' than fighting this 'very disturbing proposal' (*Inside US Trade*, 1998).

The heart of the difficulty with the ability of the WTO to deal with the issue of requests for protection from GMOs is the economic model that defines its approach to trade. As suggested above, the WTO recognises only one source of protectionism, domestic producers. This is not to say that consumer interests are ignored in the WTO, but their demands are expected to be 'legitimate'. The bias in the treatment of demands for protection is understandable because standard economic analysis predicts that on import markets consumers are winners from trade liberalisation (consumer surplus increases) while domestic producers benefit from increased protection (producer surplus increases). Of course, protectionist trade measures cause consumers to lose. The neoclassical economic analysis that predicts that consumers will be losers from protectionist measures is, however, based on the assumptions that consumers are in possession of costless perfect information and that they are rational. When asymmetric information exists or information costs are high for consumers, as in the case of GM products, then as outlined in the previous section consumers may not benefit from trade liberalisation (Gaisford and Lau, 2000). Consumers find the cost of acquiring information on GM products high, and more important, verifying the science that underlies the information is also costly. There are also high costs to verifying the credibility of the scientists charged with developing and administering food safety systems. Scientific information, scientific credentials and motivations are, essentially, credence goods that cannot be verified even after they or their services have been consumed (Hobbs and

Kerr, 1999). As a result, acceptance of credence goods is normally reputation-based. In the last quarter of the twentieth century, there were sufficient failures in the EU food safety system (for example, BSE or mad cow disease) that the reputation of the scientific community has been considerably eroded in the eyes of some EU consumers. As a result, they no longer appear to trust the scientific community and, hence, are no longer willing to accept the scientific consensus that was the basis of the SPS Agreement. While there is no accurate research on the extent of consumer distrust of the scientific community, it is of sufficient magnitude that it cannot be ignored by EU politicians.

Further, a case could be made that consumers appear to be subject to a degree of hysteria regarding food safety issues, calling into question whether their choices are rational. Consumers may also be manipulated by the media. This calls into question the strong assumption of consumer sovereignty in economic models.

The SPS and the Agreement on Technical Barriers to Trade (TBT) are the two WTO agreements that are the most applicable to the issue of GMOs. The SPS relates to trade barriers put in place to protect human, animal or plant health. The TBT deals with issues relating to consumer protection such as fraud, but not food safety. Both agreements were put in place to prevent governments from imposing bogus or overly onerous trade barriers as a means of providing covert protection to producers. The use of non-tariff barriers had become increasingly important as successful rounds of GATT negotiations closed off other avenues of extending protection. At the Uruguay Round, the TBT was strengthened and the new SPS agreement hammered out.

The centrepiece of the SPS agreement is that trade barriers put in place to protect human, animal or plant health must have a scientific basis. It was hoped that the requirement for a scientific basis would prevent the imposition of trade barriers for bogus health reasons. The use of a scientific basis to justify the imposition of trade barriers is, however, premised on the principle that the 'best available scientific information' will be used to justify their establishment and their regulatory design. The use of the 'best available' criteria for trade policy-making is centred on the principle that there exists a general consensus regarding what constitutes 'appropriate science'. While scientists may disagree on specifics, there is probably near consensus among the scientific community regarding what constitutes 'appropriate science' based on existing scientific knowledge; devising and conducting tests of those hypotheses; and establishing protocols for the ongoing monitoring of the process in a commercial environment.

There is, however, a further implicit assumption underpinning the 'appropriate science' criteria, that is that the general public will accept, or defer to, the judgement of the scientific community regarding what constitutes 'appropriate science'. As suggested above, sufficient numbers of consumers and environmentalists in some countries are no longer willing to passively accept the scientific evidence used by those scientists charged with ensuring human, animal and plant health and environmental protection. In this case, sufficient numbers means that those who hold these views cannot be easily ignored by policy-makers. However, in the absence of a direct means of dealing with consumer demands for protection, governments will be forced to attempt to use either the SPS or the TBT to justify the imposition of trade barriers.

It is important to reiterate that the obligations accepted by states in the SPS have been put in place to ensure that sanitary and phytosanitary measures are not 'misused for protectionist purposes and [do] not result in unnecessary barriers to international trade' (Stanton, 1995, p. 37). As GMOs often represent a significant technological change that provides the developer with a competitive advantage over non-GM varieties, there will always be suspicion by exporters that sanitary or phytosanitary measures, which limit market access, are protectionist measures designed to assist those who are unable or unwilling to use the improved technology. Of course, even if the restrictions are legitimate, they will confer protection upon producers of non-transgenic varieties in importing countries. The provisions of the SPS were not conceived within the dynamic context of technological change but, rather, tend to view sanitary and phytosanitary regulations as static problems relating to the purposeful imposition of a non-tariff barrier to enhance the welfare of domestic producer interests through protection.

There are three obligations of the SPS that are relevant to the case of GMOs. First, sanitary and phytosanitary trade measures are to be applied only to the extent necessary to protect human, animal or plant life or health; are to be based on scientific principles and are not to be maintained without scientific evidence (Randel, 1996). Exporters can challenge the regulations on the basis of their scientific justification. Second, the measures are to be put in place only after a risk assessment. Each country determines its own level of acceptable risk, thus allowing it to respond to the social and cultural concerns of its citizens. The factors used to assess risk and the methods used to arrive at the risk to food safety or animal or plant health must be revealed to the enquiring countries. A country can object to the assessment of risk if they perceive that it is being used as a trade barrier.

Third, countries have committed to co-operation in designing international standards for food safety, and sanitary and phytosanitary regulations. The WTO is not to be directly involved in this process. Instead, three long-standing international organisations, the Codex Alimentarius Commission (for food safety), the International Office of Epizootics (animal health) and the Secretariat of the International Plant Protection Convention (plant health) have been designated by the WTO as responsible for devising international standards. These organisations have a tradition of consensus-building deliberations.

The SPS allows countries to put trade barriers in place when insufficient scientific evidence exists. The SPS:

> clearly permits precautionary measures when a government considers the scientific evidence insufficient to permit a final decision on the safety of a product or process (Stanton, 1995, p. 40).

Although the TBT specifically defers to the SPS on sanitary and phytosanitary issues, it does cover all other quality requirements for food. Food labelling to prevent deception is one area where the TBT may apply. Technical barriers to trade must have a legitimate purpose. Further, the cost of implementing the standard must be proportional to the purpose of the standard. Labelling regulations may still lead to disputes – particularly given the onerous monitoring costs that may be imposed on exporters.

The intention of specifying a scientific basis for imposing sanitary and phytosanitary barriers to trade is to separate legitimate from capricious regulations. In the case of GMOs, however, no basis for a scientific consensus is likely to exist in the near future. In particular, as outlined in earlier chapters, there is considerable debate regarding their long-run effects on human health and the environment. There appears to be no method whereby the time required to examine the effects of toxic build-up or the possibility of long incubation periods can be shortened. Civil society groups have been lobbying governments not to license GMOs until these long-run issues can be resolved.

Depending on the strength of their civil society lobbies against GMOs, governments will license GMOs at different paces. Countries that have not licensed the products domestically will put trade barriers in place to exclude GMOs. Exporting countries may perceive this as the capricious use of trade barriers. As the long-run effects cannot be determined on a scientific basis, in the short run there is no way to determine if the application of trade barriers is capricious. If the exporting country asks for a WTO panel, the panel will have to resolve the dispute based on incomplete information or refuse to hear the case because there is insufficient information. Neither course of action is desirable. In the case of the former, the credibility of the dispute system will be called into question while in the latter, appellant countries will be frustrated, reducing their support for the WTO.

The SPS, as conceived, did not anticipate that the disputes system of the WTO would have to make judgements on scientifically complex issues or those where scientific information was incomplete. Instead, it was expected that countries would defer to the standards arrived at by the Codex Alimentarius Commission, the International Office of Epizootics or the Secretariat of the International Plant Protection Convention. These organisations seem ill-equipped to deal with the problems created by GMOs. They are, by their nature, slow careful organisations that operate on the proposition that a scientific consensus can be reached when setting standards. Given that it will not be possible to reach a short-run scientific consensus regarding long-term questions surrounding GMOs, these organisations are likely to defer setting standards until sufficient information exists.

The inability to find a consensus arises, in part, because consumers' refusal to accept the scientific evidence has politicised the process. It is not possible to have a science-based system if either a greater degree of statistical confidence or additional scientific tests can always be asked for. In effect, this means that trade barriers can always be justified because not enough science has been done – clearly an untenable situation. Dealing with consumer (or other groups') requests for protection directly rather than forcing countries to seek relief in inappropriate mechanisms like the SPS or TBT would seem to be a superior approach (Perdikis and Kerr, 1999). As currently constituted, in the absence of harmonised international standards, trade barriers can be put in place by countries on the basis of there being insufficient scientific information. As a result, extremely acrimonious disputes are likely to arise. The WTO has no apparent method to settle those disputes.

If countries choose to impose labelling regimes instead of import bans on GMOs, exporters may be faced with very large costs in certifying their labels. Given the 'soft' wording in the TBT agreement that only requires that the cost of implementing the standard must be proportional to the purpose of the standard – the latter not being definable in economic terms – no judgements will be forthcoming. It is probably ironic that the costs of labelling regimes will fall disproportionately on those who wish to sell non-GM products (Kerr, 1999). Once it is established that labelling is required, it is relatively simple to label products as containing GMOs – no one is likely to care if GM products are tainted by non-GM products. On the other hand, as discussed in Chapter 4, claims of being GM-free will have to be credible, and costly mechanisms for monitoring put in place to ensure that GM products do not contaminate the non-GM product. This will tilt the commercial advantage in favour of GM products.

The WTO seems ill-equipped to handle the trade problems that can be expected to arise with GMOs. As a result, trade in GMOs is likely to be inhibited. Given the short product life cycles that are predicted for GM products due to new innovations, access to the widest possible market is desirable. As open international access is likely to be constrained, investment in GMOs will be inhibited and the potential of the technology will not be fully realised.

7.3 INTERNATIONAL PROTECTION OF INTELLECTUAL PROPERTY

Over the last few years the proportion of the value of goods accounted for by intellectual property has been rising. Biotechnology is only one manifestation of this change. The computer and electronic communications revolutions that, along with biotechnology, underpin the new 'information' economy are to a large degree based on value attributed to intellectual property (Kerr, 2000b). Further, the large expansion of the entertainment industry over the last few decades combined with a spate of new delivery technologies has increased considerably the potential value of copyright material. Most of the innovation takes place in developed countries where intellectual property protection is relatively strong and effective. Developing countries, however, generate little intellectual property and have had little incentive to put intellectual property regimes in place or to enforce them given that most of the benefits would go to (rich) foreigners. Intellectual property piracy has become endemic in some developing countries, particularly in those countries whose technical capabilities are rising (Yampoin and Kerr, 1998). Firms investing in intellectual property sought protection for their intellectual property in developing countries but the existing World Intellectual Property Organisation (WIPO) was neither inclusive in its membership nor had any enforcement mechanism.

The governments of developed countries were also cognisant that the basis for relative economic prosperity was changing and becoming more dependent upon the ability to produce new intellectual property. Intellectual property piracy reduces the incentive to invest in its production and, hence, the absence of intellectual property protection in developing countries was seen as a threat to future improvement in their prosperity (Kerr, 2000b). As a result, an initiative was put forward at the Uruguay Round of the General Agreement on Tariffs and Trade (GATT) talks to bring intellectual property protection within the GATT's umbrella. The changes required for this to be accomplished led to an entire revamping of the international commercial policy regime. The GATT organisation was replaced by the WTO that now administered three agreements: the GATT covering trade in goods; the new General Agreement on Trade in Services; and the Agreement on Trade Related Aspects of Intellectual Property (TRIPS).

The change in structure was required for two reasons. First, the WTO administers a common dispute settlement system covering all three agreements. It was agreed that cross-agreement retaliation would be allowed through the unified disputes system. The reason for this was to allow countries to impose trade sanctions under GATT for failure to provide intellectual property protection under the TRIPS. Thus, developed countries were given an enforcement mechanism with which to induce developing countries to protect the intellectual property of their firms. Second, it was agreed that countries belonging to the WTO had to sign on to the TRIPS. In other words, to receive the trade benefits and protection of the GATT, countries had to agree to protect intellectual property under the TRIPS. The TRIPS sets out commitments regarding the establishment of domestic intellectual property regimes and their enforcement.

The effectiveness of the TRIPS, however, largely depends on the efficacy of the cross-agreement retaliation mechanism. As yet, it remains untested because developing countries were allowed a period of grace to put their intellectual property regimes in place. The international intellectual property regime will be particularly important for the biotechnology industry given it is based on intellectual property. As yet, no agreement has been reached on the penalties that can be imposed on the party judged to be in violation of its TRIPS' commitments. In the absence of either a formal WTO agreement regarding the penalties that can be imposed, or as yet precedents from disputes panels, the question arises as to what might be the retaliatory principle applied. If no agreement can be reached on compensation, the common practice when a country ignores the trade rules established by the WTO is for the injured country to be allowed to retaliate against the offending country up to the value of the trade forgone. This retaliation takes the form of a tariff or other border measures (Kerr and Perdikis, 1995). The products to which retaliatory tariffs apply are selected by the injured party.

The debates over protection of intellectual property rights are largely polarised between developed countries that are strong advocates of international protection, and developing countries that perceive that the payment of monopoly rents for the use of intellectual property is detrimental to their development process (Gaisford and Richardson, 1996; Government of India, 1989; Mansfield, 1993; Taylor, 1993). The payment of monopoly rents has been particularly contentious for agricultural inputs such as seed and for pharmaceuticals – the former because of its effect on poor farmers and the latter because of the effect on the poor's ability to afford health care. Biotechnology has, as a result, become very contentious in developing countries

While arguments are sometimes made that those in developed countries who hold the rights to intellectual property in agriculture deserve no return (Steidlmeir, 1993), most advocates of the developing countries' position would concede that those who invest in the creation of intellectual property should receive a competitive rate of return on their investment. Hence, the major contentious issue is the method used to reward the producers of intellectual property; that is, the granting of monopoly rights through patents. The granting of monopoly rights means that the rewards available from producing intellectual property are not directly related to the costs of producing intellectual property.

The monopoly returns to intellectual property that is traded internationally are appropriated in three ways: (1) directly through the prices of exports; (2) fees for use and; (3) profits of subsidiaries (Maskus, 1990). If failure to enforce intellectual property rights is instrumental in preventing the establishment of a foreign subsidiary, the use of WTO-sanctioned cross-retaliation via trade measures would not be possible. As no trade in goods has taken place, retaliation based on the value of lost trade has no effect. No loss of goods exports can be claimed by the country owning the intellectual property even though there is a loss from the failure to protect intellectual property.

The case where the foreign owner of agricultural biotechnology has the monopoly rights to its intellectual property enforced in the importing country is illustrated in Figure 7.4. This is the *worst case* for those in developing countries who object to intellectual property protection for foreign owners. For simplicity, we assume that this is a small country case where imports of the product will be supplied at a constant price whether at the monopoly price for the world market, P_M, or at a price that reflects costs, P_{NR}. The competitive export supply curve is perfectly elastic due to constant marginal cost.

Assume that a market situation exists where the developing country faces no threat of cross-retaliation as a result of non-enforcement – the situation prior to the TRIPS. A pirate industry exists in the developing country and has supply curve SP_1. When faced with non-enforcement of its intellectual property rights and competition from pirate firms, the firm which produces the agricultural biotechnology will attempt to compete with pirate firms and supply exports at a price that reflects a normal rate of return on the investment in creating intellectual property, P_{NR}. Domestic pirate firms in the developing country will supply O-K and imports will equal K-T.

Now assume that the country is a member of the WTO and either lives up to its TRIPS commitment or suffers the imposition of trade sanctions. The importing country now has a choice. It can live up to its TRIPS commitments and enforce intellectual property rights by shutting down the pirate industry or it can ignore its TRIPS commitments and suffer the cost imposed by cross-retaliation.

If the importing country chooses not to enforce, then it can expect its exports of other products to be subject to trade measures imposed by the government of the firm that holds the intellectual property rights and exports the agricultural biotechnology. Assume the lost value of exports is used to establish the size of the penalty. In Figure 7.4, the value of the trade loss is area P_M-C-J-O. It should be made explicitly clear that the export loss is not P_{NR}-G-K-O, the value of the pirates' production, but rather the value of exports once a monopoly position in the market has been obtained.

If the importing country chooses to enforce, the exporter of agricultural biotechnology will be able to set its exports so as to be consistent with the world monopoly price, P_M. Quantity O J will be imported. As price increases from P_{NR} to P_M, there will be a loss in consumers' surplus equal to P_M-C-E-P_{NR}. There will also be a loss in producers' surplus equal to

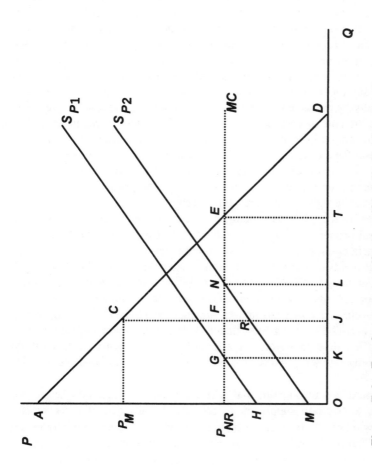

Figure 7.4 – Foreign monopolisation if intellectual property rights are enforced

211

P_{NR}-G-H from shutting down the domestic pirate industry. To this must be added the cost of enforcement. The total cost to the importing country equals P_M-C-E-P_{NR} + P_{NR}-G-H + the cost of enforcement.

Little is known about the costs of intellectual property rights enforcement. There are two aspects to enforcement costs. First, there are costs associated with identifying pirate firms and monitoring their production premises. Clearly, these costs will vary from product to product and will depend on the degree to which the capital equipment required for pirate production is fixed or mobile, the absolute size of the premises required for production, the degree of concentration in the pirate industry and so on. Second, there are factors that affect the efficacy of the enforcement effort. These include the effectiveness of the legal system in obtaining convictions, the degree of corruption in the police service and justice system and the ability of the pirate industry to influence the political will to actively pursue enforcement. One suspects that in many developing countries the cost of ensuring a degree of enforcement sufficient to satisfy developed countries will be non-trivial. Given these costs are not transparent, they will be ignored in this analysis, hence it is assumed that fully effective enforcement can be costlessly obtained. Our analysis represents the 'best case' for enforcement from the perspective of the firm which owns the rights to intellectual property.

To see if the importing country will have the incentive to enforce intellectual property rights in agricultural biotechnology in the absence of enforcement costs, one must compare the loss associated with enforcement, P_M-C-E-P_{NR} + P_{NR}-G-H with the loss associated with non-enforcement, P_M-C-J-O. As areas P_M-C-F-P_{NR} and P_{NR}-G-H are common, that is, they arise whether or not enforcement takes place, the net loss from enforcement is C-E-F while the net loss from non-enforcement is H-G-F-J-O. As drawn in Figure 7.4, H-G-F-J-O is greater than C-E-F and the importing country will have an incentive to enforce intellectual property rights in agricultural biotechnology as long as the cost of enforcement is less than H-G-F-J-O minus C-E-F.

Compare this result with that where the pirate industry is larger, for example, with pirate supply curve SP_2. In the absence of enforcement, imports will be L-T. If the importing country chooses to enforce intellectual property rights, the loss in consumer surplus remains the same as in the previous case, P_M-C-E-P_{NR} but the loss in producer surplus increases to P_{NR}-N-M. The retaliatory trade loss remains unchanged at P_M-C-J-O. The net loss from enforcement increases to C-E-N-R (from C-E-F) while the net loss from non-enforcement declines to M-R-J-O (from H-G-F-J-O). Hence, the likelihood that the importing country will have an incentive to enforce intellectual property rights in agricultural biotechnology will decline as the size of the pirate industry increases. The likelihood that enforcement will take place is further reduced because one would expect the cost of enforcement to rise as the size of the pirate industry increases.

This result is not the one desired by the owners of intellectual property in agricultural biotechnology. Presumably, they would wish for stronger incentives to enforce intellectual property rights as the size of the pirate industry increases.

It would appear that if the members of the WTO decide to follow the customary GATT practice of allowing penalties equal to the value of lost trade when they establish the cross-retaliatory penalties for TRIPs violations, then the penalties that can be imposed will not provide sufficient incentives for countries to fulfil their TRIPS commitments in all situations when violations of intellectual property rights occur. If the monopoly rents per unit output are large, the size of the potential trade penalty will not be sufficient to justify enforcing intellectual property rights. Of course, the transfer of monopoly rents to foreigners is the basis for the objections to the enforcement of intellectual property rights by developing countries.

Further, our analysis puts forward the 'best case' for enforcement because the costs of enforcement are assumed to be zero. As the size of the pirate industry increases, the likelihood that the importing country will enforce intellectual property rights to agricultural biotechnology declines. Thus, when large pirate industries exist, and firms that own intellectual property rights to agricultural biotechnology are suffering large losses, the probability of enforcement is smallest.

The use of a retaliation rule based on the value of exports lost might also have considerable practical difficulties associated with its implementation. This is because the trade loss is a counter-factual value – in other words it is not observable when a country fails to enforce intellectual property rights. Quantity O-J in Figure 7.4 cannot be determined until pirate firms are removed from the market. While it would be possible to estimate point C in Figure 7.4, it depends crucially on the slope of the demand curve. Disputes over the size of the threatened penalty would likely become endemic at the WTO.

The threatened country will also have difficulty assessing the actual harm it will suffer when the equivalent value is translated into trade restrictions on its exports. Such a lack of transparency may well reduce the effectiveness of the threat, therefore reducing the incentive to enforce intellectual property rights to agricultural biotechnology. Kerr et al. (2000) consider alternative penalties but find that no reasonable alternatives would provide a threat as large as a value based on the loss of trade. Tarvydas et al. (2000) use a different approach to modelling cross-retaliation for violations of TRIPS commitments and find a similar lack of likely efficacy.

These results suggest that the entire idea of using cross-retaliation in the WTO to induce enforcement of intellectual property rights needs to be re-examined. Cluttering trade agreements with non-trade issues is a poor precedent in any case (Kerr, 2000b). The problem of protection of intellectual property needs to be tackled directly through multinational negotiations. In the past, the problem was that developing countries had little to gain from protecting intellectual property. Now there are signs that they may see some benefit to owning property rights in the genetics of their natural flora, fauna and traditional crop varieties.

There have been movements in recent years to endow countries with ownership rights to their wild varieties and closely related weeds and previously non-commercial sources of genetic material. The debates surrounding the provision of ownership rights to genetic material are almost always couched in terms of North-South (developed-developing country) inequities.

Firms from the North who use this genetic material without paying a fee are often accused of biopiracy. The gene banks of the international centres established to preserve biodiversity are now, ironically, sometimes portrayed as an elaborate plot by Northern governments to steal Southern genetic property. Non-government organisations (NGOs) and others who argue in the name of developing countries tend to focus on the rents accruing to innovating firms from developing countries. While this may be laudable on equity grounds, as shown in Chapter 2, giving intellectual property rights to first stage collection of genetic material simply adds an additional distortion that will reduce the rate of innovation. It also begs the central question of how to redress the imbalance in the proportion of returns to global R&D that accrues to developing countries by introducing a new distortion rather than fixing the problem.

The Convention on Biological Diversity (CBD) formally recognises the sovereign rights of states over their genetic resources (but not to those in the international gene banks collected prior to the CBD). It does not, however, formally recognise 'farmers' rights' (the term for communal property rights to landrace varieties). The Conference for the Adoption of the Agreed Text of the CBD, however, also adopted a complementary Resolution 3 that identified farmers' rights as an outstanding issue not addressed by the Convention, and recognised that solutions should be sought within the Food and Agricultural Organisation's (FAO) Global System of Plant Genetic Resources (Esquinas-Alcázar, 1998). Hence, the CBD implicitly recognises farmers' rights although the details are yet to be agreed. The CBD appears to be willing to assign ownership rights to the first phase of the biotechnology process. The TRIPS, however, will not grant patent protection (Kerr and Yampoin, 2000).

With both parties having something to win from international protection of intellectual property rights, there may be the basis for an agreement. Given the agricultural biotechnology potential that lies within tropical flora and fauna, developed countries could consider compensating developing countries for their genetic material by providing technical assistance to improve their ability to generate intellectual property if the quid pro quo was better enforcement of intellectual property rights to agricultural biotechnology.

7.4 BIOTECHNOLOGY AND THE INTERNATIONAL DISTRIBUTION OF INCOME

Innovations in general are grouped in economics under the heading of 'technical progress'. Biotechnological inventions and innovations are no exception to this. Technical progress, largely the application of science and technology, transformed the agricultural economies of the eighteenth and nineteenth centuries into the industrial economies we see today. The improvements and introduction of agricultural machinery, the developments in plants, seeds and animal husbandry allowed surpluses to be generated in the agricultural sector that could then be used and applied in the industrial sphere. Technological progress in agriculture allowed countries not only to feed themselves but also provide a surplus for their growing urban populations. Today, the application of biotechnology is no different. It has the potential to increase output and generate surpluses in the same way as did agricultural developments in the eighteenth and nineteenth centuries. The questions relating to the impact of these new innovations are also the same. These are: who will gain and who will lose in both the domestic and international arenas? Economic theory shows that these questions do not have easy answers.

7.4.1   Classification of Technical Progress

Put very simply, technical progress implies that more output can be produced with a given amount of input. Another way of putting this is to say that the same level of output can be achieved with less input.

Technical progress is often classified as being neutral, capital saving or labour saving. Neutral technical progress is defined as increasing the marginal productivities of both capital and labour in the same proportion. Labour-saving technical progress increases the marginal product of capital more than it raises that of labour. Capital-saving technical progress implies the direct opposite – the marginal product of labour increasing more than that of capital.

Each of these forms of technical progress will eventually affect a country's terms of trade and its income *vis-à-vis* others. We will also discuss the impact innovation will have on the internal distribution of income. Our analysis will be based largely on the standard economic model that assumes two countries consuming and producing two goods and using two factors of production.   In such a situation, what effect will technical progress have?

7.4.2   Neutral Technical Progress, the Terms of Trade and Income Distribution

Let us begin by assuming that a country has two sectors: Y is a (physical or human) capital-intensive sector and X is a labour-intensive sector. Let us further assume that sector Y experiences neutral technical progress. While our example here refers to two distinct sectors and implies that they are totally different, that is, agriculture and manufacturing, this need not be the case. We could be looking at an advanced agricultural sector on the one hand and a traditional agricultural sector on the other. For example, the advanced sector could successfully embrace biotechnology while the traditional sector does not. What implications would this have for these two sectors? If the returns to capital and labour were to remain constant, the output of Y would increase in proportion to the increase in productivity of labour and capital. National income would rise by a smaller proportion and the output of the non-adopting sector would stay where it was.

Certain questions follow, since profits are now positive in the Y sector. For example, what are the long-term implications for outputs and factor returns? If the output of Y increases by more than consumption, which is likely for an income inelastic food product, will its price fall relative to X? If the relative price of Y stays the same, as it must in the small-country case, then as the Y industry expands further by bidding factors away from the X industry, the latter must necessarily contract. The change will, thus, tend to be anti-trade biased overall, if and only if good Y is imported.

What is the eventual, or long-run effect on the returns to the factors involved? With good Y experiencing a further expansion in production, there will be an increase in demand for both labour and capital factor inputs. With Y being a more capital-intensive industry than X, it will need to draw from X relatively more capital than labour. The demand for capital will grow relative to that of labour and as a result the return on capital will rise relative to labour. This increase in the relative price of capital will lead to a substitution of labour for capital in both sectors. The marginal productivity of capital rises in both sectors, but that of labour falls. Neutral technical progress in the capital-intensive sector will then lead to a fall in the real wage and an increase in the return to capital.

What does all this imply regarding the effect of biotechnology on the international distribution of income? Clearly, at the international level, those countries that adopt this potential cost-saving technology will benefit over those countries that do not; in particular, the owners of (physical or human) capital will gain. Within countries, it is also clear that there is the potential to affect the distribution of income in favour of the group who adopted the technology and against those who do not. Again, the benefit goes to the owners of capital and not labour. This all assumes neutral technical progress and that the country in question is a small country.

If the country is large and Y is an import-competing good, then the effect on the volume of trade depends on the balance of consumption and production effects. If imports increase and the price of Y rises, then the above distributional results will be amplified. In the likely event of an anti-trade bias, however, the decline in imports leads to a fall in the world price of Y. This will attenuate the impact of the technical change on factor returns. The results, in fact, would be reversed with the real wage rising and the real return to capital falling if the price of Y declined by a larger percentage than the unit cost. This could occur, for example, if the whole world innovates and the demand for Y is income inelastic.

In terms of the adoption of a biotechnology that represents a neutral technical change, knowledge of whether a country is small or large is very significant in working out the consequences. For the most part, developing countries can consider themselves as being in the small country category.

European countries, or more particularly the EU, could consider the large country case as being more relevant.

7.4.3 The Effect of Capital-saving Technical Progress

The effect of capital-saving technical progress on the relatively capital-intensive sector or sub-sector would be to increase its output. Why would this be the case and what would be the consequences? Again, we assume that factor returns remain unchanged to begin with. As capital saving takes place, the output of Y increases so as to reabsorb the surplus capital while the output of X declines. Profits, again, arise in the Y sector due to falling costs. This leads to a further expansion of the output of Y and a further reduction in the output of X at the initial product prices. Once again, for agricultural products it is likely that the increase in the output of Y will exceed the increase in consumption that is generated by higher national income. How are factor prices and intensities affected?

If the country is small, product prices will not change. Once again, the further expansion of the capital-intensive sector will reduce the wage relative to the return on capital. There will be an induced decline in the capital-labour ratio in sector Y beyond the direct capital-saving effect. The capital-labour ratio will also fall in sector X. As a result, labour will be worse off while capital will be better off in terms of X. Since the price Y relative to X is constant, the same must be true in terms of Y.

In the large country case, the effect of capital-saving biotechnology on the terms of trade has to be taken into account. While there is a decline in the real wage and an increase in the return on capital at constant terms of trade, these effects again tend to be at least partially offset by changes in world prices. In the likely event that the output of Y increases by more than consumption, the world price of Y will fall relative to X and tip the competitive balance back toward the X sector. Unless one knows the precise nature of the innovation, whether it is adopted in other countries and how consumption is affected, it is impossible to fully determine the distributional impact in the large country case on an a priori basis.

7.4.4 The Effect of Labour-saving Technical Progress

If innovations and the adoption of new technology lead to labour saving in the capital-intensive sector, the output of X rises at the initial factor prices, but the direction of change in the output of Y, the capital-intensive good, is indeterminate. A large reduction in the cost of producing Y, coupled with a small change in factor intensity, will lead to an increase in output, and vice versa. In either case, however, positive profits arise in sector Y.

If the terms of trade remain the same, as they must in the small country case, the profit-induced expansion of sector Y at the expense of X reduces the wage relative to the return to capital. Labour will again be made worse off while capital will be made better off. Further, at least one of the two outputs will expand overall. While the capital-labour ratio necessarily falls in the X sector, it could rise in the Y sector due to the direct effect of the labour-saving progress. Again, in the large country case it is difficult to draw general conclusions. Only when the precise nature of the terms of trade effects and their impact on the allocation of capital and labour are known, can conclusions regarding income distribution be made.

7.4.5 The Effect of Growth on Income Distribution

Thus far we have perceived the adoption of biotechnology as technical progress and our analysis has concentrated on that. We have taken this view because the developments in biotechnology and agricultural biotechnology will have major impacts on the capital-labour ratios. Growing pest-resistant crops will lead to lower inputs whether they be labour – fewer workers or labour time to carry out pest control – or less capital to apply pesticides and herbicides and so on. The adoption of advanced biotechnology could, however, be accompanied in the long run by the accumulation of capital. This, too, may indirectly affect income distribution. In the long run, if the world price of the capital-intensive good falls, the increase in capital relative to labour will lead to a fall in the return to capital relative to wages.

7.4.6 Alternative or Additional Views on Income Distribution

Our analysis has so far been limited to the standard neoclassical analysis of these issues framed within the Hecksher-Ohlin analysis (Ohlin, 1933). This analysis can be criticised on the basis that it does not deal with the feedback effects fully. It could also be said that the Hecksher-Ohlin framework is not appropriate when considering dynamic factors such as innovation and technology, especially between advanced and equally inventive countries. This is particularly the case when the innovators are multinational companies that are able to locate and relocate their activities on a global scale.

The innovations/technological theory of trade suggests that the location of high-tech innovative industries is determined more by the conditions necessary for facilitating innovations than the physical factors – labour, capital and land – that were emphasised by Hecksher-Ohlin (Posner, 1961; Vernon, 1966). Having said that, the availability of highly skilled and flexible labour is an important factor. Also important is the entrepreneurial ability of the country's businesspeople and the underlying conditions that enable this to flourish. One of the factors influencing the extent to which ideas can be turned into practical advantage is the regulatory environment. A regulatory environment that takes a relaxed view on the conduct of research and its applications will encourage the associated industries. In the longer term, the attraction of research and development activities and the knock-on effect these have on other local companies via technological transfer will have beneficial effects on the country concerned. Not only will its industries achieve first-mover advantages but the nation's other industries will benefit as well. In the Porter (1980) model of competitive advantage, countries' industries benefit greatly if their suppliers are at the leading edge. This improves the quality of the final product and allows final-goods producers to capture an advantage on their foreign rivals. The 'competitive advantage' model suggests that as long as the momentum of invention, innovation and their applications can be maintained, then countries move in a virtuous circle of development and growth. Certainly, the recent endogenous growth theory school sees research and development – invention and innovation – as being important and beneficial to the growth process.

What does the above suggest regarding the biotechnology sector? It suggests that the nurturing of the establishment and development of this sector will lead to benefits. Countries with successful biotechnology sectors will gain self-reinforcing rising incomes. Furthermore, their incomes will grow faster than those that lack these sectors. The international distribution of income will shift in favour of countries with vigorous biotechnology industries.

Developing countries may also suffer a decline in their relative welfare due to poor regulatory capability. If embargoes on GMO imports or labelling requirements for GMO imports are imposed by developed countries, developing countries may not be able to meet those requirements and may lose access to markets. In the case of import embargoes, developing countries may not have the technical capability to segregate their non-GM products and lose access to developed country markets for their exports. Even if a developing country chooses not to license GM crops, they may not be able to prove to the satisfaction of embargoing countries that their exports are GM-free and they will be faced with the loss of export markets. In these cases it may be that the only entities with the technical capacity to segregate and certify GM-free status are transnational corporations enabling them to capture a larger proportion of the income arising from exports – an outcome many developing countries would not favour.

The lower technical capability of developing countries may also mean that they will suffer to a greater extent from any negative externalities that arise from the use of GMOs. They will be less able to control the manner in which GMOs are used. They may be poorly equipped to test or otherwise assess the interaction of GMO's with the local ecosystem. They may also become dumping grounds for more risky GM products that developed countries refuse to license. Crops not licensed by importing countries due to their high-risk levels are likely to face import embargoes, further threatening developing countries' exports. On the other hand, poor technical capability may lead to import embargoes by developing countries because they are easier to administer than a licensing regime. As a result, developing countries may suffer the losses associated with import embargoes outlined earlier in this chapter. As developing countries generate little of the global R&D, their relative economic well-being is likely to decline over time.

7.4.7 Conclusion

What can we say about biotechnology and the international and internal distribution of income? Standard neoclassical economic analysis gives us mixed views depending on whether the technical change involved is neutral, capital or labour saving. Our analysis above has concentrated on technical progress taking place in the capital-intensive sector. We believe this to be a more appropriate form of analysis given the nature of innovation in the biotechnology sector. As we have indicated, the standard analysis can be modified to examine the effects in two subsections of an industry – an advanced and a traditional sector.

The standard analysis leads to the following conclusions. Where the technical progress is of a neutral type, then the real wage rate falls in terms of good X and Y while the return on capital rises in terms of both goods. The distribution of income shifts internally towards capital, and production in both sectors becomes less capital intensive. For a large country, these results continue to hold if and only if the reduction in the unit cost of Y is of a greater proportion than any fall in its price. With capital-saving technical progress, the results remain broadly similar, but with labour-saving progress, production could become more capital intensive in sector Y.

For the international distribution of income, both standard analysis and more recent alternative views suggest that inventions, innovations and their application give adopting countries a lead over others. This lead becomes self-reinforcing and results in not only an increase in national income but also a shift in the nation's favour compared to other less dynamic countries. The maintenance of dynamism is crucial to their continued advance and this itself is dependent on the nurturing of entrepreneurial spirit and freedom. With their low levels of technical capability, few developing countries will be able to reap the benefits of the biotechnology revolution and may bear a larger proportion of the costs.

NOTE

1.   The analysis in this section follows that in Gaisford and Lau (2000). The authors gratefully acknowledge discussions with C. Lau on trade and biotechnology. The authors, however, are responsible for any shortcomings in the formulations that follow.

8. Economics and the future of biotechnology

8.1 THE NATURE OF BIOTECHNOLOGICAL CHANGE

Innovation always brings change, altering the competitiveness of firms, industries, and, sometimes, nations. It challenges existing ethical beliefs and doctrines, creates opportunities and benefits for some, losses for others. Some innovations succeed, many more fail but, fundamentally, innovation has been a key driving force behind the economic development of modern society. In this sense, biotechnology is simply another facet of the wider ongoing process of technological change and innovation which has characterised the 'progress' of humankind.

Yet, in many other respects, biotechnology is different. It is these differences that set it apart from other forms of technological change, raising new challenges for economic analysis. In the agrifood sector in particular, relative to other technological innovations, biotechnological change has occurred more rapidly and at a more fundamental level, involving genetic manipulation of plants and animals. Biotechnology is also different because it affects more than just the first user of the technology. The success of previous innovations was usually driven purely by the benefits they conferred on first users. Fertilisers, for example, were adopted because of the yield benefits they brought to farmers; automobiles were adopted because of the transport benefits they gave their drivers. Agricultural biotechnology has a range of potential externality effects (both positive and negative) that extend beyond the initial user of the technology, complicating any assessment of its potential benefits, costs, and ultimately, success.

Many facets of economic theory are necessary to build a complete picture of the effects of biotechnological change – and even then, the picture is by no means 'complete'. Arising from biotechnology are economic issues concerning intellectual property, environmental impacts, consumer preferences, ethical concerns, the dynamics of industry structure and competition, the distribution of income and rents, and international trade. This book has considered each of these topics individually. While this was necessary to allow an in-depth analysis of each issue, the convenient *ceteris paribus* assumption does not apply in reality – these issues interactively affect the adoption, regulation and development of biotechnology. In practice, it is usually not possible for policy-makers, the biotechnology industry or interest groups to 'hold all else constant' in the world of biotechnology and consider one of these issues in isolation.

8.2 PUSHING THE LIMITS OF ECONOMIC ANALYSIS

Biotechnology is pushing the limits of economic theory, forcing economists to re-evaluate traditional neoclassical assumptions and to adopt non-traditional methods of applied analysis. The assumptions of homogeneous goods and homogeneous consumers clearly do not apply to markets for GM products. Increasingly, the relevant level of analysis is the 'characteristics' of the good, rather than the good *per se*. While this is not a new notion (Lancaster, 1966), the characteristics approach has not achieved the recognition and development in mainstream economic theory that is probably required to further our understanding of biotechnology. In particular, combining heterogeneous consumer preferences with heterogeneous product attributes in the presence of quality measurement costs requires further theoretical development.

Defining and analysing product 'quality' presents additional challenges to economic theory since, in the case of biotechnology products, quality is in the 'eye of the beholder'. Consumer preferences are not homogeneous. Simply adding an additional (transgenic) characteristic to a product does not necessarily result in an increase in demand. Introducing a specific characteristic through genetic engineering may make the product more or less desirable for different consumers. It may have additional externality effects, leading to market failure. Theoretical and applied economic analyses of quality draw upon concepts from the economics of information, industrial organisation and new institutional economics literatures. They involve issues of contracting, identity preservation, market segmentation and quality measurement, assurance and certification. While economists have begun to look at these issues, the area is ripe for further theoretical development and applied analysis.

Economic theory assumes that consumers behave rationally, maximising individual utility subject to a budget constraint. Usually, each individual consumer's utility is treated in isolation and is assumed not to affect another consumer's utility, except through direct externality effects. Introducing 'ethical' concerns clouds this picture and blurs the distinction between individual consumer utility functions. As discussed in Chapter 5, ethical objections to biotechnology are multifaceted. Consumer perceptions of the effects on other consumers, agricultural producers, developing countries and on nature itself, can affect consumer utility even if a consumer does not personally consume the product. Mere knowledge of the 'existence' of a biotechnology product (or more precisely, a biotechnology attribute) can create disutility. The economics of ethics has not been explored to any great depth by economists, yet it is likely to become more important as we grapple with the consequences of biotechnological change. 'Ethical economics' has applications outside biotechnology, including consumer attitudes towards farm animal welfare, environmentally-friendly production practices and other so-called 'process' attributes of food products.   In many cases, these are 'credence' attributes, further complicating the economic analysis by adding a dimension of information asymmetry. Market-based responses to ethical preferences exist already, in the form of green consumerism and eco-labelling. Whether these initiatives alone deliver the socially optimal level of environmental protection and animal welfare is not yet clear. The public good nature of these characteristics may allow some consumers to free-ride on the ethically based purchases of others, resulting in market failure. Further analysis of these issues with respect to biotechnology is needed.

The 'uncertainty' surrounding biotechnology challenges the boundaries of economic analysis. Determining effective public policy or private market responses to uncertainty is fraught with difficulty. Chapters 3 and 4, dealing with the environmental and consumer issues respectively, discussed the effects of uncertainty and the inability of private market solutions to deal adequately with this problem. As a result, decisions concerning investment in biotechnology R&D increasingly are made in an environment of uncertainty. For exporters, long-term market access is plagued by uncertainty. A comprehensive analysis of the interaction between biotechnology and uncertainty on many levels is required.

Biotechnological innovations increasingly will place pressure on regulators to incorporate formal 'risk analysis' into their product approval and regulatory processes. To some extent, this is occurring already, with emphasis placed on the three-tiered approach of risk assessment, risk management and risk communication. Clearly, the challenge for any society lies in defining 'acceptable' and economically efficient levels of risk. Economists can contribute to this debate by placing this risk analysis approach within a cost-benefit framework.

As the boundaries of economic theory are pushed outwards, they bump up against, and begin overlapping with, other disciplines. Indeed, it is difficult to contemplate a comprehensive analysis of biotechnology that does not adopt an interdisciplinary approach. While this book, by design, has focused on the economics of biotechnology, implicit consideration of the contributions of other disciplines permeates and strengthens the analysis throughout the book. In the case of biotechnology, the group of actors traditionally considered in economic analysis – consumers, firms, the government, and more recently, institutions – expands to include 'interest groups'. These interest groups lie outside the traditional consumer-producer or market player-regulator model but may have an important influence on markets and the development and adoption of policies and institutions to govern biotechnology. A number of disciplines, including political economy, sociology and law, can enrich economic analysis of the role of interest groups.

Biotechnology raises an additional set of challenges for 'applied economic analysis' of consumer preferences, particularly in the context of international trade. A variety of policy responses are emerging to deal with consumer unease over GM food, including mandatory labelling and refusal to approve GM food for production or importation. Chapter 7 explored the consequences for international trade of disagreements over the safety and acceptability of biotechnology products. A fundamental disagreement exists over whether countries should have the right to restrict imports on the basis of consumer preferences. While current WTO rules by no means give a clear answer to this question, general WTO principles suggest that the country wishing to introduce the trade restriction would have to show that the benefits to its consumers outweighed any costs imposed on exporters from other countries. Economists have a role to play in this determination by providing an objective assessment of consumer preferences and the value (positive or negative) which consumers place on the disputed product or product attribute. The economist's tool-kit contains a variety of methods for measuring consumer preferences for non-market goods that potentially could be applied in this instance. These methods include contingent valuation, conjoint analysis, hedonic pricing, experimental auctions and so on. Achieving consensus on an acceptable method of measuring consumer preferences for GM/non-GM products, however, can be expected to be a tortuous process. One only has to recall the difficulties encountered in agreeing on an acceptable definition and measurement of producer subsidy support in international trade negotiations.

Applied economic analysis, particularly of intellectual property and industry structure issues, faces substantial data challenges due to the proprietary nature of the information required. This problem is particularly important for regulators in assessing competition levels throughout the agrifood chain. Evaluating the efficacy of the institutional environment governing biotechnology, for example, intellectual property regulations and competition (antitrust) regulations, is also hampered by the absence of publicly available data. It becomes more difficult to determine whether market failure is present and to what extent government intervention would correct a misallocation of resources or create further distortions. Economists will have to adopt non-traditional methods of analysis, including survey and interview techniques to gather data. Closer co-operation between the agrifood industry and researchers in the provision and exchange of information will be required to facilitate this micro-level analysis. The analysis in this book also suggests many theoretical results that are ambiguous and, thus, require quantitative estimation to discern the relative magnitudes. All this suggests that biotechnology topics will provide a fertile field for postgraduate research in economics.

8.3 PUBLIC POLICY ROLE

A prevailing theme throughout this book has been the appropriate role for government policy. This role has many facets because there is potential market failure at many levels. In some cases, biotechnology appears to exacerbate the problem of market failure, in other cases it creates a market-driven solution to that failure. The credence nature of GMOs creates information asymmetry in the consumer market for food. Concerns have been raised about the potential negative externalities from the release of GMOs into the environment. In both cases, there is likely to be a role for public policy to ameliorate the market failure. Merger, acquisition and alliance activities have increased concentration levels throughout the agrifood chain. Whether this is indicative of an abuse of market power or is the transaction-cost efficient form of governance requires further economic analysis. Intellectual property rights protection and the specific nature of the technology have reduced the public good nature of R&D, weakening the traditional argument in favour of public sector involvement in agricultural research. As biotechnological innovations emerge, the respective roles of the public and private sectors will require constant re-evaluation. Of growing importance is the role of independent third parties as an alternative solution to market failure – primarily information asymmetry – through certification and assurance of product quality in segmented product markets.

8.4 DEVELOPING COUNTRY ISSUES

The opportunities, threats and challenges for developing countries are, in many ways, similar to those of developed countries. Certainly, all of the issues discussed throughout this book apply to developing countries. In some cases, however, the magnitude of the effects may be greater. As was suggested in Chapter 1, the potential benefits from biotechnology may have far greater economic significance for developing countries, for example, agronomically improved crops that alleviate food security problems, or foods enhanced to counteract a health-threatening dietary deficiency.

On the other hand, the magnitude of the costs may also be greater. If developing countries lack the necessary resources to adopt or enforce identity preservation and segmentation systems, their exports may be shut out of developed country markets that impose stringent labelling and identity preservation requirements on GM and non-GM food. In this scenario, biotechnology could widen the dichotomy between developed and developing countries and further regionalise international trade.

In an alternative scenario, improvements in agricultural productivity could be achieved far more rapidly in developing countries through the application of biotechnology, providing a springboard for wider economic development within these countries – thereby narrowing the gap between developed and developing countries. The effects of this type of technological change on developing countries and the role of domestic and international policies in enabling developing countries to reap the potential benefits of biotechnology deserve close attention by economists.

8.5 CRYSTAL BALL GAZING . . .

While its challenges cannot be ignored, agricultural biotechnology presents many exciting future possibilities. In many ways 'the genie is out of the bottle' with respect to scientific knowledge about biotechnology – genetic engineering in particular. It is not possible to 'unlearn' a scientific advance; instead, society needs to adapt accordingly. Of course, in some circumstances this may involve closer regulation of scientific processes and restrictions on the use of scientific discoveries that have harmful side effects. It would be hard to think of any scientific advance, however, which did not have any potential negative side effects, so a 'reasonable balance' is required.

The challenges discussed in this book notwithstanding, biotechnology research continues apace. This research holds the promise of products that reduce reliance on non-renewable resources. Environmental degradation from traditional agricultural practices could be alleviated through biological processes brought about by genetic engineering. Industrial crops grown for non-food uses may offer a method of producing pharmaceuticals at a fraction of their current cost. The fields of medical and agricultural biotechnology are converging, offering the promise of designer foods with specific medicinal properties targeted to individuals with particular medical needs. The ability to stack multiple traits in a single product revolutionises the notion of product differentiation and market segmentation.

It is right that society should question the desirability of biotechnological innovations. Change is not always good. A core principle of economics is the focus on change at the margin – an evaluation of whether the marginal benefits of a change outweigh the marginal costs. Thus, weighing the relative costs and benefits of a change is fundamental to economic analysis. Society's reaction to biotechnology is no different. Objective assessments, discussion and debate of the potential effects of biotechnological change are healthy for society. In practice, the evaluation of relative costs and benefits is by no means straightforward but that does not mean that an evaluation should not be attempted. Economics will continue to play a central role in this debate.

References

Alston, J.M., C. Chan-Kang, M.C. Marra, P.G. Pardey and T.J. Wyatt (2000), *A Meta-analysis of Rates of Return to Agricultural R&D: Ex Pede Herculem?*, Research Report 113, International Food Policy Research Institute, Washington.

Akerlof, G.A. (1970), 'The Market for Lemons: Quality Uncertainty and the Market Mechanism', *Quarterly Journal of Economics*, **84**, 488–500.

Angus Reid (2000), *The Economist/Angus Reid World Poll – International Awareness and Perceptions of Genetically Modified Foods*, 13 January, Angus Reid Group.

Arrow, K.J. (1962), 'Economic Welfare and the Allocation of Resources for Invention', in R. Nelson (ed), *The Rate and Direction of Inventive Activity: Economic and Social Factors*, National Bureau of Economic Research, Princeton University Press, Princeton.

Bagwell, K. and M.H. Riordan (1991), 'High and Declining Prices Signal Product Quality', *American Economic Review*, **81** (1), 224–239.

Barnett, A. (2000) 'Health Fears Over GM Cattle Feed', *The Observer*, 15 October, London.

Barzel, Y. (1980), 'Measurement Cost and the Organization of Markets', *Journal of Law and Economics*, **25** (1), 27–48.

Baylor Anderson, B. (2000), 'Education and Understanding: Keys to the Future of Biotech', *Agrimarketing*, January, 36–40.

Boadway, R.W. and N. Bruce (1984), *Welfare Economics*, Basil Blackwell, Oxford.

Brennan, M.F., C.E. Pray and A. Courtmanche (2000), 'Impact of Industry Concentration on Innovation in the US Plant Biotech Industry', in W.H. Lesser (ed.), *Transitions in Agbiotech: Economics of Strategy and Policy*, Food Marketing Policy Centre, University of Connecticut, pp. 153–174.

231

Burke, D (1998), Memorandum submitted to House of Lords Select Committee on European Communities, 2nd Report, 15 December, http://www.parliament.the-stationary-office.co.

Carlson, G.A., M.W. Bauer, J. Durant and N.C. Allum (1997), *The Economics of First Crop Biotechnologies*, North Carolina State University, Raleigh. (As cited in M. P. Feldman, M.L. Morris and D. Hoisington (2000), 'Genetically Modified Organisms: Why All the Controversy', *Choices*, 1st quarter, 8–12).

Caswell, J. (ed) (1995), *Valuing Food Safety & Nutrition*, Westview Press, Boulder.

Caswell, J.A. (1997), *Uses of Food Labelling Regulations*, OECD Working Papers, Vol. 5, No. 100, Organisation for Economic Cooperation and Development, Paris.

Coase, R.H. (1937), 'The Nature of the Firm', *Economica*, n.s. **4**, 386-405.

Commission of the European Communities (2000), *Communication from the Commission on the Precautionary Principle*, Brussels, 2 February http://europa.eu.int/comm/off/com/health_consumer/precaution_en.pdf.

Darby, M.R. and E. Karni (1973), 'Free Competition and the Optimal Amount of Fraud', *Journal of Law and Economics*, **16**, 67–88.

Davies, A.S. and W.A. Kerr (1997), 'Picking Winners: Agricultural Research and the Allocation of Public Funds', *The Review of Policy Issues*, **3** (3), 39–50.

Eaton, B.C., D.E. Eaton and D.W. Allen (1999), *Microeconomics*, Fourth Edition, Prentice Hall, Scarborough, Canada.

Eatwell, J., M. Milgate and P. Newman (eds) (1987), *The New Palgrave – A Dictionary of Economics*, Macmillan, London.

Einsiedel, E. (2000), *Biotechnology and the Canadian Public: 1997 and 2000*, University of Calgary, Calgary.

Esquinas-Alcázar, J. (1998), 'Farmers' Rights', in R.E. Evenson, D. Gollin, and V. Santaniello (eds), *Agricultural Values of Plant Genetic Resources*, CABI Publishing, Wallingford, pp. 207–217.

Falkner, R. (2000), 'Regulating Biotech Trade: The Cartagena Protocol on Biosafety', *International Affairs*, **76** (2), 299–313.

Fisher, A.C. and J.V. Krutilla (1974), 'Valuing Long Run Ecological Consequences and Irreversibilities', *Journal of Environmental Economics and Management*, **1**, 96–108.

Folkins, T. (2000), Personal communication based on work in progress, MA thesis, University of Calgary, Calgary.

Foltz, J., B. Barham and K. Kim (2000), 'Universities and Agricultural Biotechnology Production', in W.H. Lesser (ed.), *Transitions in Agbiotech: Economics of Strategy and Policy*, Food Marketing Policy Center, University of Connecticut, pp. 620–637.

Food Ethics Council (1999), *Novel Foods Beyond Nuffield*, London, http://www.users.globalnet.co.uk~foodeth/reportgmfood.htm.

Fulton, M. and K. Giannakas (2000), *Market Effects of Genetic Modification*, working paper, University of Saskatchewan, Saskatoon.

Fulton, M. and L. Keyowski (1999), 'The Producer Benefits of Herbicide Resistant Canola', *Agbioforum*, 2 (2), 85–93, http:www.agbioforum.org.

Gaisford, J.D. and W.A. Kerr (2001), *Economic Analysis for International Trade Negotiations: The WTO and Agricultural Trade*, Edward Elgar, Cheltenham.

Gaisford, J.D. and C. Lau (2000), 'The Case for and against Import Embargoes on Products of Biotechnology', *The Estey Centre Journal of International Law and Trade Policy*, 1 (1), 83–98, www.esteyjournal. com.

Gaisford, J.D. and R.S. Richardson (1996), 'North-South Disputes Over Protection of Intellectual Property', *Canadian Journal of Economics*, 29 (special issue), 5376–5381.

Georghiou, G.P. and A. Lagunes-Tejeda (1991), *The Occurrence of Resistance to Pesticides in Anthropods*, United Nations Food and Agricultural Organisation, Rome.

Government of India (1989), *Paper Presented by India in Uruguay Round Multilateral Talks*, Embassy of India, Washington.

Grace, E.S. (1997), *Biotechnology Unzipped: Promises and Realities*, Joseph Henry Press, Washington, DC.

Gravelle, H. and R. Rees (1992), *Microeconomics*, Second Edition, Longman, London.

Gray, R., J. McNaughton and D. Stovin (2001), 'Biotechnology and Lesser Developed Countries: An Overview of the Issues', in M. Fulton, H, Furtan, D. Gosnell, R. Gray, J. Hobbs, J. Holzman, W. Kerr, J. McNaughton, D. Stovin and J. Stevens (2000), *Taking Stock: The Benefits and Costs of Genetically Modified Crops*, Canadian Biotechnology Advisory Committee, Ottawa, pp. 89–97, http://cbac.gc.ca/documents/Richard_Gray_english.pdf.

Greenpeace Ltd (1998), Oral and written evidence to the House of Lords Select Committee on European Communities, 2nd Report, 15 December, http://www.parliament.the-stationary-office.co.

Griliches, Z. (1957), 'Hybrid Corn: An Exploration into the Economics of Technological Change', *Econometrica*, **25** (4), 501–22.

Griliches, Z. (1958), 'Research Costs and Social Returns: Hybrid Corn and Related Innovations', *Journal of Political Economy*, **66** (5), 419–431.

Hadfield, G.K. and D. Thomson (1998), 'An Information Based Approach to Labeling Biotechnology Consumer Products', *Journal of Consumer Policy*, **21**, 551–578.

Hart, M. (1998), *Fifty Years of Canadian Tradecraft – Canada at the GATT 1947–1997*, Centre for Trade Policy and Law, Ottawa.

Hayenga, M. (1998), 'Structural Change in the Biotech Seed and Chemical Industrial Complex', *AgBioForum*, **1** (2), 43–55, www.agbioforum. missouri.edu.

Henry, C. (1974), 'Investment Decisions under Uncertainty: The Irreversibility Affect', *American Economic Review*, **64** (6), 1006–1012.

Hoban, T.J. (1999), 'Consumer Acceptance of Biotechnology in the United States and Japan', *Food Technology*, **53** (5), 50–53.

Hobbs, J.E. (1996), 'A Transaction Cost Approach to Supply Chain Management', *Supply Chain Management: An International Journal*, **1** (2), 15–27.

Hobbs, J.E. (2000), 'Labelling and Consumer Issues in International Trade', in H.J. Michelmann, J. Rude, J. Stabler and G. Storey (eds) *Globalization and Agricultural Trade Policy*, Lynne Rienner, Boulder, pp. 269–285.

Hobbs, J.E. and W.A. Kerr (1999), 'Transaction Costs', in S.B. Dahiya (ed.), *The Current State of Economic Science*, Vol. 4, Spellbound Publishers, Rohtak, pp. 2111–2133.

Hobbs, J.E. and M.D. Plunkett (1999), 'Genetically Modified Foods: Consumer Issues and the Role of Information Asymmetry', *Canadian Journal of Agricultural Economics*, **47** (4), 445–455.

Hobbs, J.E. and M.D. Plunkett (2000), 'GMOs: The Economics of Consumer Issues', *Current Agriculture, Food and Resource Issues*, **1**, 11–20, http://www.cafri.org.

Holt, J.S. and H.M. Le Baron (1990), 'Significance and Distribution of Herbicide Resistance', *Weed Technology*, **4**, 141–149.

House of Lords (1998), *EC Regulation of Genetic Modification in Agriculture*, Select Committee on European Communities 2nd Report, 15 December, http://www.parliament.the-stationery-office.co.

Inside US Trade (1998), 20 February.

Isaac, G.E. (2001), *Agricultural Biotechnology and Transatlantic Trade: An International Political Economy Analysis of Social Regulatory Barriers*, unpublished Ph.D. dissertation, London School of Economics and Political Science, London.

Isaac, G.E. and P.W.B. Phillips (1999), *The Potential Impact of the Biosafety Protocol: The Agricultural Commodities Case*, a Final Report for the Biotechnology Unit of the Canadian Food Inspection Agency, CFIA Biotechnology Unit, Ottawa, March.

James, C. (1999), *Transgenic Crops Worldwide: Current Situation and Future Outlook*. Proceedings of the Conference on Agricultural Biotechnology in Developing Countries: Towards Optimising the Benefits for the Poor, organised by ZEF and ISAAA, AgrEvo and DSE in Bonn, 15–16 November, http://www.zef.de/zef_englisch/f_veranstalt_biotech.htm

Jorde, T. and D. Teece (eds.) (1992), *Antitrust, Innovation and Competitiveness*, Oxford University Press, New York.

Kalaitzandonakes, N. (1998), 'Biotechnology and the Restructuring of the Agricultural Supply Chain', *AgBioForum*, **1** (2), 40–42, http://www. agbioforum. missouri.edu

Kalaitzandonakes, N. and M. Hayenga (2000), 'Structural Changes in the Biotechnology and Seed Industrial Complex: Theory and Evidence', in W.H. Lesser (ed.) *Transitions in Agbiotech: Economics of Strategy and Policy*, Proceedings of NE-165 Conference, Food Marketing Policy Center, University of Connecticut, pp. 217–227.

Kaitzandonakes, N. and L.A. Marks (1999), *Public Opinion of Agbiotech in the US and UK: A Content Analysis Approach*, paper presented at the American Agricultural Economics Association meetings, Nashville, Tennessee, August.

Kerr, W.A. (1999), 'International Trade in Transgenic Food Products: A New Focus for Agricultural Trade Disputes', *The World Economy*, **22** (2), 245–259.

Kerr, W.A. (2000a), 'A New World Chaos? – International Institutions in the Information Age', *The Estey Centre Journal of International Law and Trade Policy*, **1** (1), 1–10, http://www.esteyjournal.com.

Kerr, W.A. (2000b), 'Is it Time to Re-think the WTO? – A Return to the Basics', *The Estey Centre Journal of International Law and Trade Policy*, **1** (2), 99–107, http://www.esteyjournal.com.

Kerr, W.A. (2001), 'The World Trade Organization and the Environment', in H.J. Michelmann, J. Rude, J. Stabler and G. Storey (eds) *Globalization and Agricultural Trade Policy*, Lynne Rienner, Boulder, pp. 53-65.

Kerr, W.A. and Hobbs, J.E. (2000), *The WTO and the Dispute Over Beef Produced Using Growth Hormones*, CATRN Paper 2000-07, Canadian Agrifood Trade Research Network, http://www.eru.ulaval.ca/catrn/beef.pdf.

Kerr, W.A. and N. Perdikis (1995), *The Economics of International Business*, Chapman and Hall, London.

Kerr, W.A. and R. Yampoin (2000), 'Adoption of Biotechnology in Thailand and the Threat of Intellectual Property Piracy', *Canadian Journal of Agricultural Economics* (forthcoming).

Kerr, W.A., R. Yampoin and J.E. Hobbs (2000), 'The TRIPS Agreement and WTO Enforcement of Intellectual Property Rights in Agricultural Biotechnology', in W.H. Lesser (ed.), *Transitions in Agbiotech: Economics of Strategy and Policy*, Food Marketing Policy Center, University of Connecticut, pp. 286–195, http://agecon.lib.umn.edu/ne165.html

Klein, B., R.G. Crawford and A.A. Alchian (1978), 'Vertical Integration, Appropriable Rents, and the Competitive Contracting Process', *Journal of Law and Economics*, **21** (2), 297–326.

Klein, B. and K.B. Leffler (1981), 'The Role of Market Forces in Assuring Contractual Performance', *Journal of Political Economy*, **89** (4), 615–641.

Klein, K.K. and W.A. Kerr (1995), 'The Globalization of Agriculture: A View from the Farm Gate', *Canadian Journal of Agricultural Economics*, **43** (4), 551–563.

Klein, K.K., W.A. Kerr and J.E. Hobbs (1998), 'The Impact of Biotechnology on Agricultural Markets', *Canadian Journal of Agricultural Economics*, **46** (4), 441–453.

Knight, F. (1921), *Risk, Uncertainty and Profit*, Houghton Mifflin Co., London.

Koziel, M.G., G.L. Beland, C. Bowman, N.B. Carozzi, R. Crenshaw, L. Crossland, J. Dawson, N. Desai, M. Hill, S. Kadwell, K. Launis, K. Lewis, D. Maddox, K. McPherson, M.R. Meghji, E. Merlin, R. Rhodes, G.W. Warren, M. Wright and S.V. Evola (1993), 'Field Performance of Elite Transgenic Maize Plants Expressing an Insecticidal Protein Derived From Bacillus thuringiensis', *BioTechnology* **4**(11), 194-200. (As cited in M.P. Feldman, M.L. Morris and D. Hoisington (2000), 'Genetically Modified Organisms: Why All the Controversy?', *Choices*, 1st quarter, 8–12).

Lancaster, K. (1966), 'A New Approach to Consumer Theory', *Journal of Political Economy*, **74** (2), 132–157.

Leibenstein, H. (1966), 'Allocative Efficiency vs. "X-efficiency"', *American Economic Review*, **56**, 392–415.

Lesser, W. (1998), 'Intellectual Property Rights and Concentration in Agricultural Biotechnology', *Agbioforum*, **1** (2), www. agbioforum.org.

Loader, R. and J.E. Hobbs (1996), 'The Hidden Costs and Benefits of BSE', *British Food Journal*, **98** (11), 36–45.

Mansfield, E. (1986), 'Patents and Innovation, an Empirical Study', *Management Science*, **32**, 173–194.

Mansfield, E. (1993), 'The Case for and against a Uniform Worldwide Intellectual Property Rights System', in M.B. Wallerstem, M.E. Mogee and R.A. Schoen (eds), *Global Dimensions of Intellectual Property Rights in Science and Technology*, National Academy Press, Washington, pp.18–39.

Marks, L.A., B. Freeze and N. Kalaitzandonakes (1999), 'The AgBiotech Industry – a U.S.–Canadian Perspective', *Canadian Journal of Agricultural Economics*, **47** (4), 419–431.

Marks, L.A., W.A. Kerr and K.K. Klein (1992), 'Assessing the Potential Impact of Agrobiotechnologies on Third World Countries', *Science, Technology and Development*, **10** (1), 1–32.

Maskus, K.E. (1990), 'Normative Concerns in the International Protection of Intellectual Property Rights', *The World Economy*, **13**, 18–39.

Mavroidis, P.C. (2000), 'Trade and Environment After the Shrimps–Turtles Litigation', *Journal of World Trade*, **34** (1), 73–88.

Mayer, H. (1999), *The Economics of Transgenic Herbicide-tolerant Canola*, unpublished M.Sc. thesis, University of Saskatchewan, Saskatoon.

Milgrom, P. and J. Roberts (1986), 'Price and Advertising Signals of Product Quality', *Journal of Political Economy*, **94** (4), 796–821.

Miller, J.R. and F. Lad (1984), 'Flexibility, Learning and Irreversibility in Environmental Decisions: A Baysian Approach', *Journal of Environmental Economics and Management*, **11**, 161–172.

Ministry of Agriculture, Fisheries and Food (MAFF) (1996), *Report of the Committee on the Ethics of Genetic Modification and Food*, Her Majesty's Government, London, http://www.gn.apc.org/pmhp/dc/genetics/cegmods.htm

Monsanto (1999), Open Letter from Monsanto CEO Robert B. Shapiro to Rockefeller Foundation President Gordon Conway, 4 October, http://www.monsanto.com/monsanto/gurt/default.htm.

Mooney, S. and K.K. Klein (1999), 'Environmental Concerns and Risks of Genetically Modified Crops: Economic Contributions to the Debate', *Canadian Journal of Agricultural Economics*, **47** (4), 437–444.

Moschini. G. (2001) 'Biotech – Who Wins? Economic Benefits and Costs of Biotechnology Innovations in Agriculture', *Estey Centre Journal of International Law and Trade Policy*, **2** (1), 93–117, www.esteyjournal.com.

Moschini, G. and H. Lapan (1997), 'Intellectual Property Rights and the Welfare Effects of Agricultural R&D', *American Journal of Agricultural Economics*, **79**, 1229–1242.

Moschini, G., H. Lapan and A. Sobolevsky (2000), 'Roundup Ready Soybeans and Welfare Effects in the Soybean Complex' *Agribusiness*, **16**, 33–55.

Mulongoy, K. (1997), 'Different Perceptions on the International Biosafety Protocol', *Biotechnology and Development*, **31**, June, 33–38.

Nagy, J.G. and H. Furtan (1978), 'Economic Costs and Returns from Crop Development in Canada', *Canadian Journal of Agricultural Economics*, **26** (1), 1–14.

Nelson, G.C., T. Josling, D. Bullock, L. Unnevehr, M. Rosengrant and L. Hill (1999), *The Economics and Politics of Genetically Modified Organisms in Agriculture: Implications for WTO 2000*, Bulletin 809, College of Agricultural, Consumer and Environmental Sciences, University of Illinois at Urbana-Champaign, Urbana-Champaign.

Nelson, P. (1970), 'Information and Consumer Research', *Journal of Political Economy*, **78** (2), 311–329.

Nelson, P. (1974), 'Advertising as Information', *Journal of Political Economy*, **82**, 729–754.

OECD (Organization for Economic Cooperation and Development) (2000), *Regulatory Developments in Biotechnology in OECD Member Countries*, OECD, Paris, http://www.oecd.org/ehs/country.htm.

Ohlin, B. (1933), *Interregional and International Trade*, Harvard University Press, Cambridge, MA.

Oxley, J.E. (1997), 'Appropriability Hazards and Governance in Strategic Alliances: A Transaction Cost Approach', *The Journal of Law, Economics, and Organization*, **13** (2), 387–409.

Paillotin, G. (1998), 'The Impact of Biotechnology on the Agro-food Sector', in OECD, *The Future of Food: Long Term Prospects for the Agro-food Sector*, OECD, Paris, pp. 71–89.

Palmeter, D.N. and P.C. Mavroidis (1998), 'The WTO Legal System: Sources of Law', *American Journal of International Law*, **92** (3), 398–413.

Pearse, A. (1980), *Seeds of Plenty, Seeds of Want: Social and Economic Implications of the Green Revolution*, Clarendon Press, Oxford.

Perdikis, N. (2000), 'A Conflict of Legitimate Concerns or Pandering to Vested Interests?: Conflicting Attitudes Towards the Regulation of Trade in Genetically Modified Goods – the EU and the US', *The Estey Centre Journal of International Law and Trade Policy*, **1** (1), 51–65, http://www.esteyjournal.com.

Perdikis, N. and W.A. Kerr (1999), 'Can Consumer-based Demands for Protection be Incorporated in the WTO? – the Case of Genetically Modified Foods', *Canadian Journal of Agricultural Economics*, **47** (4), 457–465.

Perring, C. (1991), 'Reserved Rationality and the Precautionary Principle: Technological Change, Time and Uncertainty in Environmental Decision Making', in R. Constanza (ed.), *Ecological Economics*, Columbia University Press, New York, pp. 153–166.

Peterson, W. and Y. Hayami (1977), 'Technical Change in Agriculture', in R. Martin (ed.) *A Survey of Agricultural Economics Literature*, University of Minnesota Press, Minneapolis, pp. 443–460.

Phillips, P.W.B and W.A.Kerr (2000), 'Alternative Paradigms – the WTO Versus the Biosafety Protocol for Trade in Genetically Modified Organisms', *Journal of World Trade*, **34** (4), 63–75.

Plunkett, M.D. (2000), *Are Genetically Modified Foods Good? The Welfare Implications of Biotechnology*, unpublished MA thesis, University of Calgary, Calgary.

Plunkett, M.D. and J.D. Gaisford (2000), 'Limiting Biotechnology: Information Problems and Policy Responses', *Current Agriculture, Food and Resource Issues*, **1**, 21-28, www.cafri.org.

Porter, M.E. (1980), *The Competitive Advantage of Nations*, Macmillan, London.

Posner, M.V. (1961), 'International Trade and Technical Change', *Oxford Economic Papers*, **13**, 323–41.

Randel, A. (1996), 'Sanitary and Phytosanitary Issues – Protecting Human, Animal and Plant Life and Health while Facilitating Trade', *Zemedelska Ekonomika*, **42** (6), 285–88.

Rissler, J. and M. Mellon (1996), *The Ecological Risk of Transgenic Crops*, MIT Press, Cambridge, Massachusetts.

Shapiro, C. (1983), 'Premiums for High Quality Products as Returns to Reputations', *Quarterly Journal of Economics*, **98**, 659–679.

Sherwood, R. M. (1990), *Intellectual Property and Economic Development*, Westview Press, Boulder.

Shieh, S. (1993), 'Incentives for Cost-reducing Investment in a Signaling Model of Product Quality', *Rand Journal of Economics*, **24** (3), 466–477.

Shimoda, S. (1998), 'Agricultural Biotechnology: Master of the Universe?', *AgBioForum*, **1** (2), 62–68, http://www.agbioforum.missouri.edu.

Schumpeter, J.A. (1942), *Capitalism, Socialism, and Democracy*, Harper, New York.

Spillane, C. (2000), 'Could Agricultural Biotechnology Contribute to Poverty Alleviation?', *AgbiotechNet*, **2** (March), www.agbiotechnet.com/reviews/march00.html/spillane.htm.

Stanton, G.H. (1995), 'Understanding the GATT Agreement on the Application of Sanitary and Phytosanitary Measures', *Food, Nutrition and Agriculture*, **11**, 36–42.

Steidlmeier, P. (1993), 'The Moral Legitimacy of Intellectual Property Claims: American Business and Developing Countries' Perspectives', *Journal of Business Ethics*, **12**, 157–164.

Streinz, R. (1998), 'The Precautionary Principle in Food Law', *European Food Law Review*, **4**, 413–432.

Tabashnik, B.E. (1994), 'Evolution of Resistance to Bacillus thuringiensis' *Annual Review of Entomology*, **39**, 47–49.

Tarvydas, R., J.D. Gaisford, J.E. Hobbs and W.A. Kerr (2000), 'Agricultural Biotechnology and Developing Countries: Will It Be Technology Transfer Through the Market or Piracy?', in W.H. Lesser (ed.) *Transitions in Agbiotech: Economics of Strategy and Policy*, Food Marketing Policy Center, University of Connecticut, pp. 407–424, http://agecon.lib.umn.edu/ne165.html

Taylor, M.S. (1993), 'TRIPS, Trade and Technology Transfer', *Canadian Journal of Economics*, **26**, 625–37.

Teece, D., R. Rumelt, G. Dosi and S. Winter (1994), 'Understanding Corporate Coherence: Theory and Evidence', *Journal of Economic Behavior and Organization*, **23** (1), 1–30.

Trachtman, J. (1999), 'The Domain of WTO Dispute Resolution', *Harvard International Law Journal*, **40** (3), 333–365.

Varian, H. (1992), *Microeconomic Analysis*, Third Edition, Norton, New York.

Vernon, R. (1966), 'International Trade and International Investment in the Product Cycle', *Quarterly Journal of Economics*, **80**, 190–207.

Western Producer (1999a), 'EU Closed to Modified Food', 25 February.

Western Producer (1999b), 'Rat Tests of Modified Potatoes Flawed', 27 May.

Williamson, O.E. (1971), 'The Vertical Integration of Production: Market Failure Considerations', *American Economic Review*, **61**, 112–123.

Williamson, O.E. (1979), 'Transaction-cost-economics: The Governance of Contractual Relations', *Journal of Law and Economics*, **22**, 233–262.

Yampoin, R. and W.A. Kerr (1998), 'Can Trade Measures Induce Compliance with TRIPS?, *Journal of the Asia Pacific Economy*, **3** (2), 165–182.

Index

accommodating pricing 106-7, 110-12, 123, 144
acquisition(s) 27-8, 39-40, 173-6, 178, 185, 227
Advanced Informed Agreement (AIA) 84-5
adverse quality effect 7, 101, 108, 110-14, 124-5, 136, 139, 142-3, 166, 189, 191, 198
adverse selection 24, 94, 96,
Agreement on Technical Barriers to Trade (TBT) 203-6
Agreement on the Application of Sanitary and Phytosanitary Measures (SPS) 202-6
Agreement on Trade Related Aspects of Intellectual Property (TRIPs) 26, 208, 210, 213-5
agrifood chain 173-4, 227
allergenic 11-12, 16-7, 90, 159-60
Animal Plant Health Inspection Service (APHIS) 159
animal welfare 95, 113, 152, 166, 199, 201, 225
antibiotic resistance 90, 159
appropriate science 187, 203, 204
asset specificity 177, 184-6
asymmetric information 6, 21-2, 24, 94-7, 99, 107, 112, 126, 202, 225, 227-8
    see also information asymmetry
autarky 191

Bacillus thuringiensis (Bt) 10, 11, 19, 55, 62-3, 87, 158, 165, 181

Baha'i Faith 152
barriers to entry 175, 180-82, 185
Bayes' Rule 64, 98
Betrand 121, 144
Biodiversity 23-4, 42, 51, 56, 61, 63, 84-5, 87, 158, 163, 199, 214
Biopiracy 51, 214
Biosafety Protocol (BSP) 82-7
Bovine Somatotropin (rBST) 4, 11
Bovine Spongiform Encephalopathy (BSE) 92, 94, 113-14, 159, 203
Buddhist 152

canola 4, 5, 10, 12, 33-4, 55, 86, 93, 95
    see also rapeseed
cheating 126, 128, 135-6, 138, 140, 143, 146, 161, 163, 166, 198
Christian 152-3
civil society 201, 205
cloning 4, 22
Codex Alimentarius Commission 205-6
Competency theory 175, 178
consumer attitude 89, 98, 151, 225
consumer preferences 31, 200, 224, 226-7
contamination 24, 33, 56, 77, 90, 92, 161, 166
contestable 52, 180
contract(s) 22, 97, 172, 174-9, 182-3, 224
Convention on Biological Diversity (CBD) 83, 214-15

corn (see also, maize) 4-5, 10, 21,
33, 41, 51, 55, 62-3, 87, 93,
95, 157-9, 165, 174, 181-3
cotton 5, 11, 28, 33, 55, 174
Cournot 121, 144
credence attribute 94, 98, 126, 145,
147, 202-3, 225, 227
cross-breeding 43, 152
cross-pollination 53, 158, 160

decision rule 54, 57
developing countries *xii*, 9, 13-14,
24-6, 33, 35, 48, 51, 85, 86,
207-10, 212-15, 217, 220-22,
225, 228
disease resistance 10, 13
distribution of income
see also income distribution
215-22, 224
DNA 2-4, 6, 16, 165
drought resistance 10, 13

economies of scale 36, 126, 146,
180, 215
enforcement costs 36, 127, 131, 139,
143, 176-77, 179, 185
see also monitoring and
enforcement costs
Environmental Protection Agency
(EPA) 59
evolution 27, 152
external benefits 61, 75, 77
external costs 61-5, 67-8, 70, 72, 74-
5, 77, 79, 82, 163, 198, 199
externality 7, 9, 13-14, 19-21, 23, 34,
54, 59, 61, 64, 68, 70, 75, 77,
82, 157, 163, 165-6, 187, 199,
221, 223-5, 227

field trial 40, 43, 144, 168
first-mover advantage 23, 155, 220
Food Ethics Council 155, 157, 158
food processing 4, 11, 92, 159, 173,
176, 182, 184-5
food retailing 11

food safety *xii*, 11, 87, 90-93, 96,
113, 159, 161, 163, 165, 202-
3, 205
Food Standards Agency 92
Frankenstein food 2, 15-16, 30
free rider problem 43
Friends of the Earth 31
functional food 12, 182-3

gene bank 35, 42, 51, 214
gene isolation 51
gene mapping 5-6, 42
gene splicing 2, 179
General Agreement on Tariffs and
Trade (GATT) 200-201, 203,
208, 213
genome 2-3, 51
genomics 2
germplasm 174, 177
governance 176-7, 179, 227
grain handling 184
Green Revolution 21, 33, 35
Greenpeace 31
growth hormones 113, 201

habitat 19, 58, 158
herbicide resistant 28, 158, 181
herbicide tolerant 5, 9, 10-11, 13, 18,
181
Hindu 152-3
hold-up 177, 186
human genetic modification 152-3
Human Genome project 3, 51

identity preservation system (IPS)
96, 126-8, 131-2, 134-6, 138-
40, 142-6, 166, 188
imperfect information 94-5
import embargo 188, 191-2, 194-6,
199-200, 220-21
income distribution 216, 219
see also distribution of income
incomplete information 21, 63, 94-5,
98, 160-61, 206
industrial crops 12, 229
information asymmetry 24, 94-5,
225, 227-8

see also asymmetric
   information
information cost 203
innoculent 176
innovation *xiv*, 21, 29, 36, 38-41, 43-
   5, 48, 51, 56, 86, 97, 102-3,
   106-7, 110-14, 122, 124-5,
   128, 134, 144, 155, 169, 171-
   2, 175-7, 179-81, 192, 207,
   214-16, 218-23, 225, 228-9
input-trait 11, 13, 19, 92, 96, 99,
   123, 165, 176, 182, 184
insect resistance 28
   see also pest resistance
International Office of Epizootics
   205-6
irreversibility 58
isolation cost 47-8

Jewish 153, 165
joint venture 38, 173-4, 176-8, 183-4

lacewing 17, 158
landrace 35, 42, 48, 214
lemons problem 96, 112-4, 126, 143
licensing *xiii*, 17, 23, 26, 31, 33, 41,
   43, 86, 151, 182, 201-2, 205,
   221
life science 28-30, 39-40, 93, 172-4,
   182-5

maize 5, 33, 95, 157
   see also corn
marginal cost pricing 80
marker gene 17, 90
measurement cost 183, 224
media 15, 56, 67, 91, 93, 144, 203
merger(s) 27, 40-41, 173, 175-6,
   178, 185, 227
Miami Group 85
micro-propagation 2
Monarch butterfly 19, 56, 61-3, 87,
   158, 165
monitoring and enforcement costs
   36, 127, 131, 139, 143, 176,
   179, 185, 205, 207
   see also enforcement costs

monoculture 23, 56
monopoly pricing 52, 97, 103, 107,
   110, 112, 123
monopoly profit 47, 179
monopoly rent 41, 45, 209, 213
Monsanto 27-8, 41, 172-4, 181-3
moral hazard 94, 179
multinational 51, 93, 73, 219
Muslim 152-4, 165

Nash equilibrium 106, 108, 121-3,
   144-5
negotiation costs 176, 179
Non-Government Organisations
   (NGOs) *ix*, 51, 214
novel food 16, 93
nutriceutical 12

opportunistic behaviour 81, 186
organic 18, 26, 31, 55, 158-9
outcrossing 18, 56
output-trait 11, 18, 99, 161, 182-4

patent 2, 6, 36, 40-45, 51, 90, 172,
   175, 178-9, 181-2, 209, 215
pest resistance 5, 9, 56, 62, 219
   see also insect resistance
pharmaceutical *xiv*, 5, 12, 25, 29, 31,
   56, 63, 173-4, 209, 229
Pigouvian subsidy 77
Pigouvian tax 67-8, 70, 72, 77, 79,
   82, 199-200
piracy 25, 207-8
plant breeders' rights 172
pooling equilibrium 96, 99, 115,
   134, 143, 166
potato 12, 16, 32-3, 51, 95, 98
precautionary principle 60, 61, 84-6,
   93-4, 155
pre-emptive pricing 103, 107, 110-
   12, 123
private good(s) 43, 171, 188, 198
Product Life-Cycle Theory 25, 45,
   175, 207
protectionism 23, 202, 204

public good(s) 21, 29-30, 35-9, 41-3,
    47-8, 51-2, 61-3, 65, 75, 140,
    169, 171, 198, 225, 228

quasi-rent 184, 186

rapeseed 5, 33, 86, 95,
    see also canola
rice 5, 14, 33, 53
risk analysis 91, 225-6
risk assessment 60, 84-5, 91, 204,
    226
Roundup Ready 9-10, 182

sanitary and phytosanitary 204-5
    see also Agreement on
    Sanitary and Phytosanitary
    Measures (SPS)
search costs 176
Secretariat of the International Plant
    Protection Convention 205,
    206
segregation 24, 26, 33, 182, 184,
    220-21
selective breeding 3, 152
separating equilibrium 96, 128, 192,
    194, 196
Sikh 153
soil erosion 9-10, 62
sorting costs 183, 194, 196
soybeans 5, 10-11, 33, 41, 90, 172,
    174, 181-3
strategic alliance 173-4, 176-8,
    183-4
stress-tolerant 19

tariff 200-201, 209
technology-use agreement 172, 181
terminator gene 37, 56, 172
tissue culture 2
tradable permits 67
trade barriers 23, 25, 85, 201, 203-6
trade disputes 187
trade liberalisation 202
Trade Related Aspects of Intellectual
    Property (TRIPS) 26, 208,
    210, 213-15

    see also Agreement on Trade
    Related Aspects of Intellectual
    Property Rights
trade sanctions 208, 210
Transaction Cost Economics (TCE)
    176, 178
transaction cost(s) 68, 70, 75, 80, 82,
    126-7, 131-2, 140, 143, 175-9,
    185
transgenic 2-4, 17, 34, 42, 53, 56, 90,
    97, 107, 172, 176, 179, 204,
    224
transnational 22, 26-29, 31, 33, 171,
    221

United Nations 83
United States Department of
    Agriculture (USDA) 59
Uruguay Round 26, 201, 203, 208
US Federal Trade Commission 41,
    181

vaccine 14
vertical co-ordination 173, 176, 178,
    183-5
vertical integration 173-4, 176-7,
    179, 184

weed control 9, 18
wildlife 18, 58, 158
World Intellectual Property
    Organisation (WIPO) 208
World Trade Organisation (WTO)
    23, 25-6, 30, 83-5, 87, 200-
    203, 205-10, 213-14, 226

X-inefficiency 179